Economics and Personal Finance Education

National Business Education Association Yearbook, No. 47

2009

Editor
William J. Wilhelm
Indiana State University
Terre Haute, Indiana

Associate Editor
Allen D. Truell
Ball State University
Muncie, Indiana

Published by

National Business Education Association
1914 Association Drive
Reston, VA 20191-1596
(703) 860-8300 • Fax: (703) 620-4483
www.nbea.org

Economics and Personal Finance Education

Copyright © 2009 by the National Business Education Association

National Business Education Association
1914 Association Drive
Reston, VA 20191-1596

ISBN 0-933964-72-2

Any views or recommendations expressed in this book do not necessarily constitute official policy of the National Business Education Association.

The Web addresses listed were accurate when this book was written but may have changed since publication.

TABLE OF CONTENTS

PREFACE

As this publication hits the presses, world economies are in dire straits, with the U.S. economy suffering through the severest recession since the Great Depression. U.S. unemployment is approaching double digits, the financial markets are frozen, consumer and corporate spending has dropped alarmingly, and tens of thousands of homeowners are already in or are facing foreclosure on their mortgages. The global financial crisis was brought on by vast numbers of complex and sometimes predatory home mortgage loans that were issued to U.S. borrowers who were incapable of making their monthly payments on homes that many could not afford. Contrary to previous decades when home loans were held by savings and loans and other banking institutions until maturity, mortgage loans today are packaged and sold as secure investments to institutional investors. Investor institutions, being risk averse, bought "insurance" in case they were not able to collect on the moneys due from the borrowers. That put the risk of mortgage defaults on the insurers. These "insurance policies" are referred to as credit default swaps.

When the values of homes began to decrease and borrowers began to default on their mortgage loans, investors found that they could lose substantial amounts of money on their securitized mortgage investments, and they turned to the insurers to get their money. In many instances, the insurer companies did not have the cash reserves to pay their obligations to the investors. That left the investors holding securitized assets that were rapidly losing value and thus becoming "toxic."

The problem of the toxic securitized mortgage investments affected a wide number of investment companies not only in the United States, but throughout the world since these securitized investments were bought and sold by global investors. Since the companies holding the toxic assets could not get their money from either the homeowners or the insurers, they were also faced with cash (liquidity) problems and could not raise capital to pay their debts—in many cases, money they borrowed to finance the purchase of the mortgage-backed securities. Then it became a situation of institutions that lent money they had borrowed not being able to pay back their own debts.

The result of this massive toxic debt debacle is that no one wants to lend money to anyone because of the fear that they will not be repaid. That situation is what has been referred to as the *frozen financial markets* and was the focus of the outgoing Bush Administration and the Federal Reserve in trying to unfreeze the credit markets through massive infusions of capital. After the Bush Administration spent $350 billion to shore up financial institutions in a highly debatable allocation of tax dollars to banks with no oversight of how those dollars would be used, the new Obama Administration has pushed the U.S. Congress to approve an economic stimulus package of close to $900 billion of tax cuts and spending to boost the economy out of recession. Central banks throughout the world are also trying to remedy the situation internationally by infusions of capital into the credit markets and, in many instances, taking steps to nationalize commercial banks.

Congress is investigating the events that have lead up to this crisis and have so far uncovered evidence of malfeasance in securities regulation, lending practices, and government oversight, but little attention has yet been paid to the fact that many U.S. home buyers signed extremely complex and often financially risky mortgage agreements. How is it that these high-risk mortgages would be agreed to by homeowners? How can individuals sign loan documents that bind them to the largest purchases of their lives without seeing the potential dangers of some of the loans they were committing to? How can consumers submerge themselves in debt so much beyond their abilities to repay that they stand to lose everything if housing markets turn? Unfortunately, in far too many cases, the answer is consumer ignorance.

Personal financial and economic literacy education in this country is severely lacking. While many school districts mandate economic education in high school, person finance is generally not mandated. Both economic and personal financial skills and competencies are needed for citizens to even begin to understand how to manage money given the complexities inherent in today's national and global economies. As stated by Mark Zandi, chief economist and cofounder of highly influential Moody's Economy.com, in his 2009 book *Financial Shock:*

Financial illiteracy was a fundamental cause of the subprime financial shock…The nation's general financial illiteracy contributes to a wide range of poor decisions on borrowing, saving, and investments…It is both bizarre and tragic that American high schools today are more likely to offer students cooking classes than personal finance courses. Such courses should be required – period.(pp. 236-237).

Now, more than ever before, it is imperative that our schools teach our young people about the mechanisms of money. That is what the *2009 National Business Education Association Yearbook* is all about: economics and personal financial literacy concepts.

The *Yearbook* is divided into two parts: Economics and Personal Finance. Authors were selected based on their knowledge of their chapter topics, and they represent a broad range of business professionals in the areas of economics and financial education. Professionals from the Federal Reserve Bank, state councils on economic education, state departments of education, universities, community colleges, and public schools are among the authors who have contributed to this endeavor. Chapter authors present not only discussions about the economic and personal finance topics entified as important for all students by the National Business Education Association, the National Council for Economic Education, and the Jump$tart Coalition, they also present instructional strategies and resources that classroom teachers can use at various grade levels.

Each chapter in this yearbook is structured to directly address the economics and personal finance standards established by the National Business Education Association. Chapter 1, Importance of Economics and Personal Finance, lays the foundation for the need to teach economics and personal finance in our schools, and differentiates between the two concepts so that it is clearly understood that economics is not the same as personal finance. The author emphasizes that concepts in *both* disciplines need to be taught to our students in order for them to be successful in their careers and their lives.

The chapters in Part I, Economics, closely follow the NBEA standards for economics. Chapter 2, Allocation of Resources, presents a discussion of the rational decision-making processes used to effectively allocate resources, and discusses the differences in incentives between needs and wants and why one concept has precedence over the other in economic decision-making. Economic Systems and Institutions are covered in Chapter 3. The author discusses how societies at various levels of developmental maturity and under the control of differing political structures develop different types of economic systems based on the decision-making processes used to allocate limited resources. Chapter 4, Market Structures, Pricing and Productivity, presents an analysis of how beliefs about human intentions, motivation, and behavior have shaped various political systems throughout history, and how these political systems in turn shape economic structures that support markets for the exchange of goods and services. The author of this chapter also discusses the differences between the types of market structures and the effects they have on price determination and the quality of the goods and services produced.

The Role of Government is the focus of Chapter 5, which points out that governments are not just participants in an economy as both consumers and producers of goods and services and purchasers of factors of production, they are also the primary formulators of economic policies. From providing for the national defense to stabilizing markets, many aspects of economic activity are affected by policies and controls established by the government.[1] Chapter 6, Global Economic Concepts, addresses absolute and comparative advantages that some countries have in terms of economic trade with other countries that have contributed significantly to current concerns over

---

[1] Since yearbook chapters were submitted by the authors, edited, and approved for publication before the apex of the global financial crisis in the fall of 2008, this chapter does not cover the U.S. government's role in the crisis.

globalization. These concerns—both positive and negative—have been brought on not only by disparities in the standards of living and infrastructures of various trading partner countries, but also by the world-flattening effect of modern technology. This chapter examines the role of trade, protectionism, and monetary markets in the global economy. Chapter 7, Aggregate Supply and Aggregate Demand, is the final chapter in Part I. The author discusses how decisions to buy, sell, save, and invest made by millions of participants in an economy have cumulative effects on subsequent decisions to buy, sell, save, and invest. The author makes clear why this aggregation of decisions affects national and global supply and demand, and why these concepts are important for individuals to understand, not just economists.

Part II of the *Yearbook* focuses on Personal Finance. The first chapter in this section, Personal Decision-Making (Chapter 8), carefully scrutinizes personal decision-making processes and includes effective techniques for assessing opportunity costs and trade-offs in personal financial decisions. Resources for obtaining good financial information are explained and referenced with examples. The authors of Chapter 9, Earning and Reporting Income, discuss the lifeblood of an individual's economic well being: income, whether it derives from earning a wage, investing in the stock market, renting or leasing assets already owned, or living on interest generated from a retirement portfolio. Occupational interest considerations and the concept of supply and demand in the job market are also addressed in this chapter. Managing Finances and Budgeting, Chapter 10, presents best practices for developing plans for spending and saving, methods and sources for recording and tracking expenditures and investments, and life-cycle variations in spending and savings plans. While Chapter 10 discusses the mechanics of managing finances and budgeting, Chapter 11, Saving and Investing, focuses specifically on the importance to individuals of saving and investing not just for the long term, but to achieve intermediate goals as well. The authors compare the advantages and disadvantages of earning compound interest through savings plans as opposed to investing in the stock market, and discuss how one analyzes these options.

Perhaps the most confusing part of buying goods and services in the United States today is the vast array of alternatives to choose from. Chapter 12, Buying Goods and Services, focuses on how to make shrewd buying, renting, or leasing decisions for goods and services and discusses methods for smart management of finances and budgeting to develop prudent buying behavior. The authors of Banking and Financial Institutions, Chapter 13, discuss why banks today are lauded as facilitators for providing loans for entrepreneurial ventures, as well as demonized as predatory lenders of questionable mortgages and providers of credit card contracts fraught with opportunities for spiraling personal debt. The authors also discuss types of banking institutions and identify the array of financial services individual consumers expect to receive from them. One of the most prominent banking services, credit, is discussed in Chapter 14, Using Credit. This chapter focuses on the advantages and disadvantages of obtaining and using credit, identifies the types of loans available through lending institutions, nd discusses what an individual needs in order to borrow and repay a loan safely. Finally, Chapter 15, Protecting Against Risk, examines risks that we all face and discusses a variety of methods by which these risks can be mitigated throughout one's life.

The 2009 *NBEA Yearbook* was written by 22 dedicated business professionals who spent many hours researching, writing, and revising their manuscripts. Their dedication to this important publication will be appreciated by all who use this yearbook for increasing student knowledge about these critical concepts. A special thank you goes to the 37 reviewers of the manuscripts for this publication for their insightful and valuable contributions that helped the authors and editors develop the chapters to their fullest potential. I also wish to acknowledge and thank my associate editor, Allen Truell, professor at Ball State University, who shared the arduous editing task with me in the preparation of the chapters for publication. Finally, I would like to express my appreciation to the NBEA Publications Committee for their guidance and suggestions and to Susan O'Brien, former NBEA editor, for her advice and assistance.

While I hope that all readers of this yearbook will find the chapters informative and insightful, I especially hope that the educators who read this publication will find it helpful in developing interesting, engaging, and valuable lessons in economics and personal finance for their students.

REFERENCES
Zandi, M. (2009). *Financial shock*. Upper Saddle River, NJ: Pearson Education, Inc.

William J. Wilhelm, Editor
Indiana State University
Terre Haute, Indiana

Economics and Personal Finance Education

ACKNOWLEDGMENTS

The following individuals graciously contributed their time and talents to review manuscripts for *Economics and Personal Finance Education.*

Mary Ellen Adams

Marcia A. Anderson

Stephen M. Avila

Glenn Bailey

Carol Blaszcynski

Cecil Bohanon

Michael Bronner

Julie Chadd

John Conant

Clarence Deitsch

Karen Drage

John Fitzgerald

Robert Guell

Barbara Hagler

Janice C. Harder

Virginia Hemby

Debra Israel

Susan Jaderstrom

Burton Kaliski

John Lightle

Richard Lotspeich

Linda McGrew

Peter F. Meggison

Wayne Moore

Larry Pagel

Donald Richards

Denise L. Roseland

Jim Rucker

Lisa Gueldenzoph Snyder

Chari Sowers

Lila Waldman

William Warfel

Cheryl Wiedmaier

Kelly Wilkinson

Dawn Woodland

DeVon Yoho

Jensen Zhao

Importance of Economics and Personal Finance Education

John E. Clow
National Council on Economic Education
New York, New York

Today U.S. citizens are being barraged with a bewildering set of economic developments. Losing jobs because of outsourcing, needing to accumulate retirement nest eggs because employers no longer provide pensions, determining whether free trade is a positive or a negative, and analyzing the positions of candidates who want the government to do more or less for the citizenry are some of the many challenges facing U.S. citizens today. Confusion in knowing which decisions to make when faced with such issues often occurs because people have little background in economic and personal finance principles.

This chapter focuses on defining economic and personal financial literacy, analyzing why economics and personal finance must be taught, and delineating the conceptual content of economics and personal finance. The chapter will look at the relationship between the concepts of economics and personal finance, analyze findings from studies that focus on student learning of economics and personal finance, and explain the role that business education has played in teaching these two concepts. A brief mention of general resources available for teaching economics and personal finance is also included.

DEFINING ECONOMIC AND PERSONAL FINANCIAL LITERACY

Economic literacy, as defined by Meade and Sandene in *The Nation's Report Card: U.S. Economics 2006* (2007), "...includes understanding how economies and markets work, what the benefits and costs of economic interaction and interdependence are, and that people have to make choices because resources are limited" (p. 1). This definition includes not only developing knowledge and skills, but also being able to use that knowledge and those skills in making decisions.

Financial literacy, as defined by the Jump$tart Coalition for Personal Financial Literacy (2007), is "…the ability to use knowledge and skills to manage one's financial resources effectively for lifetime financial security…Financial literacy refers to an evolving state of competency that enables each individual to respond effectively to ever changing personal and economic circumstances" (p. 1).

The focus of economic literacy is to equip the individual to deal with economic experiences using the concepts traditionally found in microeconomics and macroeconomics. Financial literacy *is not* synonymous with economic literacy. Financial literacy is the ability to manage one's own financial resources, which involves developing money management skills. Developing an understanding of various financial products, governmental interventions, and consumer markets is a part of developing financial literacy. As will be pointed out in more detail later, economic and personal financial education interrelate and complement one another.

IMPORTANCE OF ECONOMIC AND PERSONAL FINANCIAL LITERACY
One of the primary purposes of education is to prepare students with the skills, knowledge, and attitudes necessary for leading lives that are productive and enjoyable. In our country, freedom of the individual is highly prized. Freedom, for example, means that individuals can choose their occupations, determine how to spend and save their money, and decide how to vote for their representatives and for public policy issues.

The U.S. economic and political systems respond to individuals' choices. People make their wishes known by voting in two ways—in the polling booth and in the marketplace. Those candidates who gain the most votes win the privilege to represent citizens in governmental institutions, wherein decisions are made about how various public resources are used. By voting in the marketplace, consumers choose which goods and services to purchase. If enough consumers agree to buy a good or service at a price that is sufficiently profitable to the supplier, the good or service will be produced. Conversely, if a good or service is not purchased, suppliers will not expend resources to produce it.

With this emphasis on individual decision-making, the important element for the health and welfare of the economy and society is that individuals have the knowledge, skills, and attitudes necessary for making informed decisions by casting those votes in the polling booth and in the marketplace. Without an informed citizenry, economic resources can be easily wasted, therefore not promoting the welfare of the society, the dividual, or the family. For an intelligent and sustainable citizenry, then, economic nd personal financial literacy are very important.

Current Economic and Personal Financial Issues

Making the case for more and better economic and personal financial education s increasingly important today because individual households and the nation as a whole are faced with several serious challenges. These challenges include the following factors:

Low level of savings. Today individuals are increasingly called upon to provide for their own retirement. Gone are the days when many employers provided generous retirement packages. Revell (2008) indicated that in 2005, only 18% of employers in the private sector provided defined benefits pensions, whereas in 1980 the percentage was 39%. Thus, building a nest egg or creating wealth for the future must be accomplished by the individual, and he or she needs to have the knowledge, skills, and attitudes about setting aside and investing money for the future. Reyes (2008) points out that half of the population over 50 years of age have $100,000 or less in their savings set aside for retirement. Without economic and personal financial literacy, people will not see the need for nor be capable of accomplishing the necessary preparation for a comfortable retirement.

The United States is no longer a society of savers. Nancy Register of the Consumer Federation of America stated in an article in the *Christian Science Monitor* that "In two generations it seems that we've lost the culture and habit of savings" (Marks & Scherer, 2006, p. 1). Financial planner Procter agrees when he states, "For some reason we've gotten away from feeling that saving is our responsibility" (Bruce, 2006, p. 1). Indeed, the statistics provided by the U.S. Bureau of Economic Analysis (2007) support these comments. In 2005 personal savings as a percentage of disposable income was -0.4%; in 2006 it was -1.1%, which means that U.S. citizens were spending more than they earn in income. Prior to 1993, our personal savings percentage was generally much above 5%. For each year after 1993, the savings percentage has been less than 5%.

A lack of savings affects not only the household unit but also the entire economy. From the savings of individuals and groups comes the monetary capital to plow back into the economy so that financial institutions can provide credit to businesses for the purchase of capital goods. While the United States has been fortunate that foreigners who hold U.S. dollars have been willing to invest in U.S. enterprise for the last several years, we cannot be assured that foreigners will continue to do this, especially if they become concerned about U.S. creditworthiness. Former Federal Reserve Chairman Alan Greenspan warned that "the low savings rate is impairing the nation's long-term economic prospects. An improved savings rate would provide investment money for businesses, which would create jobs" (Marks & Scherer, 2006, p. 1).

Overuse of credit. Another problem is the U.S. overreliance on the use of credit. One indication of the overuse of credit was the rate of home foreclosures in 2007. *Money News* reported ("Foreclosures Jump," 2008) that the number of homeowners facing foreclosure jumped 57% in January 2008 compared to a year earlier. The American Bankruptcy Institute ("Personal Bankruptcies Up," 2008) cited that personal bankruptcy filings climbed substantially from January to February 2008. As Register of the Consumer Federation of America indicated, today's consumers want everything now, and if they don't have the money, they just use a credit card (Marks & Scherer, 2006).

The overuse of credit not only creates family discord but also has a negative effect on society. Home values declined precipitously in areas of the United States with high percentages of subprime mortgages when debtors defaulted. Many people walked away from their mortgages because the value of their homes had fallen below the amount of their mortgages. Tax revenues also fell in those communities, which, in turn, adversely affected support for schools and other public services provided by government. Bankruptcies also affect the costs of goods and services, because consumers have to pay more for those goods and services to compensate sellers for the additional costs of bad debts from non-paying or delinquent customers. Overuse and improper use of credit, therefore, is not only a personal problem but also a societal one.

Increased global competition. A third reason why economic and personal financial literacy are especially important relates to competitiveness in the global job market. Gunderson, Jones, and Scanland (2004) contend that the average U.S worker is in an international labor market instead of a local, state, or national labor market. U.S. workers in many instances have to consider competition for jobs not only from workers in the local area, but also from China, Ireland, or Eastern European countries. Futurists predict that people will not only have multiple job changes during their lifetime, but also multiple career changes. The workers of today and tomorrow must realize the nature of the labor market and develop and market the skill sets that will support them in a changing world.

This phenomenon of increased global competition has societal implications. The United States must make certain that it continues to be competitive in the 21st century. The rest of the world is catching up to or surpassing our country in education and technology. More and more countries are opening their doors to increased trade. More U.S. jobs are being outsourced—from low- to high-skill levels—because of lower labor costs and, in some cases, equal or higher quality production capabilities available in other countries. On the other hand, U.S. consumers enjoy many goods and services that come from other countries—generally with lower price tags than if the same goods were produced domestically. Individuals need to understand the advantages and disadvantages of increased competition and make decisions that will benefit them and the nation in the long run.

IMPORTANT CONTENT FOR DEVELOPING ECONOMIC AND PERSONAL FINANCIAL LITERACY EDUCATION

As shown by the standards for economic and personal finance, experts in both economic education and personal financial literacy education believe that the disciplines are developmental in nature, which means that students can and should be introduced to economic and personal finance content early in their educational experience. Economic and personal finance issues not only affect adolescents and adults, but also affect those in the lower grades. Therefore, many teachable moments are available for teaching young people economics and personal financial concepts at the early grades.

Several organizations dedicated to the advancement of economic and personal financial literacy have developed standards for both economics and personal financial literacy that focus on starting instruction at the early grades and extending it through twelfth grade and into the postsecondary level. The leading organizations promoting economics and personal financial literacy education and offering academic curriculum standards to support such efforts are the National Business Education Association (NBEA), the National Council on Economic Education (NCEE), and the Jump$tart Coalition for Personal Financial Literacy.

NBEA Academic Achievement Standards

NBEA's *National Standards for Business Education* (2007) contain academic achievement standards for both economics and personal finance. The NBEA economics standards identify nine conceptual areas of understanding, encompassing four levels of proficiency (grades 4, 8, 12, and 14). These conceptual areas include knowledge and understanding of allocation of resources, economic systems, economic institutions and incentives, markets and pricing, market structure, productivity, the role of government, global economics, and aggregate supply and aggregate demand. The personal finance standards identify eight conceptual areas of understanding (also encompassing the four levels of proficiency). The conceptual areas covered by these standards include personal decision making, earning and reporting income, managing finances and budgeting, savings and investing, buying goods and services, banking and financial institutions, using credit, and protecting against risk.

NCEE Academic Standards

NCEE, which has been promoting economic education in the schools since 1949, has identified 20 national content standards (NCEE, 1997) in economics. These standards relate to the conceptual areas of scarcity, decision-making, economic systems, economic incentives, voluntary exchange, specialization of trade and production, markets and pricing, reasons for price changes in a market, competition, economic institutions, functions of money, the role of interest, sources of income, entrepreneurship, investment in human and physical capital, the role of government, the costs of government, measures of economic health, societal economic problems, and fiscal and monetary policy. Each of the content standards has benchmarks at the fourth-, eighth-, and twelfth-grade levels. For each standard and for each set of benchmarks at a grade level, there are activities that students should be able to do if they have mastered the standard or the benchmarks. The focus is not only on the understandings that should be developed, but also what students should be able to do after mastering the content described in each standard.

Jump$tart Coalition Academic Standards

Jump$tart Coalition for Personal Financial Literacy is a coalition of business, government, labor, and educational institutions established in 1995 that are concerned about the rampant personal financial illiteracy in the United States. A major goal of the coalition has been to bring to the forefront of our schools the need for personal financial literacy. As part of that goal, Jump$tart developed its *National Standards in K-12 Personal Finance Education* (2007), which includes 29 standards in six conceptual areas: financial responsibility and decision-making, income and careers, planning and money management, credit and debt, risk management and insurance, and savings and investing. The Jump$tart Standards, like the previously mentioned NBEA and NCEE standards, have expectations of content mastery at proficiency levels for the fourth, eighth, and twelfth grades.

The standards identified by NBEA for economics and personal finance correlate well with those developed by NCEE and the Jump$tart Coalition and therefore clearly delineate what should be covered at various educational levels for grades K-12.

THE RELATIONSHIP BETWEEN ECONOMICS AND PERSONAL FINANCIAL LITERACY

The standards previously mentioned demonstrate that economics and personal finance are two distinct but interrelated disciplines. Each discipline contributes to a better understanding of the other.

Contribution of Economics to Personal Finance

The understanding and use of economic concepts can contribute to personal financial literacy in several ways. First, the discipline of economics provides the foundation for understanding our economic world. Comprehending why the price for a good or service changes in a market economy can enable consumers to rationally choose when to purchase a good or service. For example, many consumers waited to buy a personal computer until the demand was sufficient such that, when suppliers reached production economies of scale and there was considerable competition among suppliers, prices for computers became quite affordable. Understanding how and why the Federal Reserve increases or decreases interest rates can assist the consumer in planning when to refinance a house. These are just two simple examples of how economics supports an understanding of personal finance concepts.

Another contribution of economics to an understanding of personal financial management is that economic concepts demonstrate the interrelatedness of institutions within an economy and, thereby, society. For example, economic instruction about the circular flow in an economic system shows how households, businesses, and government depend upon one another to exist successfully and for the benefit of all in a society. Individuals need to understand other relationships, such as the relationship between savings and credit, between increased global competition and their job security, and between consumer aggregate decisions in the marketplace and what is produced by businesses. If individuals understand these relationships, they can better grasp why specific economic changes occur, which can assist them in making better decisions about how to deal with those changes. For example, an understanding of increased global competition in the labor market can lead to more informed choices about preparing for an occupational area that will not become obsolete or outsourced.

Economics is important to personal finance because it identifies the importance of rational decision-making and opportunity cost, i.e., realizing that making one choice means giving something else. Economics is all about making choices and analyzing the costs and benefits that relate to those choices before making them.

Contributions of Personal Finance to Economics

Personal finance contributes to economic understanding by providing many opportunities for students to use their economic understandings to make individual decisions. Using cost/benefit analysis to determine whether to go to college or to work after high school is one example. Buying stocks over bonds in a period of inflation as a result of understanding the nature of inflation and how stocks generally maintain "purchasing power" better than bonds during inflationary times is another example. A third example is understanding how extensive advertising can lead an otherwise unwary consumer to consider only one brand of product, such as a hamburger or a cup of coffee, over perfectly good and more economical substitutes.

Both Disciplines Enhance Each Other

Lewis Mandell (2006) in his latest Jump$tart Coalition study of personal financial literacy among U.S. youth found that high school students who had taken either a course in economics or a course in personal finance did not do very well on a test of personal finance. He postulated that economics teachers did not provide much attention to personal financial decision-making. From Mandell's point of view, many ways exist to show the application of economic principles through personal decision-making. On the other hand, he believed that personal finance teachers focus primarily on teaching facts and procedures and do not teach the economic and institutional contexts that are necessary for making informed choices. Mandell is, in effect, indicating that the teaching approaches in the two disciplines can enhance each other, should be interrelated, and are both necessary for educating informed consumer citizens.

PUBLIC PERCEPTIONS OF IMPORTANCE

There are several good indicators of the public's perception of the importance of economic and personal finance education. These indicators include state curriculum requirements, the nationwide studies of adults, the recent recognition of economics by a national testing group, and a statement by the National Association of State Boards of Education about the importance of personal financial literacy.

The NCEE has surveyed the states for a number of years regarding their emphasis on economics and personal finance education. Its most recent survey (2008) indicates that there has been an increased emphasis on economic and personal finance instruction over the last 10 years in our nation's schools. All 50 states have included economics in their academic standards, while 40 states require some standards in personal finance. Economics is emphasized more than personal finance, which is not surprising, considering that economics has been a part of the curriculum for more years than personal finance. Neither discipline is viewed as being important enough by a majority of the states to have a separate required course for all students. Less than 50% of the states require student competency in both content areas.

The NCEE Survey of Economic Literacy conducted by Louis Harris and Associates (Harris, 1999) found that that most of the adults surveyed believed that economics should be a part of the school curriculum. The study was replicated by Harris Interactive (2005) and they found virtually the same result—100% of the adults believed that economics should be included in high school education.

Another indication of the increasing importance of economics is its acceptance in 2000 as a discipline to be tested by the National Assessment of Educational Progress (NAEP), the national organization commissioned by the government to determine how students are doing in various subject matter areas over a period of time. The first national assessment of economics completed by this group was done in 2006.

The Jump$tart Coalition for Personal Financial Literacy, as noted above, was started in 1995 because many people in business, education, and government believed that there was insufficient emphasis on personal finance in the schools. Through its 10-plus years of existence, this national coalition has established a network of state coalitions that has garnered support within individual states for promoting more and better personal financial education in the schools.

In a 2006 report of the National Association of State Boards of Education (NASBE) entitled *Who Will Own Our Children*, all of the recommendations relate to the inclusion of more and better quality financial literacy and investor education in the schools. NASBE represents local school boards comprised of members of the local community. This study is saying that the lay leadership of our schools believes that personal finance is important.

DEGREE OF EDUCATIONAL SUCCESS

Because of the interest in economic and personal financial literacy, a number of research studies have focused not only on the literacy levels of students but also that of adults. Some generalizations can be made from these studies, even though there is some variance in the findings regarding the effect of a separate course in personal finance.

Studies Measuring Economic Literacy

The Louis Harris and Associates study (Harris, 1999) completed for NCEE surveyed students and adults to determine their knowledge and understanding of economic concepts. They found that adults had a mean score of 57% on the test, whereas students had a mean score of 48%. Students who were taught economics in school generally did better than those who had no instruction in economics. The study was replicated by Harris Interactive (2005) and found that adults received a mean score of 70 % for their knowledge of economics, with the student mean score being 53%. Students who were taught economics in high school were more likely than those without economics instruction to have received what would be considered a passing grade in their schools.

A study completed by the National Assessment of Educational Progress (Meade & Sandene, 2007) assessed the economic literacy of 11,500 twelfth-grade students in public and nonpublic high schools. Forty-two percent of the students performed at the proficient level, which is defined as a level at which students are able to "identify and recognize a broader set of economics concepts and relationships that are important for solid understanding of the market economy, national economy, and international economy" (p. 9). In this case, most of the students had exposure to economic instruction.

As the data in these studies show, improvement has been made in the economic literacy of U.S. youth. The student averages on the tests, though, are still deficient. Much more needs to be done to develop the economic literacy of all students.

Studies Measuring Personal Financial Literacy

The Jump$tart Coalition for Personal Financial Literacy supported testing of high school seniors for personal financial literacy throughout the last decade. Studies were conducted in 1997, 2000, 2002, 2004, and 2006, each by Lewis Mandell. Each student in the sample was given a survey instrument that included a 30-item test geared to the standards for personal financial literacy developed by the Jump$tart Coalition. The questions were a mix of knowledge and application questions.

The average score in 2006 was 52.4%, which is the best average score since 2000. For most of the years, a one-semester high school personal finance course did not seem to make much difference in the scores of the students. The same finding regarding the effect of a separate course in personal finance was found in the 1999 Youth and Money Survey (American Savings Education Council, 1999), where high school and college students were surveyed. Those who took a course in personal finance did not seem to have better financial behavior than those who did not take such a course.

There is some research that paints a different picture as far as the effect of a separate personal finance course. Bernheim, Garrett, and Maki (2001) looked at whether a mandated high school financial curriculum had an effect on savings in the long term, one important competency area of personal financial literacy. They found that a mandated personal finance course had a long-term positive effect on the savings patterns of those who took the course.

The personal financial literacy of our youth is gradually improving, but they are still getting a failing grade. Much more needs to be done in order to ensure that all students are financially literate.

STUDENT ATTITUDES ABOUT PREPAREDNESS

Some research studies have shown that students are overconfident about their financial skills, do not realize the value of school-based personal finance, and have no interest in economics. Teachers should be aware of these perceptions in order to deal with them in a positive way.

Mandell (2002) reported that those who were "very sure" of their ability in the area of money management did poorer on the 30-item test than those who were somewhat confident. The study of high school and college students by the American Savings Education Council (1999) shows that only a little over one quarter of those who thought they did a good job of managing their money believed that saving regularly was important. This overconfidence may explain why some students don't get very serious about mastering personal finance concepts. They may believe they already know all that they need to know. The challenge for the teacher is to show the students that they do not have as much competency as they believe that they do.

Also in the American Savings Education Council study (1999), 62% of students indicated that their current school or a prior school offered a course in personal finance, but only 34% of them took the course. The same study reported that students relied on their friends and family members for financial advice more than schools. Studies conducted by Mandell (1998, 2002) showed that high school seniors believed that their parents as well as their own experiences were much more influential than school in learning personal finance concepts. Because personal finance is a life skill, perhaps students believe they are doing fine in managing their resources if they are not bankrupt or behind on their credit payments. A need exists to show them how using sound personal financial knowledge can lead to satisfying more of their wants and needs, and can lead to a more satisfactory life.

In the Harris Interactive Study (2005), which surveyed U.S. students in grades 9-12, half of the students indicated that they had no interest in economics. They did have an interest in economics if they had taken an economics course, however. With an elective course in economics in a school, which is quite common, students should be clearly shown why economics is very important for their future, which would encourage them to enroll in the class.

Understanding student perceptions with regard to learning economics and personal finance competencies is very important in order for parents, teachers, administrators, and legislators to emphasize these skills in educational curricula and to motivate students to learn and value these skills. In the case of both personal finance and economics, a need exists to show students the value of both skill sets.

THE ROLE OF BUSINESS EDUCATION

Business education began as a discipline at the high school level and beyond, focused on educating people for business—a vocational objective. Bahr and Wegforth (1976) pointed out that consumer education, which is very similar to personal finance, got its major push and gained momentum in business education in the 1930s. Business education thus adopted a general education component—moving the discipline to having two major thrusts—general education and vocational education. Many business educators were actively involved in the consumer education movement that gained momentum during the 1930s.

As pointed out by Price, Hopkins, and Duff (1972), economic education as defined in this chapter was accepted as a major objective of business education starting in the 1960s. Two major publications cosponsored by NBEA and the Joint Council on Economic Education (now called the JCEE) focused on economic education and the business educator: *A Teachers Guide to Economics in the Business Education Curriculum* (Olson, Price, Swearingen, Garrison, Yerian & Bahr, 1963) and *Two Decades of Partnership in Economic Education* (Bahr, 1969).

Offerings of semester-long or full-year courses in economics and personal finance in the business education curriculum vary from school to school. However, many courses in the business education curriculum have had components of personal and economic education on a continuing basis for a long time. For example, the general business or introduction to business courses generally have contained economics and personal finance components for several decades. The high school accounting course has also had some personal financial components, such as how to fill out an income tax form.

Economics and personal finance education have been a part of the business education curriculum for decades. NBEA in its standards documents has always recognized that economics and personal finance are integral parts of the business education curriculum. Business educators can and should continue to play an important role in promoting economic and personal financial education in the schools.

GENERAL TEACHING RESOURCES

A large number of resources are available for teachers of economics and personal finance. NBEA's professional journal, *Business Education Forum,* includes articles about economics and personal finance on a continuing basis. Other NBEA resources for teaching economics and personal finance are listed on its website (www.nbea.org).

The Jump$tart Coalition for Personal Financial Literacy operates a clearinghouse where a teacher can learn about the vast array of materials that are available in teaching personal finance (www.jumpstart.org). The clearinghouse includes a description of each of the entries that is listed.

The NCEE website (www.ncee.net) lists lesson plans in the areas of economics and personal finance for different grade levels, as well as curriculum materials that can be purchased. It also has interactive computer simulations for students and lists of materials from other groups, such as the Federal Reserve. Many private firms such as banks and nonprofits also have published materials. The chapters in this yearbook will specify a number of resources for use in teaching economics and personal finance at various educational levels.

SUMMARY

There is a tremendous need for more and better economic and personal financial literacy education in our nation because of the important role that the individual plays in making decisions in our economy and political system. This need is increasing in importance because of major economic challenges faced by individuals in our economy—today—challenges such as increased international competition, the overextension of debt, decreased emphasis on savings, and an increased responsibility for workers to plan their own careers and retirements.

The economic and personal finance competencies that should be developed at various grade levels have been specifically identified by several professional organizations. The public is very supportive of more and better economic and personal finance education, and the schools are moving toward greater inclusion of these disciplines in the curriculum. Still, more emphasis needs to be placed on these areas, as evidenced by test scores of high school seniors and adults. Unfortunately, students don't always see the importance of studying economics and personal finance. While the disciplines are separate in the world of making economics decisions, both are necessary and interdependent. Economics and personal finance education have been goals in business education for many years, and there is no lack of classroom materials that teachers can use to teach these competencies and skills.

REFERENCES

American Savings Education Council. (1999). *Youth and money survey.* Washington DC: Author.

Bahr, G. (Ed.) (1969). *Two decades of partnership in economic education.* New York: National Council on Economic Education.

Bahr, G., & Wegforth, R. P. (1976). A historical development of an economic emphasis in business education. In Ruth B. Woolschlager and E. Edward Harris (Eds.), *Business education yesterday, today, and tomorrow* (pp. 20-37). Reston, VA: National Business Education Association.

Bernheim, B. D., Garrett, D. M., & Maki. D. M. (2001). Education and saving: The long-term effects of high school financial curriculum mandates. *Journal of Public Economics, 80,* 435-465.

Bruce, L. (2006, March 8). Is negative savings rate a problem? *Bankrate.com.* Retrieved February 21, 2008, from http://www.bankrate.com/brm/news/sav/20060308e1.asp

Foreclosures jump 57 percent since 2007. (2008, February 26). *Money News.* Retrieved March 7, 2008, from http://archive.moneynews.com/money/archives/articles/2008/4/15/081210.cfm

Gunderson, S., Jones, R., & Scanland, K. (2004). *The jobs revolution.* Washington DC: Copywriters, Inc.

Harris Interactive. (2005). *What American teens & adults know about economics.* New York: National Council on Economic Education.

Harris, Louis & Associates. (1999). *Survey of economic literacy.* New York: National Council on Economic Education.

Jump$tart Coalition for Personal Financial Literacy. (2007). *National standards in K-12 personal finance education (3rd ed.).* Washington, D C: Author

Mandell, L. (1998). *Our vulnerable youth: The financial literacy of American 12th graders.* Washington, DC: Jump$tart Coalition for Personal Financial Literacy.

Mandell, L. (2001). *Improving financial literacy: What schools and parents can and cannot do.* Washington, DC: Jump$tart Coalition for Personal Financial Literacy.

Mandell, L. (2002). *Financial literacy: A growing problem.* Washington, DC: Jump$tart Coalition for Personal Financial Literacy.

Mandell, L. (2004). *Financial literacy: Are we improving?* Washington, DC: Jump$tart Coalition for Personal Financial Literacy.

Mandell, L. (2006). *Financial literacy: Improving education.* Washington, DC: Jump$tart Coalition for Personal Financial Literacy.

Marks, A., & Scherer, R. (2006, January 30). U. S. savings rate falls to zero. *Christian Science Monitor.* Retrieved February 21, 2008, from http://articles.moneycentral.msn.com/Investing/Extra/USSavingsRateFallsToZero.aspx?pa

Meade, N., & Sandene, B. (2007, August). *The nation's report card: U.S. economics 2006.* Washington, DC: National Assessment of Educational Progress.

National Association of State Boards of Education. (2006). *Who will own our children: The need for financial literacy standards.* Alexandria, VA: Author

National Business Education Association. (2007). *National standards for business education: What America's students should know and be able to do in business.* Restor VA: Author

National Council on Economic Education. (1997). *Voluntary national content standards in economics.* New York: Author.

National Council on Economic Education. (2008). *Survey of the states – Economic, personal finance education ad entrepreneurship in our nation's schools in 2007: A report card.* New York: Author.

Olson, M. C., Price, R. G., Swearingen, E. L., Garrison, L. L., Yerian, T., & Bahr, G. (1963). *A teachers guide to economics in the business education curriculum.* New York: Joint Council on Economic Education.

Personal bankruptcies up 15 percent since January. (2008, March 5). *Huffington Post.* Retrieved March 7, 2008, from http://www.huffingtonpost.com/2008/03/05/personal-bankruptcies-up-_n_89931.html.

Price, R. G., Hopkins, C. R., & Duff, T. B. (1972). In Leroy Brendel and Herbert Yangel (Eds.), *Changing methods of teaching business subjects* (pp. 2-3). Reston, VA: National Business Education Association.

Revell, J. (2008). Survival strategies. *Money, 37*(1), 90.

Reyes, K. W. (2008, March and April). Still working after all these years. *AARP The Magazine, 51*(2B), 98.

U. S. Bureau of Economic Analysis. (April, 2007). Personal income and its disposition. Retrieved February 21, 2008, from http://www.census.gov/compendia/stabab/tables/08s

Allocation of Resources

Jody Hoff
Federal Reserve Bank of San Francisco
San Francisco, California

A quotation by Thomas Sowell (1993) nicely summarizes the fundamental constraint that is the basis for the study of economics and underpins the responsibility of each society: "The first lesson of economics is scarcity: There is never enough of anything to satisfy all those who want it. The first lesson of politics is to disregard the first lesson of economics" (p. 131). What makes this quotation so interesting is the way in which it captures the juxtaposition of economic reality and political expediency. There is no escape from the constraint of limited resources. Societies develop institutions to deal with the inevitable need to choose among alternatives in an effort to make best use of limited resources. The role and responsibility of the decision-making authority and the need for efficient outcomes are often difficult to reconcile. The tension between the unlimited needs of humanity and limited available resources has been and continues to be a driving force behind issues of growth, decay, and development. The potential is high for this conundrum to engage students on multiple levels, both in its applicability to their personal lives and the degree to which it is manifest in the world every day. This chapter is designed to cover the basic premise of economics, which is to study the allocation of scarce resources to meet the needs of society. The topics of scarcity, opportunity cost, rational decision-making, factors of production, and economic allocation mechanisms will be discussed with suggestions for teaching strategies.

SCARCITY

Scarcity is the condition that exists when human wants exceed available resources. This predicament is the foundation for the study of economics and the entry point for discussion and analysis of how best to satisfy unlimited wants in a world of limited resources. The human condition is to want things, including basic items such as food, clothing, education, and medical care. People also want items like cars, time off for leisure, and movie tickets. They may also want more knowledge, friendships, freedom, and excitement. Is it possible to have it all, to satisfy both material and non-material wants? Unfortunately, offsetting our unlimited desires is the opposing constraint of limited resources. Resources, in this context, comprise the inputs used to produce goods and services. Oil reserves, arable land, clean water, and time, money, and memory are diverse examples of resources. What they share in common is a limited ability to satisfy the wants of all people. Scarcity exists whenever the available resources are unable to meet all of these wants.

Unlimited Wants, Limited Resources

The two components of scarcity—unlimited human wants and limited resources—apply to everyone, everywhere, because people simply cannot have all the goods and services they desire due to limits on the amount and availability of resources. The circumstance of scarcity in an African refugee camp is a world away from the financial analyst facing a scarcity of street parking in San Francisco, and light years from the constraints faced by Warren Buffet, ranked by Forbes magazine as the "world's richest man" (Kroll, 2008), and his $62 billion fortune. The relative level of scarcity does not change the fact of its existence and, although the effects of scarcity vary greatly among individuals and societies, the condition itself is inescapable.

Teaching about Scarcity

Economics is essentially the study of how to manage the condition of scarcity. In helping students understand and appreciate the ubiquitous nature of scarcity, an effective strategy is to begin a discussion with the personal experiences of students followed by more generalized situations and conditions related to unlimited wants and limited resources. Also, the distinction between wants and needs is often covered in secondary textbooks, although most economists consider this to be a "false" distinction (Leets & Lopus, 2003) and not an effective use of instructional time.

The following are several suggestions for teaching about scarcity at the postsecondary and secondary levels. Postsecondary level teaching suggestions include having students prepare a list of personal items, both material and non-material, that they anticipate consuming within the next 24 hours and to speculate on how the content and the volume of the list will change over time as they age. The objective of the list is to demonstrate the unlimited and ongoing nature of human wants. Additionally, teachers can assign the article "Betting on the Planet" (Tierney, 1990) and apply the nclusion found on page eight to the current concerns about global oil supplies. The objective of this reading is to emphasize that the concern about limited resources is not a new phenomenon and that it has multiple viewpoints and a variety of corresponding solutions. Secondary-level teaching suggestions include introducing the topic of scarcity with the quotation, "Why abundance sucks, and other unexpected lessons of the game economy" (Castronova, 2006). Teachers can define the term "abundance" and add the following: "What if everything in life were free? You'd think we'd be happier. But game designers know better: We'd be bored" (Castronova, 2006, ¶1). Guide students in a discussion about their personal experience with video games by identifying common goals and objectives of the games they have played. Connect the game goals and objectives to the concept of abundance or the opposite condition of scarcity. Castronova's article *Why Abundance Sucks, and Other Unexpected Lessons of the Game Economy* can be assigned for further reading. The objective of this discussion is the connection between video game design and the topic of scarcity, which serves as an interesting and unexpected entry point for students in the introduction to economics and how game designers attempt to model reality through the concept of scarcity.

CHOICE

The consequences of scarcity are profound. The quality of life available to individuals and collectively to society is dependent on the day-to-day negotiation to satisfy unlimited wants with limited resources. This negotiation manifests in one of the most fundamental of all human capacities, the ability to choose. Consider the volume of choices an individual is confronted with in a single day: What to have for breakfast? Which pair of shoes to wear? Which route to take to work? Whether to answer that incoming cell phone call? Whom to include in a memo? Paper or plastic? The list of these choices is endless and directly related to the condition of scarcity. Choice can be characterized as a response to the condition of scarcity. The impact of choice, at the individual level and at the level of a society, is related to both sides of the scarcity issue. The diversity of global living standards reflects the difficulty in satisfying the unlimited wants within a specific set of resource limitations and provides insight into consequences of choice. Economics provides a set of tools and concepts to understand and predict the consequences of choice and methods by which to improve the outcome of these choices.

Trade-Offs and Opportunity Cost

The use of choice to solve the scarcity issue involves a well-known and often painful aspect of the decision-making process, called the trade-off. Trade-offs represent those items that will be given up in order to gain something else. Every time a choice is made, something else (the trade-off) must be given up, forgone, and left behind. If a family decides to buy a new plasma TV this year, they may not be able to afford to take a summer vacation. If an individual decides to spend Saturday morning reading the paper, he or she may not have time to clean out the garage. If a firm decides to give bonuses to their employees this year, they may not be able to afford to develop a new product. And a child living in a developing country who spends his or her day in search of food and water may be unable to attend school. Identifying the trade-offs o the alternatives involved in a choice does not provide the answer to what should be done, but it improves the likelihood of a good decision when the options are more clearly understood. The inevitable *giving-up* aspect involved in the decision-making process is critical for understanding the choices that people and societies make.

Identifying trade-offs is the first step in the process of choosing. The next step involves comparing the costs and benefits of each alternative. Once a decision has been made, the cost of the decision is defined in terms of what was given up. The term for the alternative not selected whenever a choice is made is called the *opportunity cost* The term "opportunity" implies the *potential* involved with the alternatives, and "cost" implies that something has been given up or lost. Revisiting the examples above, the opportunity costs in each of the three cases are represented by the alternative not selected. The family's opportunity cost for the summer vacation taken is the plasma TV foregone. The individual's opportunity cost for taking the time to read the paper on Saturday morning is the time foregone for cleaning out the garage. The firm's opportunity cost for paying employee bonuses is sacrificing the capital necessary for new product development. In each case, the choice is expressed as the alternative not selected. The key to the analysis is to understand the true costs and benefits of the alternatives. A further refinement in fully developing the costs and benefits of a decision is the idea of marginal thinking.

Marginal Thinking

Marginal thinking, or thinking on the margin, is a key element in effective decision-making. In this context, the term "marginal" refers to the incremental change or adjustment in a decision. The quality of decision-making is greatly enhanced by under-standing and appropriately assigning costs and benefits to the incremental aspect of an alternative. It is interesting to note that most decisions can be enhanced by examining information at the margin. In an earlier example, the question was whether or not to purchase a new plasma TV. Once the decision is made to buy the TV, thinking about the purchase on an incremental or marginal basis enhances the quality of the decision. As an example, how much additional benefit will be derived by spending an additional $500 for the higher resolution TV model? When cleaning out the garage, how much additional benefit will be derived from spending an additional 90 minutes washing the concrete?

Another example of how thinking on the margin helps decision-makers is to look at the hotel industry. Consider the situation of a hotel with an average cost of a room at $200 and, during a slow week, the hotel is underbooked and rooms are available. Does it make sense for the hotel to accept a Priceline.com bid of $100 or let the room go empty? On the margin, the additional $100 in benefit may well offset the marginal osts of an extra hotel guest. In general, the cardinal rule of decision-making states that the optimal choice is always the alternative in which the marginal benefit exceeds he marginal cost. Given the marginal costs and the corresponding marginal benefits, he choice between alternatives appears to be very straightforward. However, the neart and soul of quality decision-making, and often the most difficult aspect of the process, is correctly assigning appropriate costs and benefits to the alternatives under consideration. In economics, a common assumption is that individuals act in a rational manner throughout the decision-making process.

Rational Decision-Making

One of the key assumptions about human behavior in economic analysis is that individuals always act in ways that benefit their own situation. In essence, the assumption is that individuals consistently act in accord with their own best interests. It follows that people only make choices that they believe will benefit them or improve their lives and that people generally do not choose alternatives that make them worse off. This corresponds to the previous discussion on decision-making: people choose the alternative wherein the benefit is greater than the cost. Applying this principle to the concept of marginal thinking, individuals only pursue choices when the marginal benefit is greater than the marginal cost. The individual who makes use of the "snooze" function on an alarm clock that goes off at 6:00 a.m. is utilizing the concept of marginal decision-making. This decision involves an expectation that the benefit of an extra 10 minutes of sleep outweighs the cost of 10 fewer minutes to get to work or school on time. These benefits and costs are estimates of potential future value and represent what might reasonably be expected to occur, but are not a guarantee of what may actually occur. The key to effective decision-making is to accurately estimate both the marginal benefits and marginal costs in any given decision.

It might be argued that smoking cigarettes is an irrational choice given what is known about the consequences of tobacco smoke to good health. However, in economics the decision to smoke is assumed to be rational in that individuals, for reasons of their own, have determined that the marginal benefit of smoking is greater than the marginal cost. The rationality assumption assumes that individuals are able, based on their own preferences, to assign marginal costs and benefits to any given decision. Is it possible to alter an individual's preference for a particular preference such as smoking? Influencing decisions is a matter of modifying the costs and benefits of a decision through the use of incentives.

Incentives

When people behave rationally by pursuing an activity in which the marginal benefits are greater than the marginal costs, they are responding to the incentives related to the expected costs or benefits. When the price of gasoline rises, people tend to find ways to buy less gasoline; they buy cars with higher fuel efficiency or hybrid automobiles, they make fewer trips, or they carpool and use public transportation.

The change in behavior is based on the increased marginal cost relative to the marginal benefit of driving a car.

Prices, wages, taxes, and subsidies are examples of economic incentives that influence either the expected benefits or expected costs of a decision. Ethanol is an excellent example of the potency of an incentive, in this case in the form of a government subsidy, to alter decision-making. An ethanol subsidy effectively reduces the cost to produce ethanol. This artificial reduction in the cost to produce ethanol radically alters the marginal cost-benefit analysis and the corresponding decision-making in many industries. The consequences of the recent ethanol subsidy have been documented by various organizations including the United Nations, which recently blamed the incentive for producing a global food shortage because of the large quantities of corn needed to produce ethanol (BBC News, 2008).

Incentives can be characterized as either positive or negative in terms of encouraging or discouraging a decision to engage in a particular behavior. The example of the ethanol subsidy is a positive incentive designed to encourage the production and utilization of biofuels. Incentives can also be utilized in prohibitive ways that discourage production and consumption. Negative incentives operate by increasing the marginal cost or decreasing the marginal benefit. User fees, pollution taxes, and fines are all examples of negative incentives. The fact that people generally respond to incentives in predictable ways is a powerful concept that completes the framework for decision-making. Scarcity forces individuals to choose between alternatives. An effective decision-making framework for dealing with the condition of scarcity includes understanding trade-offs, identifying costs and benefits, thinking on the margin, and recognizing the role of incentives.

Teaching about Choice

Human beings cope with the condition of scarcity through the process of choosing. The decision-making framework just discussed is one way of dealing with choice in situations of scarcity. A number of strategies can highlight this decision-making framework. An interesting way to illustrate the ubiquitous nature of decision-making and the nature and components of choices is to ask students to record 10 decisions they have already made that day. To get students started, a few examples could be provided, followed by a brief discussion of their responses. The strategy behind this simple list is to engage students by personalizing the content before moving into the instructional aspect. From these lists, students will be able to identify the trade-offs, the opportunity costs, the marginal nature of their decisions, and the incentives involved in the decision-making process.

The following are additional suggestions for teaching about choice specific to postsecondary and secondary-level students. Postsecondary students could be assigned to ind and summarize an article related to marginal cost-benefit analysis or incentives. Another teaching strategy would be to have students read *Psychology of Economic Behavior* (Wolozin, 2002), discuss the topic of rational thinking, and contrast the author's conclusion about what traditional economic decision-making involves.

Students could participate in a classroom simulation of the Prisoner's Dilemma and identify the incentives to either cooperate or defect. A simple in-class version of this simulation utilizing playing cards demonstrates the decision-making process (Holt & Capra, 2000). An online version of the Prisoner's Dilemma offers an alternative format in which the students individually play the game against a computer (Daniels, n.d.). The objective of these simulations is to provide students with a hands-on experience with decision-making.

Secondary-level students need practice identifying trade-offs, recognizing opportunity costs, and assigning costs and benefits in the decision-making process. The National Council on Economic Education (NCEE) (http://www.ncee.net/resources) and the Foundation for Teaching Economics (FTE) (http://www.fte.org) have excellent lesson plans for secondary-level students. NCEE lessons are located on the EconEd-Link website, which contains an extensive database of lesson plans searchable by grade level and topic. *Keep Your Eye on the Margin: A Lesson on Marginal Analysis* (Crain, 2004) is an example of a lesson plan that provides students with an opportunity to explore thinking on the margin. FTE also has a variety of proven lesson plans that focus on active learning and real-world applications, with teacher resources located on its website. *Lesson One: Scarcity and Choice* (Foundation for Teaching Economics, n.d.), provides an excellent lesson plan that incorporates the fundamental structure of decision-making into a well-formulated lesson. These activities provide both practice in applying the decision-making framework and examples of quality instruction.

FACTORS OF PRODUCTION

Managing the condition of scarcity is the basic premise for the study of economics. The ability to fulfill the wants of an individual or a society, also known as the standard of living, is dependent on the capacity to produce goods and services. A country's capacity to produce goods and services is directly related to the availability of resources. The term "resources" has a fairly broad definition and includes any input used to generate another good or service. The variety, quality, and quantity of inputs are critical to the production process and the ensuing fulfillment of human wants. Inputs to the production process are typically categorized into four areas: land, labor, capital, and entrepreneurship. The manner in which these factors of production are utilized in the production of goods and services represent what is available to meet the wants of people.

Land

Land is a large category that encompasses the natural resources of the environment, often referred to as "gifts of nature." These types of inputs exist prior to and without human effort. Arable land, minerals, fossil fuels, water, and forests are examples of land inputs that can be utilized in the production of other goods and services. For example, the quality and availability of soil greatly influences the production of food. Deposits of copper and aluminum are extracted and incorporated into the production of assemblies ranging from computer chips to aircraft engines.

Labor

Labor is the mental and physical effort of people in the production of goods and services. Labor is produced when people develop code for a new video game, operate a printing press, or drive a school bus, among other efforts. All of these activities represent the various contributions of labor to produce goods and services. Investment in training and education are keys to improving the quality of labor and thus the productive capabilities of a country. The strong correlation between the quality of labor and standard of living is well documented and a focus of economic development in many countries (Ratner & Siems, 2006).

Capital

Capital represents the equipment and structures utilized in the production process. Tools, machines, office buildings, and factories are all examples of capital that are needed to produce goods and services. The decisions to invest in improvements and new technology have the potential to create more goods and services in the future. Capital also plays an important role in economic development and, in the long term, can substantially influence living standards (Ratner & Siems, 2006).

Entrepreneurship

Entrepreneurship is the process of innovatively combining land, labor, and capital to produce goods and services. The development of new opportunities in the production of goods and services often occur due to unique and creative combinations of land, labor, and capital. The importance of entrepreneurship is demonstrated when small business is credited with being a driver of U.S. economic growth. In addition, a recent report by the Global Entrepreneurship Monitor highlights the correlation between economic development and entrepreneurship worldwide (Bosma, Jones, Autio, & Levie, 2007). The role of each factor of production contributes to the output of goods and services in providing individuals with the opportunity to fulfill their economic wants.

Teaching about Factors of Production

Land, labor, capital, and entrepreneurship are the building blocks of the production process and ensure that goods and services are available to meet the wants of a society. The resource side of the scarcity issue is one that students may not be as

amiliar with in comparison to their obvious role as consumers. Teaching suggestions
or the postsecondary level could involve students considering the key role of the
ntrepreneur in economic development by having them read the article *Innovative
Entrepreneurs Drive Economic Growth* (Chumra, 2005) and summarize the key points
n relationship to the factors of production. Also having students access the Global
Entrepreneur Monitor website (*http://www.gemconsortium.org*) to review the 2006
Financing Report and explore the connection between capital formation and entrepreneurship is a viable teaching option for postsecondary students. The objective of these
activities is to connect the factors of production to real-world applications that
profoundly affect the economic development of individual countries.

At the secondary level, students often find studying the factors of production to be
abstract and of low relevance to their lives. Teaching suggestions at this level might
include conducting a simple production process simulation to connect students to the
important interaction of land, labor, and capital. Widget Production, Lesson Seven
(ECONnections, 2003) provides a good description of a simple production simulation.
The discussion question can be adapted to fit a high school audience with a focus on
the application of the factors of production. Researching a local entrepreneur and
preparing a presentation describing the innovative or unique combination of land,
labor, and capital used to develop the product or service that the entrepreneur created
is another teaching opportunity for use with secondary students. The objective of
these activities is to introduce the production process, stress the importance of the
inputs that go into the production process, and increase awareness of the role of the
entrepreneur.

RESOURCE ALLOCATION DECISION-MAKING

The collective wants of human beings far outpace the limited resources available to
satisfy those wants. The production process combines land, labor, capital, and entrepreneurship to produce goods and services. The issue of scarcity, however, cannot be
avoided regardless of the quality of decision-making or the quantity of goods and
services produced. The essential issue becomes a matter of deciding how best to
allocate scarce resources among people. This is the fundamental premise of economics
and is characterized by three key questions: (1) What to produce? (2) How best to
produce? (3) For whom to produce? Scarcity requires every society to answer these
three questions regardless of each country's resource endowment, the size of its
population, or its political structure. The broad diversity in living standards throughout the world is a reflection of how each country has answered these three questions,
which are discussed next.

What to Produce?

The question of what should be produced in a country will be answered by who
owns and controls the resources of land, labor, capital, and entrepreneurship.

Ownership of the factors of production is generally divided between two groups: individuals and governments. The relative mix of resource ownership within a given country, often characterized as the economic system, provides important clues to how the country is organized politically and the degree to which individuals and the government share economic power. Economic systems are typically characterized by the concentration of economic power, reflected in ownership of productive resources, between individuals and government. One way to look at the division of ownership and, consequently, economic power is to think of a continuum in which government owns all the factors of production at one extreme and individuals own all the factors of production at the other extreme. The situation in which ownership and control of the factors of production lie exclusively in the hands of government is commonly known as a command economy. In the other extreme, known as a market economy, ownership lies exclusively with individuals. In reality, there are very few examples of countries at either extreme. More commonly, economies have a combination of government and individual ownership of the factors of production, and consequently both groups make decisions about what to produce. These types of systems are termed mixed economies and can be visualized as being located more toward the middle of the continuum. When the mix between government and individual ownership of the factors of production are more heavily weighted on the side of government, the economy would be located closer to the command side of the continuum. Mixed economies with a heavier concentration of individual ownership of the factors of production would be located closer to the market side of the continuum. In all three classifications, the decision about what goods and services to produce is contingent on both the availability of resources and the quality of the decision-making entities, be they individuals or governments.

How Best to Produce?

The second allocation question deals with how best to produce goods and services in an environment of scarcity. The concept of "best" refers to the desire to make the most out of the available resources. The objective is to maximize limited resources in a manner that produces the greatest output of goods and services. The term "efficiency" is generally used when discussing how best to utilize resources in the production process. An efficient use of the factors of production is dependent on the quantity and quality of land, labor, capital, and entrepreneurship utilized in producing goods and services. How countries answer this complex question determines the standard of living available to their inhabitants. Economic development is an effort to improve the inputs in the production process to enhance the efficiency in which goods and services are produced. This enhanced efficiency can be in the form of developing new extraction methods for acquiring and utilizing natural resources, developing greater skill levels in the workforce, providing greater access to equipment and facilities, and providing an appropriate environment where innovative ideas can result in development of new and improved goods and services (Ratner & Siems, 2006).

ʾor Whom to Produce?

The last fundamental question to consider is who will actually have access to the ;oods and services produced within a country. How will the output of the economy be distributed among the people? In other words, who gets what? This is the definitive allocation question, and every society develops mechanisms and institutions to determine the distribution of goods and services throughout its economy. In general, income and prices are utilized to allocate resources among the people. How income and prices are determined answers the allocation question. Within a command economy, a central planning authority makes decisions regarding the allocation of economic output by setting prices for goods, services, and wages. In a market economy, the interaction of supply and demand in the marketplace determines prices for goods, services, and wages. In a mixed economy, allocation of goods and services is determined by a combination of the marketplace and governmental institutions.

The answers to the economic questions of what to produce, how to produce, and for whom to produce influence the level of the living standards a country achieves. The diversity of global living standards reflects both the challenge of responding to the issue of scarcity and the array of decision-making combinations between government institutions and market mechanisms for the allocation of resources.

Teaching about Resource Allocation

Resource allocation decision-making involves application of the basic economic concepts of scarcity and choice to the issues of production. Exploring resource allocation in other countries provides an opportunity for students to evaluate a country's ability to meet the needs of its people. Many good examples of resource allocation simulations will give students a hands-on experience of the challenges in developing mechanisms for distributing scarce resources and goods and services. Postsecondary-level teaching suggestions include conducting a simulation on the allocation of communication licenses using a non-price allocation method entitled *Rent Seeking and the Inefficiency of Non-market Allocations* (Goeree & Holt, 1997). Exploring the correlation between living standards and the quality of governance through the use of the World Bank's Worldwide Governance Indicators is another postsecondary teaching idea (Kaufmann, Kraay, & Mastruzzi, 2006). Reviewing and discussing the essay *Command Economy* (Erikson, 2008), which reviews the basic allocation methods of a command economy and explores the demise of the former Soviet Union, is another teaching option.

At the secondary level, students are encouraged to explore specific allocation methods including price and non-price mechanisms and the costs and benefits of each. Suggestions for teaching about resource allocation include students reflecting and writing about their own personal experiences with resource allocation in terms of how the process operates within their families. Examples for consideration might include ways in which families allocate resources such as Internet access, video games, lawn mowing, who sits in the front seat of the car, and who has priority for selecting TV programs to watch. The Foundation for Teaching Economics provides a video demonstration of the different allocation methods and an interesting case study, accessible via the FTE website. FTE also has an interesting instructional unit "The Demise of the Former Soviet Union" that examines the use of a central planning authority to allocate resources. The unit is also available on the website and contains a number of effective lessons on comparative economic systems and resource allocation. "Comparative Economic Systems" is another excellent resource for comparing economic systems and can be found on the EconEdLink site (http://www.econedlink.org/lessons/index.cfm?page=teacher&lesson=EM322). The objective of these activities is to apply the concepts of resource allocation to personal lives and understand their application and effects in societal applications.

SUMMARY

Economics is the study of how to allocate scarce resources to meet the unlimited needs and wants of society. This chapter presented the basic concepts of scarcity, choice, and allocation, and highlighted teaching suggestions to engage students in the basic content of the material.

The first section discussed the basic tension between the unlimited wants of individuals and the reality of limited resources. The condition of scarcity forces individuals and societies to choose between alternatives. The second section discussed the basic framework for decision-making that includes recognizing trade-offs, defining the cost of a decision in terms of what was given up, identifying the marginal costs and benefits in evaluating trade-offs, and exploring the power of incentives to influence decisions. The third section discussed the production of goods and services in terms of inputs to the production process. These inputs, known as the factors of production, are critical in producing goods and services. The factors of production are generally divided into the four categories of land, labor, capital, and entrepreneurship. The fourth section covered the allocation of goods and services produced throughout a society's economy. Three fundamental questions are considered in the allocation concept: what to produce, how to produce, and for whom to produce. The manner in which a country addresses these fundamental questions determines, to a great extent, the standard of living available to its inhabitants.

The concept of allocating scarce resources is the fundamental basis upon which economics is grounded and is the foundation on which all economic theory rests. An understanding of scarcity, the decision-making process, and issues of allocation provide students with a solid basis upon which to apply economic theory to their own lives and to understand the broader world.

REFERENCES

BBC News. (2008). World Bank tackles food emergency. Retrieved April 14, 2008, from http://news.bbc.co.uk/2/hi/business/7344892.stm

Bosma, N., Jones, K., Autio, E., & Levie, J. (2007). Global Entrepreneurship Report, Executive Summary. Retrieved April 20, 2008, from http://www.gemconsortium.org/download/1210605403829/GEM_2007_Executive_Report.pdf

Castronova, E. (2006). Why abundance sucks, and other unexpected lessons of the game economy. Retrieved June 20, 2008, from http://www.wired.com/wired/archive/14.04/gecon.html

Chumra, M. (2005). Innovative entrepreneurs drive economic growth; Entrepreneurs in middle income countries play catch-up, tap into New Technologies. Retrieved April 20, 2008, from http://www3.babson.edu/Newsroom/Releases/globalgem11206release.cfm

Crain, C. (2004). Keep your eye on the margin: A lesson on marginal analysis. Retrieved April 20, 2008, from http://www.econedlink.org/lessons/index.cfm?lesson=EM571&page=teacher

Daniels, M. (n.d.). Prisoner's dilemma. Retrieved April 20, 2008, from http://www.princeton.edu/~mdaniels/PD/PD.html

ECONnections, McGraw-Hill. (2003). Lesson 7, Widget production. Retrieved May 10, 2008, from http://www.e-connections.org/lesson4/widget.pdf

Ericson, R. (2008). Command Economy. Retrieved May 10, 2008, from http://econ.la.psu.edu/~bickes/rickcommand.pdf

Foundation for Teaching Economics (n.d.). Lesson One: Scarcity and Choice. Retrieved May 10, 2008, from http://www.fte.org/teachers/programs/efl/lessons/lesson1.htm

Goeree, J., & Holt, C. (1997). Rent seeking and the inefficiency of non-market allocations. *Southern Economic Journal, 65,* 603-610.

Holt, C., & Capra, M. (2000). Classroom Games: A Prisoner's Dilemma. *Journal of Economic Education, 31*(3), 229-236.

Kaufmann, D., Kraay, A., & Mastruzzi, M. (2006). Governance Matters V: Aggregate and Individual Governance Indicators for 1996-2006. World Bank Policy Research Department Working Paper No. 4280. Washington, DC: World Bank.

Kroll, L. (2008). Special report: The world's billionaires. Retrieved March 5, 2008, from http://www.forbes.com/lists/2008/03/05/richest-people-billionaires-billionaires08-cx_lk_0305billie_land.html

Leets, D., & Lopus, J. (2003). Ten Observations on High School Economics Textbooks. Retrieved March 5, 2008, from http://www.csufresno.edu/cerecc/documents/leet_Ten_Observations_HS_textbooks.pdf

Mankiw, G. (2006). *Principles of microeconomics.* Mason, OH: South-Western Thomson Learning.

McAfee, R. (2006). Introduction to economics. Retrieved January 20, 2008, from http://www.introecon.com

Ratner, A., & Siems, T. (2006). Strengthening globalization's invisible hand: What matters most? *Business Economics, 41,* 45-46.

Sexton, R. (2002). *Exploring economics*. Mason, OH: South-Western Thomson Learning.

Sowell, T. (1993). Student loans. In *Is reality optional? and other essays*. San Francisco: Hoover Institution Press.

Tierney, J. (1990). Betting on the planet. Retrieved May 10, 2008, from http://courses.washington.edu/anwr/readings/BettingonthePlanet.pdf

Wolozin, H. (2002). The individual in economic analysis: Toward a psychology of economic behavior. *Journal of Socio-Economics, 31*, 45-57.

Economic Systems and Institutions

Martha C. Yopp
University of Idaho
Boise, Idaho

Allen Kitchel
University of Idaho
Moscow, Idaho

Societies at different levels of maturity and under the control of unique political structures develop various forms of economic systems based on the decision-making process used to allocate limited resources. The United States has developed the free enterprise system of economic decision-making. In order to function as conscientious active citizens, students need to understand the important characteristics and benefits of the U.S. free enterprise system and the institutions that enable it to function. They also should be able to compare and contrast these characteristics with other economic systems. This chapter reviews relevant achievement standards and examines the functions, types, and advantages and disadvantages of different types of economic systems. In addition, the chapter will discuss economic institutions and the role of the entrepreneur as an important component in the free enterprise economic processes of production and distribution. Identification of best practice teaching methods and references to quality teaching materials support the chapter's concepts.

TEACHING ABOUT ECONOMIC SYSTEMS—WHY AND HOW

The breakup of the Soviet Union, the collapse of communism in Eastern Europe, the ascendance of globalization, and the free market reforms underway in many nations exemplify the changing economic environment in which U.S. citizens and businesses must compete. Successful competition requires citizens to understand the functions of the U.S. economic system and their interaction with other economies. Traditional pedagogical approaches to this topic may not capture the variety and complexities of the economic environment that is present in the world today. A comparative systems approach can better address these issues and provide benefits for students. A comparative systems approach asks students to consider some fundamental questions:

- What is the economic basis and consequence for private or public ownership of land and other productive resources?

- What are the advantages and disadvantages of centralized and decentralized decision-making in an economy?

- What is the appropriate extent of and what are the appropriate limits to competition and legislated forms of cooperation in an economy?

- What should be the basic functions of government in a market economy, particularly concerning public goods, market failures, and externalities?

- What can or should the government do in an economy when people demand economic security and employment for low-income families?

- How much inequality of income is acceptable in a labor market where workers are free to make decisions about human capital investments and their careers?

Many tools are available to enhance the study of economic systems and institutions. Internet resources allow students to explore, compare, and contrast attributes of economies around the world. Current statistical data can be accessed from sources such as The Heritage Foundation (www.heritage.org/index), The World Bank (www.worldbank.org), and the Federal Reserve System (www.federalreserve.gov).

Controversies exist about economic systems that can help generate interest and enthusiasm for the study of this topic; controversial issues include those related to the limits of economic freedom in markets, the influence of religion, and government involvement and control. Discussions of current economic events occur daily through the news media and provide another opportunity to engage students in the study of economic systems and institutions.

In response to the need for up-to-date information for teaching economic systems at the secondary level, the National Council on Economic Education commissioned a publication entitled *Focus: Economic Systems*, which is a valuable tool in the teaching of economic systems (McCorkle, Meszaros, Odorzynski, Schug, Watts, & Horwich, 2001). In the preface, the authors write that they hope the text will assist teachers who want to teach about one of the most enduring questions of all human history: What kind of economic system delivers the goods and the way of life that people want most? The answer to this question will shape the economic and political environment in the future as it has in the past.

Educational Standards

Education in the United States is based on standards that promote rigor, consistency, and accountability. Toward that end, teachers can design and defend activities and lessons that align with National Council on Economic Education (NCEE, 2000) and National Business Education Association (NBEA) standards (2007). NCEE's Content Standard 3: Economic Systems states, "Students will understand that: Different methods can be used to allocate goods and services. People, acting individually or collectively through government, must choose which methods to use to allocate different kinds of goods and services" (NCEE, 2000, p. 5).

Content Standard 3 is divided into benchmarks that students should reach by the completion of grade 4, grade 8, and grade 12. These benchmarks can serve as the basis for developing objectives and measurable outcomes for students in elementary school, middle school, and high school.

NBEA achievement standards for teaching economic systems and institutions (National Business Education Association, 2007) include the following—

- Explain why societies develop economic systems, identify the basic features of different economic systems, and analyze the major features of the U.S. economic system;

- Analyze the role of core economic institutions and incentives in the U.S. economy;

- Analyze the role of government in economic systems, especially the role of government in the U.S. economy;

- Apply economic concepts when making decisions for an entrepreneurial venture;

- Analyze how forms of business ownership, government regulations, and business ethics affect entrepreneurial ventures.

Historical Perspective

Before the advent of modern societies, there was little, if any, specialization or division of labor. Without division of labor, the family served as the primary economic unit, meaning that it was essentially self-sufficient, providing and managing all elements of production in order to satisfy its needs and wants (Stephens, Leach, Jones, & Taggart, 1998). As societies evolved and distribution systems emerged, individuals, families, and communities began to specialize in those activities in which they were most efficient (Heilbroner & Millberg, 2008).

Division of labor or specialization results in economic efficiency because economic units focus production resources on the activities they do best or at a competitive advantage. The resulting increase in productivity improves the lives of individuals and society as a whole, while at the same time increasing interdependence upon each other. This interdependence is the root of the rise of economics and economic systems. Economics is the study of "the process of providing for the material well-being of society" (Heilbroner & Millberg, 2008, p. 1) and examines the ways in which society answers questions related to production and distribution of goods and services, which in turn influence the type of economic system in place.

ECONOMIC SYSTEM FORMATION

The type of economic system is defined by how a country's economy is organized and by how it uses and controls its productive resources. Scarcity of productive resources, including natural resources, labor resources, and capital resources, necessitates that every country have a formal structure in place to answer three important economic questions.

Economic systems are determined by the way a society answers three basic economic questions: what to produce, how to produce, and for whom will products be produced (Arnold, 1999; Rosser & Rosser, 2004). A fourth question, how are these decisions made, is embedded within each of the three basic economic questions (Stiglitz, 2000):

- What to produce? No nation can produce every good it wants in the quantity it would like. Countries must make production choices. The choices made dictate the products produced as well as the products not produced.

- How to produce? Society must identify the resources used, the forms of production, and who will do the producing, e.g., to produce privately or publicly.

- For whom to produce? Decisions related to taxing, welfare programs, and public versus private goods determine who will be able to obtain the products produced (Stiglitz, 2000).

TYPES OF ECONOMIC SYSTEMS

An economic system can be thought of as "a set of institutions for decision making and for the implementation of decisions concerning production, income, and consumption ..." (Gregory & Stuart, 2004, p. 19). Economists refer to three types of theoretical systems: traditional, command, and market economies (Heilbroner & Millberg, 2008; Pennington, 2003; Rosser & Rosser, 2004). When forming a conceptual framework about economic systems, it is not only valuable to understand the theoretical description of each, but also to recognize that real systems are mixed economies and include elements from more than one theoretical system (Gardner, 1998).

Traditional Economies

In a *traditional* economic system, economic decisions are made locally, and production and distribution rely on historical procedures and the influence of customs and beliefs. Trade is facilitated through barter, fathers pass their jobs on to their sons, men and women specialize in unique endeavors, and the production problem is addressed before the distribution problem.

Traditional economies exist in the rural parts of developing countries and affect approximately four billion people, mainly Indians, Chinese, Latin Americans, and Africans (Hart, 2006). In these economies, the family or local community produces most of its own goods, they meet their basic needs directly from nature, and they do not rely on modern forms of currency (Hart, 2006; Smith, 2000). Traditional systems are limited in their ability to coordinate economic activities and cannot serve the needs of dynamic and growing economies (Gardner, 1998).

Command Economies

In a *command* economy, a central government authority controls the forces of production and distribution by determining what, how, and for whom products will be produced. Command economies emerge when a traditional system is taken over by a central power that dictates how productive resources are used and how products are distributed. This control can increase society's production and distribution capability, as was evidenced by the ability of the government to create the great civilization of ancient Egypt with all its roads, temples, and pyramids (Heilbroner & Millberg, 2008).

Within these systems, the degree of government control and the types of incentives vary. Two forms of command economies are planned socialism and market socialism. Planned socialism involves governmental ownership of the factors of production, with decision-making based on a central plan and the desires of the controlling authority. Market socialism involves governmental ownership of the factors of production but differs from planned socialism in that decision-making is decentralized and directed by market forces (Gardner, 1998; Gregory & Stuart, 2004).

Market Economies

In a *market economy,* otherwise known as capitalism or free enterprise, there is limited or no central governing authority that dictates the economic activities of the population. Instead, market forces of supply and demand created by buyers and sellers provide signals that trigger decisions by individuals related to the production and distribution of goods and services. Individuals and private organizations are free to decide what, how, and for whom products will be produced, and do so based on how they interpret market signals. Characteristics of a market economy include the following:

- Private ownership has control of the factors of production.

- Decentralized decision-making mechanisms reside with the owners of the factors of production.

- Market forces provide information for decision-making.

- Participants are motivated by material incentives.

- Democratic political institutions determine public choices (Gregory & Stuart, 2004).

Market economies are based on the premise that each entity should be free to determine its own economic choices and that its decisions will be influenced by supply and demand for goods and services (Heilbroner & Millberg, 2008). Individual freedom to make decisions about resource allocation is a precondition for economic success in a market economy (Gardner, 1998).

Mixed Economies

In reality, economies are *mixed economies* whereby some economic activities are market based and some are controlled by government (Guell, 2007). The U.S. economic system is a mixed economy containing many elements of a market economy that empowers individuals to make decisions, while concurrently employing some elements of a command economy in order to provide an equitable and safe environment for people to engage in economic activity. Elements of a command economy in the U.S. system include the government's role in controlling, regulating, and providing citizens with court-enforced legal rights, national defense, education, homeland security, welfare and social services, interstate highways, and other needed goods and services that would not be effectively provided for through free market activities (Stiglitz, 2000).

Alternate Economies

In some of the world's developing economies, religion is a dominant influence on economic activities. These traditional or *alternate* economies are a mixture of traditional, market, and command forces that conform to the dictates of the dominant religion. Examples of new traditional economies include Buddhist economies, Hindu economies, and Islamic economies, although others may exist (Gregory & Stuart, 2004; Rosser & Rosser, 2004).

SHIFTING ECONOMIC SYSTEMS

Recent history has seen numerous command economies integrate features of the market system. An example is Russia, which was declared a market economy in 2002 (Gregory & Stuart, 2004); however, it should be noted that Russia maintains more features of a command economy than most western nations. These emerging economies, or economies in transition, have many opportunities and challenges. As evidenced by the demise of the Soviet Union in 1991, highly centralized authoritarian command economies tend to be inefficient because of a lack of competition among industry and agricultural production units and a lack of innovative activities by workers. As these emerging economies adopt market approaches, they have the opportunity to see the benefit that competition and innovation can have on productivity and ultimately the standard of living of the population (Gregory & Stuart, 2004).

In order for economies in transition to take advantage of the opportunities provided by adopting market economic attributes, challenges must be overcome. Examples of these challenges include major structural adjustments such as the creation f nongovernmental institutions for conducting economic activity, the introduction of a high degree of transparency for economic and political institutions, the transfer of state assets to private ownership, and the creation of an environment that permits private enterprise and multiple political parties (Estes, 2007).

Index of Economic Freedom

The degree of economic freedom within an economy determines the extent to which the economic system can improve the lives of the citizens though economic efficiency and increased productivity. The Heritage Foundation/Wall Street Journal's *Index of Economic Freedom* has documented the role that economic opportunity plays in economic prosperity (The Heritage Foundation and Dow Jones & Company Inc., 2008). The index is composed of 10 measures: business freedom, trade freedom, fiscal freedom, government size, monetary freedom, investment freedom, financial freedom, property rights, freedom from corruption, and labor freedom. A review of the 2008 ranking shows that the top five individual country ratings from highest to lowest are Hong Kong, Singapore, Ireland, Australia, and the United States. A general conclusion is that economic freedom is positively correlated with economic performance and the level of prosperity of a given country.

The U.S. Free Enterprise System

Each economic system has strengths and weaknesses. A society's values, traditions, and goals will influence which elements from each system are adopted to form the framework of a country's economic system. Freedom to own, use, and exchange property for economic gain is an important characteristic of the U.S. free enterprise system. The interaction and existence of buyers, sellers, and competition is a stimulus for greater productivity and leads to economic efficiency. This efficiency arises from the influence that price has on decisions involving production and consumption made by workers, businesses, and consumers.

The U.S. free enterprise system is characterized by the right to own private property, the right to dispose of private property through individual self-interest, competition, a price system determined between buyers and sellers, and limited government regulation (Lopus & Willis, 2003). Over time, the existence of private ownership and the profit motive promote entrepreneurship, self-reliance, and responsibility in people. Competitive labor markets reward education, hard work, and performance. Financial institutions encourage saving, which in turn allows them to lend money that helps other businesses to grow and expand.

Teaching about Types of Economic Systems

Lopus and Willis (2003) devote a chapter to economic decision-making with an activity on Economic Systems that explains to students the different ways of classifying economic activities. The chapter includes a visual on economic systems and suggests dividing the class into small groups to categorize group-allocation decisions by the type of economic system. For example, if the group decides to sell an item to the highest bidder, it would be a market economy. If the group lets one person decide what to buy or sell, it would be a command economy. If the group decides to allocate resources based on what has been done in the past, it may resemble a traditional system (Lopus & Willis, 2003).

A comprehensive instructional tool for teaching about economic systems is the McCorkle text commissioned by the NCEE, which includes 12 individual lessons on Teaching Economic Systems (McCorkle et al., 2001). Other resources and lessons that have appropriate teaching ideas and activities for students in grades K-2, 3-5, 6-8, and 9-12 are included in the NCEE Virtual Economics 2005 V.3 CD (NCEE, 2005).

It is important for learners to understand that every individual and every society must contend with the problem of scarcity. Every society must have an economic system to determine how to use its limited productive resources to answer the three basic economic questions of what, how, and for whom to produce (Day, 2006).

ECONOMIC INSTITUTIONS
The word "institution" refers to any formal or informal rules, beliefs, or behaviors that facilitate carrying out an organized activity. Markets are institutions, as are private and public institutions, called enabling institutions, that help to establish a market economy and make it work efficiently and humanely (Horwich, Leet, Odorzynski, Suiter, VanFossen, & Watts, 2003).

Economic institutions represent the constraints that shape the interaction and incentives for economic activity within an economy. These institutions include organizations tasked with collecting and studying economic data or providing a product important to the economy, as well as established cultural economic arrangements and structures. Economic institutions in the U.S. economy include households, businesses, financial institutions, government agencies, labor unions, and nonprofit organizations. Examples of economic arrangements and structures include competitive markets, the banking system, a system of property rights, types of incentives and other rules, and customs and enforcement mechanisms that affect the exchange of goods and services (Gregory & Stuart, 2004; NCEE, 2000; Rosser & Rosser, 2004; Stretton, 1999; The Library of Economics and Liberty, 2008).

Households and Businesses
Households and businesses have tremendous economic power in the United States and their economic activities are inexorably linked. Businesses study consumer behavior carefully in an effort to predict what to produce. Businesses are also consumers of products and services in the operation of their businesses. Production is important, as is the distribution system used for moving goods from production to the final consumer. The distribution system can be particularly complex as it must allow goods

o be moved from one place to another, often with several stops in between; however, they must arrive on time, in excellent condition, and at a cost that is competitive.

Governmental Institutions

The U.S. government, as well as state and local governments, play a limited role in the free enterprise system because most goods and services can be freely and efficiently produced in the private sector (Lopus & Willis, 2003). In some instances, however, government intervention is necessary. Economists and the public generally agree that the role of the government is to provide a legal system, provide public services, correct market failures, maintain competition, redistribute income, and stabilize the economy by reducing unemployment and inflation and promoting economic growth (Lopus & Willis, 2003; Rosser & Rosser, 2004). A legal system provides a structure to enforce contracts and protect property rights. The right to own and use property is one of the most basic characteristics of a market economy and represents an essential economic institution.

Providing public services is necessary when the private sector cannot adequately provide for society's needs. Public services are by definition non-excludable, meaning they are available to everyone, and non-rival, meaning no diminishment of the amount of the service available to one person results from the use of it by another. Examples of public services include national defense, law enforcement, fire fighting, roadways, clean air, and street lighting.

Markets do not always provide optimum prices and quantities of goods and services. Market failures occur due to external costs or benefits. Environmental factors such as pollution and diminished water quality are examples of external costs. If a factory disposes of its waste in the air causing pollution, it imposes costs on others and therefore does not pay for all of its production costs. External *benefits* may also exist. For example, if farmers spray their trees to get rid of pests and the spraying helps both their trees and those of everyone else in the area, the result is an external benefit to farmers and others who did not pay.

Competition is vital in a market economy because it leads to lower production costs and prices. Businesses and organizations without competition, i.e., monopolies, can have negative effects on society. Laws, in the form of antitrust legislation, empower the government to regulate monopolies and to promote free trade.

Governments redistribute income primarily through taxing mechanisms. Taxation takes portions of income from some citizens and redistributes it to others in need. The redistribution of income, or transfer of payments, occurs in the form of social welfare programs, retirement payments to federal workers and military personnel, disability payments, food stamps, Medicaid, Medicare, and agricultural subsidies. In addition to taxing, the government can redistribute income in other ways. Examples include restrictions on imports that result in a transfer of wealth from consumers to domestic producers, and agricultural restrictions that force artificially high prices and transfer wealth from consumers to farmers.

The government attempts to *stabilize* the economy and achieve steady economic growth and low levels of unemployment and inflation through fiscal and monetary policy. Fiscal policy involves taxing and spending levels by the government. Monetary policy seeks to stabilize the economy through the control of the money supply. The Federal Reserve System (discussed in more detail in Chapter 5) is the primary economic institution used for manipulating the money supply through open market operations and interest rate levels in an attempt to promote economic stability.

Taxation is a means by which the government can discourage or encourage various economic activities. High taxes discourage activities deemed to have negative effects on society, e.g., tobacco taxes. Tax incentives encourage activities deemed positive to society, e.g., for improving energy efficiency of homes.

Teaching about Economic Institutions

When teaching about the role of economic institutions, teachers can compare and contrast popular points of view to address and reflect about pros and cons of government policies that interfere with the market economy. Tax policies and the use of tax revenues are examples of topics viewed differently by many people, including politicians and even economists, and discussed in the media regularly. While addressing this topic, it is important to discuss the fiscal restrictions that exist for individuals and state and local governments that do not exist for the U.S. federal government. If the federal government chooses, it can spend without limit, incurring annual deficits that add to the national debt. This deficit spending occurs for a variety of reasons that include the need to pay for a war or to meet the demands of citizens for social services. Questions of particular relevance include asking who will have to pay for the deficit spending, what justifies passing debt to future generations, and whether there a time limit for which deficit spending can occur.

Property Rights in a Market Economy and The Role of Government in a Market Economy are lessons 4 and 5 in an NCEE publication entitled *Economics in Action: 14 Greatest Hits for Teaching High School Economics* (Lopus & Willis, 2003). These lessons are particularly well developed and will increase student understanding about economic systems and institutions.

The most comprehensive publication for teaching economic institutions at the secondary level is an NCEE publication entitled *Focus: Institutions and Markets* (Horwich et al., 2003). This publication provides teachers with new approaches for teaching

bout the role of institutions and their effects in a market economy. It contains an
ntroductory essay on institutions for building a market economy, along with 12
ndividual lessons with curriculum.

THE CIRCULAR FLOW OF ECONOMIC ACTIVITY

Economists use the *circular flow of economic activity model* to illustrate how different economic institutions, most notably businesses, government, and households,
interact in a market system. The model represents the flow of money in one direction,
and the flow of commodities of value in the other.

There are two markets within the circular-flow model in which economic transactions take place: the products (goods and services) market and the factor (factors of
production) market. Within the product market, all actors in the circular-flow model,
i.e. households, businesses, and government, buy and sell goods and services amongst
each other. For example, households buy goods and services from businesses and pay
money for those products. Households also buy services from the government
(defense, roads, education, etc.) and pay for them with taxes. The government makes
similar purchases of goods and services from businesses and households, and
businesses do likewise from households and the government.

In the factor market, the same "actors" buy and sell factors of production amongst
each other (land, labor, capital, and entrepreneurship). Households sell their labor and
entrepreneurial ideas, invest their capital, and provide natural resources (land) to both
businesses and the government in return for income in the form of payroll, salaries,
and interest and dividends. Businesses sell factors of production to the government,
and the government also provides factors of production to businesses in the form of
mineral lease rights, forestry rights, and other licenses and rights (Horwich et al., 2003;
Pennington, 2003).

Wages and Prices

Labor supply and demand determines the wages or salaries paid to workers in a
market economy. In general, the more education individuals have, and the more
specialized and in demand are the skills they offer, the higher their wages. Supply and
demand for products determine prices. In a market economy such as the U.S. free
enterprise system, the government influences prices through various forms of taxation
such as sales and excise taxes and tariffs. Although these interventions raise the price
of goods in the marketplace, there is a benefit to society in that they provide funding
for public goods and services. The way wages and prices are set in a market economy
differs from the mechanism used in other systems. In a command economy, the
government sets both wages and prices. In a traditional economic system, facilitation
of exchange occurs through non-monetary means such as barter.

Private Ownership, Profit, and Competition in a Market Economy

Private ownership, profit, and competition are all characteristics of a market economy and directly influence the flow of economic activity. These characteristics create incentives that lead to economic progress. People who use their own property tend to be more motivated and productive than workers in economies that do not have ownership rights. Profit is an incentive for business people to enter into or continue operating in a trade or industry. Free and fair competition promotes the efficient use of resources and provides an incentive for innovation, product development, and cost savings (Gwartney, Stroup, & Lee, 2005).

Teaching about the Circular Flow of Economic Activity

Simulations and hands-on activities engage students to learn about the circular flow of economic activity. Lesson 1 in *Focus: Institutions and Markets* (Horwich et al., 2003) and Lesson 10 in *Economics in Action* (Lopus &Willis, 2003) provide valuable teaching resources with hands-on activities for learning about the circular flow model.

The Horwich et al. lesson addresses markets and market systems, and it includes an excellent description of the circular flow model along with diagrams and student activities. The authors provide materials for use when time is limited that present a circular flow model that only includes households and businesses. They also provide a more in-depth approach when time is not limited that includes households, businesses, and government.

The Lopus and Willis lesson provides materials for students to read about market interactions and includes a simulation for enhancing instruction related to the circular flow model. The simulation involves transactions between households and businesses in both the products and factor markets, and allows for discussion of how the government fits into the model. Students can be divided into two groups of households and businesses. Cards that represent the factors of production are provided to the households, and businesses are provided currency in order to buy the factors of production. The goal of the businesses is to produce products and then sell them back to the households in order to generate a profit. The production of a single product unit requires the business to have a card for each of the factors of production. The goal of the households is to buy as many product units as possible using the income generated from the sale of the factors of production. At the conclusion of the simulation, teachers can use the discussion questions provided to review, clarify, and reinforce the important concepts addressed in the lesson.

ENTREPRENEURSHIP IN A MARKET ECONOMY

The U.S. economy includes millions of small businesses that employ fewer than 20 people. In fact, almost 90% of the businesses in the United States are small businesses. Men and women who own, operate, and take the risk of business ownership are known as *entrepreneurs* (Greene, 2006). Free enterprise systems promote entrepreneurship by providing material incentives, protecting private ownership and property rights, and fostering competition to control quality and value.

Entrepreneurship has many rewards, but it also involves hard work and risks. Entrepreneurs tend to invest long hours while facing the possibility of irregular and uncertain income, the loss of money, and, in worst-case scenarios, bankruptcy. Important questions that these business people must address include how to get into the business market, what products or services to sell, where to locate the business, and what form of ownership to adopt.

Business Opportunities

Purchasing an existing business is one way in which a person may become a business owner. Benefits of purchasing an existing business may include established earnings, an existing customer base, good will, and the existence of inventory and supplies. When buying an existing business, it is important to understand the financial condition and reputation of the business, as well as market conditions, in order to establish a fair purchase price.

A franchise is one type of business that entrepreneurs may purchase. A franchise is a legal agreement to operate under an established name with a recognized and identifiable product or service. Initial franchise fees may be high, and the owner must usually pay promotional fees, a percentage of the profits, and other costs to the parent organization.

As an alternative to buying a business, new business owners may elect to start their own business from scratch. Starting from scratch may have benefits in terms of start-up costs and control, but requires the entrepreneur to make all business decisions without the guidance gained from buying an existing business or a franchise. Much thought and planning should take place before deciding to start a small business (Greene, 2006).

Forms of Ownership

A sole proprietorship is a business owned exclusively by one person or family unit. This form of ownership is the least complicated and most prevalent in the United States. A sole proprietorship may be either a small or large business, although many start out as small businesses and grow over time. A serious consideration for sole proprietors is that they are accountable for all of the business debts and activities. Thus, if the business fails, the entrepreneur's private assets are subject to forfeiture in order to satisfy any business debts.

A partnership involves ownership of a business by two or more people. For partnerships to work well, each partner must understand and fulfill their responsibilities to the business. In a partnership, all partners are responsible for the business decisions of the others, as well as any debts the business incurs.

A corporation is a legal entity of its own with the legal rights of a person. Ownership is in the form of stock. Stocks represent the value of the business and voting rights. Each corporation is overseen by a board of directors, and profits are distributed as dividends to the stockholders. The management and operators of the business may or may not also be stockholders, and earn compensation through wages and benefits. The corporate form of ownership can be complicated and costly but provides the owners/investors with limited liability and the ability to raise capital. Stockholders are not personally liable for the business's debts (Greene, 2006).

More than 5.8 million small businesses contribute billions of dollars each year to the U.S. economy. They employ more workers than all of the large corporations combined. Small businesses are often more creative and flexible than their bigger counterparts. For this reason, small businesses play an increasingly important role in the U.S. economy (Greene, 2006).

SUMMARY

Economic systems and institutions represent a good starting point from which to begin a discussion about scarcity, the allocation of resources, and opportunity cost. An introduction to the characteristics of a market economy versus a command economy can facilitate a discussion for comparing and contrasting free markets with planned markets. A discussion of prices, profits, competition, and economic institutions encourages students to understand and appreciate the choices they have in terms of employment, consumer spending, and entrepreneurship. In addition to these concepts, this chapter also discussed the importance of economic incentives and the role of government in providing economic stability, the distribution of income, a legal system, public goods, and fiscal and monetary policies.

Economics is very important—more so today than perhaps ever before. The world has become an interconnected marketplace, and today's students need to know how to survive and prosper. When exposed to interesting and practical lessons and activities, students enjoy and appreciate economics. Economics relates to the real world, offers countless opportunities for exploration and inquiry, and helps students understand the U.S. economy and its interconnectedness to economies around the world.

REFERENCES

Arnold, R. A. (1999). *Economics in our times.* Cincinnati, OH: West Educational Publishing Company.

Day, H. R. (2006). *What economics is about: Understanding the basics of our economic system.* New York: National Council on Economic Education.

Estes, R. J. (2007). Developmental challenges and opportunities confronting economies in transition. *Social Indicators Research, 83*, 375-411.

Gardner, H. S. (1998). *Comparative economic systems* (2nd ed.). Orlando, FL: The Dryden Press.

Greene, C. L. (2006). *Entrepreneurship: Ideas in action* (3rd ed.). Mason, OH: South-Western Publishing Company.

Gregory, P. R., & Stuart, R. C. (2004). *Comparing economic systems in the twenty-first century* (7th ed.). Boston and New York: Houghton Mifflin Company.

Guell, R. C. (2007). *Issues in economics today* (4th ed.). New York: McGraw-Hill/Irwin.

Gwartney, J., Stroup, R. L., & Lee, D. R. (2005). *Common sense economics*. New York: St. Martins Press.

Hart, S. L. (2006). Worlds in collision. *Journal of Organizational Excellence* (summer), 13-25.

Heilbroner, R. L., & Millberg, W. (2008). *The making of economic society* (12th ed.). Upper Saddle River, NJ: Pearson/Prentice Hall.

Horwich, G., Leet, D. R., Odorzynski, S. J., Suiter, M., VanFossen, P. J., & Watts, M. (2003). *Focus: Institutions and markets*. New York: National Council on Economic Education.

Lopus, J. S., & Willis, A. M. (2003). *Economics in action*. New York: National Council on Economic Education.

McCorkle, S., Meszaros, B. T., Odorzynski, S. J., Schug, M. C., Watts, M., & Horwich, G. (2001). *Focus: Economic systems*. New York: National Council on Economic Education.

National Business Education Association. (2007). *National standards for business education: What America's students should know and be able to do in business*. Reston, VA: Author.

National Council on Economic Education. (2000). *National content standards in economics*. New York: Author.

National Council on Economic Education. (2005). Virtual economics V.3. New York: Author.

Pennington, R. L. (2003). *Economics*. Austin, TX: Holt, Rinehart and Winston.

Rosser, J. B., Jr., & Rosser, M. V. (2004). *Comparative economics in a transforming world economy* (2nd ed.). London: The MIT Press.

Smith, A. W. (2000). *Demystifying economics*. Naples, FL: Ironwood Publications.

Stephens, P., Leach, A., Jones, H., & Taggart, L. (1998). *Think sociology*. Cheltenham, United Kingdom: Nelson Thornes.

Stiglitz, J. E. (2000). *Economics of the public sector*. New York and London: W.W. Norton & Company.

Stretton, H. (1999). *Economics: A new introduction*. London: Pluto Press.

The Heritage Foundation and Dow Jones & Company Inc. (2008). *2008 index of economic freedom executive summary*. Retrieved May 29, 2008, from www.heritage.org/index

The Library of Economics and Liberty. (2008). *Economic institutions*. Retrieved May 27, 2008, from http://econlib.org/Library/Topics/HighSchool/EconomicInstitutions.html

Market Structures, Pricing, and Productivity

Paul Johnso
University of Alask
Anchorage, Alask

The global economy is characterized by the central role of markets in determining prices, production, and distribution. Markets facilitate trade, which permits specialization, and specialization is essential for productivity and economic growth. How well a particular market performs this role depends, in part, on its structure. This chapter describes the specific forms of market structure and the associated concepts of specialization, productivity, and factors of production. These concepts are part of the following economics standards from the *National Standards for Business Education* (NBEA, 2007): IV (Markets and Prices), V (Market Structures), VI (Productivity), and VIII (Global Economic Concepts). The major topics discussed in this chapter are the determination of price and quality of goods and services under the four types of market structures, the four factors that determine productivity, and globalization in the context of market structures and productivity.

MARKET STRUCTURES

Market structures, pricing, and productivity lie within the realm of microeconomics. Unlike macroeconomics, microeconomics is characterized by a high degree of agreement among economists regarding basic theory. The microeconomics of firms is the analysis of profit maximization given the constraints of production costs and consumer preferences.

Definition of Market Structure

A market's *structure* is determined by the number of buyers and sellers in the market and the degree to which individual sellers can differentiate their products from those of competitors. The study of market structure addresses questions such as these: Do individual buyers or sellers exercise a degree of influence on the market price? Does the market price and quantity differ from the socially desirable price and quantity? Should government regulate markets to create more competition?

The Four Types of Market Structure

The rationale for classifying markets by structure arises from the economic consequences for society when individual firms have a degree of influence over the price they can charge buyers. If individual firms have a significant degree of price control, the market will be less efficient than when firms are constrained by the force of competition to charge a single market price. The four types of market structure presented in this section are competitive markets, monopolies, oligopolies, and monopolistic competition.

Competitive markets. Competitive markets are markets with many buyers and sellers of an identical product. The nature of the product is such that product differentiation is not possible. *Product differentiation* has the same meaning in economics as it does in marketing—distinguishing the differences of a product in such a way as to make it more attractive to a target market than competitors' products. Within a competitive market, the intensity of competition forces all firms to sell their product at the same price. The markets for globally traded commodities are examples of a competitive market (e.g., wheat). Quality differentiation does not occur within competitive markets since, by definition, all sellers produce an identical product.

Monopolies. Monopolies occur when there is one seller and many buyers of a product. Product differentiation is unnecessary, in this case since there are no competitors. A necessary characteristic of a monopoly is that there are significant barriers to entry. *Barriers to entry* are obstacles in the path of firms that desire to enter the industry. These barriers may be regulatory or economic in nature. A power company that has been given the exclusive right to supply electricity to a city is a monopoly. Monopolies have the least incentive to provide high-quality products or services, since they have no competitors.

Oligopolies. Oligopolies are markets with sufficiently few sellers of the same product that firms have some degree of control over their own product price. A local market for gasoline is an example of an oligopoly because each gas station sells essentially the same product but still has a limited degree of control over price. Oligopolies are characterized by firms reacting to the pricing actions of competitors by changing their own prices. Oligopolies produce an identical product, so there is no product differentiation.

Monopolistic competition. Monopolistic competition exists when many sellers can successfully differentiate their own product from those of their competitors and thereby avoid having to compete only on price. Manufacturers of consumer products such as clothing and electronics use advertising, branding, and design features in this way. Monopolistic competitors have the greatest incentive to distinguish their products through higher quality.

Competitive markets are also referred to as markets with *perfect competition*, while monopoly, oligopoly, and monopolistic competition are *imperfectly competitive* markets. These definitions of market structure assume that there are many buyers. This assumption is reasonable for most goods and services markets. Labor markets sometimes have a *monopsony* structure, characterized by a single large buyer and many sellers. Workers selling their labor services to a large employer may face a situation where the buyer, not the seller, has the major influence over the price.

Classroom Lesson: An Introduction to Market Structure
The concept of market structure can be illustrated using a classroom lesson that requires students to classify industries by market structure. For high school and postsecondary classes, teams of students could be asked to give examples of local firms they patronize, such as fast-food restaurants, department stores, supermarkets, and video stores. Half the teams then rate each type of firm according to how much variation there is locally in the prices and products among competing stores. The other teams are assigned to classify each type of firm according to market structure at the national level. The importance of structure in influencing firm behavior can be demonstrated by bringing the teams together to compare and discuss their findings. For example, the proliferation of styles and labels in local clothing stores can be explained as a consequence of the monopolistically competitive nature of that industry at the national level. Middle school students are less likely to have direct purchasing experience with many local firms, but they can be asked to work through a simple classification exercise and discuss their perception of the number of different sellers in each market and the relative importance of price versus quality in their own consumer decisions.

In summary, goods and services markets have four types of structure. Competitive markets have so many buyers and sellers that firms are forced to charge the same price. Monopoly, oligopoly, and monopolistic competition are imperfectly competitive. It is under monopolistic competition that firms have the greatest incentive to compete on quality and other product characteristics.

PRICE DETERMINATION IN COMPETITIVE MARKETS
The analysis of competitive markets is the foundation of the theory of price determination in market economies. Critical elements of price determination are presented in this section.

Competitive Market Equilibrium

In a competitive market, the market price is determined by the interaction of buyers and sellers, but no individual buyer or seller is able to exert a significant influence on the price. The theory of *supply and demand* is the accepted model for explaining how prices and quantities are determined by this interaction. The supply and demand model predicts that values for prices and quantities will equal the *equilibrium* values. An equilibrium point is that price point wherein agreement between suppliers and consumers is such that all supplies of a good or service are bought, and all demand for that good or service is likewise satisfied. Equilibrium in economics is the state where economic forces have reached a balance, so that in the absence of new outside forces, there is no tendency for variables to change.

Classroom Lesson: Supply and Demand

A strategy for teaching supply and demand is to derive the *demand curve*, followed by the *supply curve*, and then place these two curves together on the same diagram and "solve for" the equilibrium price and quantity. Once students understand the concept of equilibrium in the supply and demand model, they should work through *comparative statics* exercises to learn how to apply the model to actual world markets. Comparative statics is the comparison of two economic equilibrium states, before and after the market has been "shocked" by changes in one or more economic variables.

The *demand curve* is best explained through building up from the story of a typical consumer product that is familiar to students such as music CDs. As the price for this good rises, the hypothetical consumer will choose to consume less of this product. Adding across all the consumers in the market, *quantity demanded* is inversely related to market price. This is the *law of demand*. The law of demand is represented graphically by the familiar downward sloping demand curve diagram with market price and quantity on the y (vertical) and x (horizontal) axes respectively.

Once students understand the concept of "moving along" a demand curve in response to changes in the market price, they need to learn the factors influencing the position of the demand curve, such as income, prices of related products, tastes, expectations about the future, and number of buyers (Mankiw, 2007). The supply curve should be derived through a similar argument. Supply is a more challenging concept because few, if any, students have experience as sellers in a market. As the market price rises, individual sellers will be willing to sell greater quantities of their product, and adding across sellers *quantity supplied* is positively correlated with the market price, producing the upward sloping *supply curve*. The supply curve is represented in its own diagram with market price and quantity on the y (vertical) and x (horizontal) axes respectively.

The position of the supply curve is influenced by four factors: input prices, technology, expectations about the future, and the number of sellers. Students must understand how each one shifts the supply curve, increasing or decreasing supply

(Mankiw, 2007). The supply and demand diagram in Figure 1 shows the demand curve and supply curve together, and the intersection of the curves at price P* and quantity Q*.

Figure 1. Supply and Demand Diagram

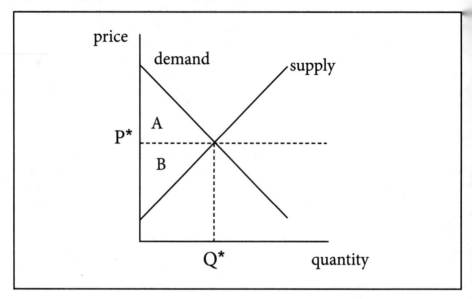

Equilibrium price. The equilibrium price P* is the price at which quantity demanded and quantity supplied are equal. If the price is higher than P*, then *excess supply* will induce sellers to offer a lower price. If the price is lower than P*, *excess demand* will cause the price to be bid up by buyers. P* is the equilibrium price since it is the only price where there is no tendency for the price to change for either the suppliers or the buyers.

Equilibrium output. The equilibrium quantity Q* is the quantity of the goods that will be bought and sold when the market price is P*. The total output of firms in this industry will be Q*. Q* is the *socially efficient* level of output because Q* maximizes the sum of *consumer surplus* and *producer surplus*. In the diagram, consumer surplus is represented by the area A and producer surplus is represented by the area B. Consumer surplus is the value buyers place on their total consumption of the good in excess of what they paid for it. Producer surplus is the revenue producers receive in excess of their total cost of production.

Classroom Lesson: A Competitive Market Auction
A classroom auction is very effective for demonstrating the concepts of demand, supply, competitive equilibrium, and surplus. Two students are assigned to serve as

auctioneers, and the remaining students are divided equally into buyers and sellers. The teacher assigns each seller and buyer a value for a hypothetical product, such as a book. For each buyer or seller, this value represents the benefit that they receive from possession of a book.

Each buyer and seller is given a unique "value." The pattern of values for buyers follows a demand curve, and sellers' values follow a supply curve. Students are only allowed to know their own value as a buyer or seller during the auction. They are not allowed to communicate privately with other students during the auction. Students are not told that this is a "demand and supply" activity—they will trade without knowing what is "supposed" to happen. Figure 2 shows an example of a set of values for 12 students or 12 teams of students with buyers' and sellers' values intersecting at a value of 6.

Figure 2. Competitive Market Auction Example Bids/Asks

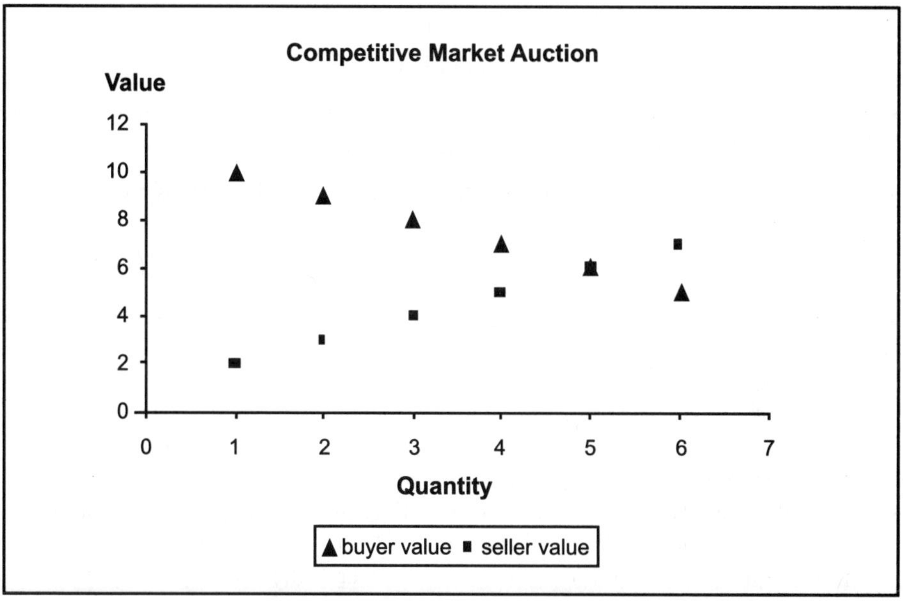

The auction has a few simple rules. There are five rounds of two minutes each. During each round, sellers can sell one book. If a book is not sold, it does not carry over to the next round. Buyers can buy only one book each round. Sellers make a profit equal to the excess of the sale price over the seller's value for a book. Buyers make a profit equal to the excess of the buyer's value over what they paid for a book. Students cannot trade at a loss. Students must keep a record of completed transactions.

The auctioneers will allow buyers and sellers to make bids (for buyers) and asks (for sellers). The current bid and ask will be displayed on the board. A new bid will only replace the current bid if it is an improving (higher) bid. Likewise, a new ask will only replace the current ask if it is improving (lower). When there is a matching bid and ask, the auctioneers announce that a trade has occurred, record the name of the buyer and seller as well as the price, clear the board of the current bid and ask, and open up trading again for the rest of the round.

If the students are motivated to achieve profit by some reward (such as a candy bar), the market price will trend toward the equilibrium value. By the end of the last round, the market price will be very close to the predicted value.

The debriefing following the auction is just as important as the activity itself. The auction results illustrate important facts about competitive markets:

- The intersection of the demand and supply curves determines an equilibrium price, and the market price will converge on that price.

- The competition for profit drives the price in the *right* direction.

- By moving books from sellers (with a low value for books) into the hands of buyers (with a high value for books), a *surplus* (new wealth) is generated for society.

- The sum of the buyers' and sellers' profits is a measure of the surplus created.

- Profits are not "exploitation"—they are the reward for participating in wealth creation.

- Buyers and sellers do not have to "know everything" and superhuman rationality is not required for the market to work.

Holt (1996) provides a further description of this classroom pit market, including a discussion of the best debriefing strategies. This auction has been used successfully with students from middle school through the postsecondary level. Middle school students will generally not be expected to learn the concept of supply and demand curves, but will still benefit from learning how trade in a market generates wealth, and how profit represents the division of new wealth and not the rearrangement of a "fixed pie."

Classroom Lesson: Comparative Statics

The analysis of a competitive market's response to external forces on supply and demand is called *comparative statics*. Students need to practice the application of the model to analyze the effects of different shocks. Once students have a clear under-standing of the nature of equilibrium in the supply and demand framework, they should work through a comparative statics lesson. The students should be divided into eight teams. Each team will be given one case to analyze and present to the class. There are nine potential permutations of change in demand and supply curves, since the demand and supply curves can each change in three ways (increase, decrease, or no change). The case where neither curve shifts is of no interest, which leaves eight permutations to solve.

The application of supply and demand to the analysis of the effects of external shocks to the market is a four-step process. Students can determine how equilibrium price and quantity will respond to a shock by answering these questions:

1. Who are affected by the shocks, buyers and/or sellers?

2. Which curves move?

3. Which directions do the curves move?

4. How does the new equilibrium price and quantity differ from the initial equilibrium price and quantity?

The students should be able to fill in Table 1 with the correct answers for predicted equilibrium price and quantity changes.

Table 1. *Comparative Statics Outcomes*			
Permutations	**Increase in supply**	**No change in supply**	**Decrease in supply**
Increase in demand	P ambiguous Q increases	P increases Q increases	P increases Q ambiguous
No change in demand	P decreases Q increases	P no change Q no change	P increases Q decreases
Decrease in demand	P decreases Q ambiguous	P decreases Q decreases	P ambiguous Q decreases

For more practice, Morton and Goodman (2003) present comparative statics problems in a graphical format, with hypothetical goods that require plotting coordinates and calculating exact numeric values for the changes in equilibrium price and quantity. The model of supply and demand is the accepted theory for explaining the determination of prices and quantities in a competitive market.

PRICE DETERMINATION UNDER IMPERFECT COMPETITION

Imperfect competition is the study of monopoly, oligopoly, and monopolistic competition.

Monopoly

A monopoly is a market with only one seller. There are several reasons why a market may be a monopoly:

- Average costs of production continuously decrease with production volume;

- Government regulation protects a monopolist from competition;

- A single firm controls a key resource.

A monopolist's output is the entire supply in the market, and so this firm sets the market price through its choice of output quantity. If a monopolist increases the quantity supplied (and demand is not changing), the market price will fall. A monopolist's output quantity will be lower than the socially optimal level. By keeping the price high, the monopolist will gain more than enough profit to offset the profit forgone by producing at a level below the socially optimum output. In an attempt to minimize the efficiency loss to society from monopolies, governments have implemented antitrust laws and regulatory policies. The U.S. Department of Justice and the Federal Trade Commission enforce antitrust law. The principal statutes and their purposes are as follows:

- The Sherman Act prohibits the formation of a monopoly, whether individually or in combination with competing firms.

- The Clayton Act prohibits anticompetitive actions, including mergers that may substantially lessen competition.

- The Federal Trade Commission Act prohibits "unfair" competition. Subsequently, the Robinson-Patman Act strengthened the Clayton Act's prohibition on price discrimination

When government regulatory bodies should apply anti-trust regulation is controversial. The "structural" approach to antitrust equates a small number of firms in a market with a concentration of economic power and the ability to extract excess profits. The Chicago School views the objective of antitrust policy as a way to accomplish economic efficiency. This view allows that there may be sound economic reasons for having a small number of firms in an industry. Hemphill (2005) discusses the challenges of applying antitrust law in the modern economy.

Oligopoly

In an oligopoly a small number of firms sell identical products. An oligopolist has to take into account rivals' reactions if it should change its own product's price. The oligopolists in a market will maximize their joint profits if they can cooperate in such a way as to act as a single monopoly. The challenge for the members of this coalition (or *cartel*) is how to cooperate in pricing without violating antitrust laws proscribing price collusion. One solution is for the *market leader* (usually the largest firm) to set a price. If the other oligopolists follow this firm and set the same price, they are acting as a cartel even though no inter-firm communication (collusion) has occurred.

Monopolistic Competition

Under monopolistic competition there are many sellers with differentiated products. Monopolistic competition is the closest type of competition to the everyday retail experiences of students. Each firm has the option to create a price premium for its product by differentiating its products according to the principles of business marketing. Differentiation can be achieved through modifying the attributes of the product itself, branding and otherwise promoting a product, or having a superior product distribution system. Under monopolistic competition, total output is below the social optimum. On the other hand, consumers benefit from the variety of product choices and the competitive pressures on firms to differentiate their products through innovation and improving product quality.

Classroom Lesson: When There Is Not Pure Competition

Watts, McCorkle, Meszaros, and Schug (2001) provide an activity that requires students to evaluate the role of non-price competition and explain the tendency toward price collusion in imperfectly competitive markets. Students play the role of a buyer or seller in a market for crude oil, with the instructor gradually increasing the opportunities to collude and share information. As the market becomes less competitive, students observe the increasing price and decreasing quantity that arises from their own behavior in the market. It also includes discussion and activities regarding properties such as the interdependence of firms. Although this activity is targeted at high school, it could also be used in an introductory postsecondary course.

Imperfect competition is the study of monopoly, oligopoly, and monopolistic competition. Prices will be higher and quantities lower than in the competitive market. Monopolistic competition does provide a benefit that competitive markets do not: a greater variety of products for consumers and an incentive for firms to improve quality and design in order to differentiate themselves from competitors.

PRODUCTIVITY

Productivity is defined as output per unit of labor. When applied to the national level, it explains most of the difference in economic growth rates among nations. Productivity is determined by physical and human capital, technological knowledge, and natural resources.

Physical capital. Physical capital is the equipment and structures used to produce goods and services. Government policies can increase productivity by encouraging saving and investment to facilitate the creation of physical capital.

Human capital. Human capital is the accumulation of knowledge and skills acquired through education and on-the-job training. Public support for education contributes to the growth of human capital. A country has to save and invest in order to create human capital.

Technological knowledge. Technological knowledge of the best way to produce goods and services is created through research and development. The creation and maintenance of protection for intellectual property through patents and patent enforcement by governmental agencies encourages research through granting the innovator a limited property right over their invention. Openness to international trade and investment allows foreign resources, technology, and ideas to contribute to technological knowledge.

Natural resources. Natural resources are inputs into production that nature provides, such as land and mineral resources. Natural resources can be renewable (such as wood) or nonrenewable (such as oil). Abundant natural resources can be helpful, but they are not essential for productivity, as the example of Japan, which imports its resources from abroad, demonstrates.

Globalization and Productivity

Globalization (discussed in more detail in Chapter 6) is the integration of national economies through trade, foreign direct investment, capital flows, migration, and the spread of technology. Globalization raises living standards as countries specialize in the production of goods and services according to their *comparative advantage,* and investment flows to projects that are the most productive.

The principle of comparative advantage demonstrates that even if a country has no absolute advantage over all other countries in the production of any product, that country can still benefit from specializing in and exporting the products for which it has the lowest *opportunity cost* of production. For example, the country that can produce wheat with the lowest per unit sacrifice of other products (opportunity cost) can profitably export wheat, even though it may not have the *lowest* absolute costs of wheat production. Appleyard, Field, and Cobb (2008) provide a more detailed explanation and diagrams illustrating comparative advantage.

Factors of production will determine a nation's relative productivity across industries. As a country accumulates physical capital, human capital, and technological knowledge, it will not only become more productive overall, but also its mix of exports will shift toward products that are more technologically advanced. Globalization allows nations to best exploit their natural and acquired productive factors through specialization and trade.

Classroom Lesson: The Malthusian Fallacy

An example of the importance of technological growth is provided by the "Malthusian Fallacy." Thomas Malthus predicted that economies could not continue to grow over time because population growth would outstrip food production. While present-day students may not have been exposed to the Malthusian Fallacy in its original form, they may be exposed to the idea that large families are intrinsically wrong (or even immoral) because population growth "uses up" natural resources and causes poverty.

Morton, Shaw, and Stroup (1997) describe a structured teaching activity designed to help students gain insights into the causes and effects of population growth. Students start out with a discussion of the costs and benefits of having children, then move on to an examination of the reasons for large family size in poor countries, followed with statistics for 20 nations to analyze according to 10 specific questions. Finally, six discussion questions draw students to a data-based consideration of the hypothesis that population growth is the greatest threat to the environment and living standards. Instructors may wish to update the economic statistics for this activity.

Classroom Lesson: Comparative Advantage and Trade in a Global Economy

Lopus and Willis (2003) provide a lesson suitable for all class levels in which pairs of students engage in a role-play where one student is more productive at both of two activities. Students complete a worksheet and discover that specialization and trade can benefit everyone, not just the lowest cost producer.

A website of the Levin Institute (http://www.globalization101.org) provides excellent current news items, briefs, and materials for teachers and students to discuss multidisciplinary aspects of globalization within the context of recognizing the fundamental benefits of trade.

Productivity is determined by physical and human capital, technological knowledge, and natural resources. The principle of comparative advantage demonstrates that all nations can benefit from trade within a globalizing world.

SUMMARY

Goods and services markets are divided into competitive markets and imperfectly competitive markets. Firms in imperfectly competitive markets are classified as monopolies, oligopolies, or monopolistically competitive. Competitive market firms compete intensely on price to differentiate their products. Monopolistically competitive firms exhibit product differentiation through competition in design, quality, branding, and advertising. Monopolistic competition offers the consumer variety in product features and quality. Monopoly and oligopoly are characterized by a firm's power to raise prices above the socially efficient minimum price, and antitrust legislation is designed to curb this monopoly power.

The model of supply and demand is the basic tool for analyzing the principles of price determination in competitive markets. Students must learn how to use the comparative statics approach in order to predict the effect of external forces on the market price.

Productivity and economic growth are functions of the four factors of production: physical capital, human capital, technological knowledge, and natural resources. The principle of comparative advantage in productivity demonstrates that a country can trade profitably with the rest of the world even if it is not the lowest absolute cost producer in any particular market. The globalization of trade offers nations the opportunity to exploit their production factors to maximum advantage through engaging in production specialization through the advantages afforded through international trade.

REFERENCES
Appleyard, D. R., Field, A. J., Jr., & Cobb, S. L. (2008). *International economics* (6th ed.). New York: McGraw-Hill/Irwin.
Hamermesh, D. S. (2004). *Economics is everywhere.* New York: McGraw-Hill/Irwin.
Hemphill, T. A. (2005). Modernizing U.S. antitrust law: The role of technology and innovation. *Business Economics, 40*(2), 70-74.
Holt, C. A. (1996). Classroom games: Trading in a pit market. *Journal of Economic Perspectives 10*(1), 193-203.
Lopus, J. S., & Willis, A. (2003). *Economics in action: 14 greatest hits for teaching high school economics.* New York: National Council on Economic Education.
Mankiw, G. N. (2007). *Principles of economics.* Mason, OH: Thomson Higher Education.
Morton, J. S., & Goodman, R. (2003). *Advanced placement economics microeconomics: Student activities* (3rd ed.). New York: National Council on Economic Education.
Morton, J. S., Shaw, J. S., & Stroup, R. L. (1997). Overpopulation: Where Malthus went wrong. *Social Education, 61*(6), 342-347.
National Business Education Association. (2007). *National standards for business education: What America's students should know and be able to do in business.* Reston, VA: Author.
Watts, M., McCorkle, S., Meszaros, B. T., & Schug, M. C. (2001). *Focus: High school economics.* New York: National Council on Economic Education.
Weiner, R. (2007). Globalization101.org: A free web site for teaching about globalization. *Journal of Economic Education, 38*(2), 254.

The Role of Government

Judee A. Timm
Monterey Peninsula College
Monterey, California

In an era of rising oil prices, subprime mortgage failures, and increasing global competitive threats, the role of government in the U.S. economy has taken center stage. What is the role and purpose of the U.S. government in keeping the economy vibrant and productive? What tools are available for government to affect positive economic changes? How do the challenges created by politics, social needs, and globalization affect economic decisions?

This chapter focuses on answering these questions in the context of educating students for their future roles as consumers, entrepreneurs, and U.S. citizens. What do students need to know about our government's influence on the economy and how it affects their personal lives? What is a citizen's responsibility in a democracy to ensure that government economic policies and strategies reflect the will of the electorate? Standards of achievement developed by the National Business Education Association (NBEA) (2007) and the National Council on Economic Education (NCEE) (1997) address the competencies needed by students at various levels in honing their economic literacy skills. As noted by Federal Reserve Chairman Ben Bernanke (2008), "Financial literacy and consumer education—coupled with robust consumer protection —makes the financial marketplace effective and efficient, and better equips consumers to make tough yet smart financial decisions" (p. 1). In a society of legislators, judges, corporate executives, managers, small business owners, teachers, and voters, among others, it is imperative for each individual to understand the trade-offs, constraints, and limitations of the economic system in which they live. In other words, society needs informed and thoughtful citizens. Teaching strategies that focus on developing needed economic competencies will provide educators ideas that can be used to make economic literacy real and relevant for all Americans.

ROLE AND PURPOSE OF THE U.S. GOVERNMENT

The role and purpose of government in the U.S. economy has evolved throughout history in response to the needs, threats, and opportunities of the time. This section reviews the history that has laid the foundation for government's role in a free market society. The following discussion will also show how the creation of regulatory agencies and the development of a legal and physical infrastructure have encouraged competition, economic stability, social welfare, and innovation.

Historical Evolution

The U.S. economic system was built on the belief of individual responsibility with little government intervention. Our founding fathers supported the belief of 18th century economist Adam Smith that as long as markets were free and competitive, individuals would work together for the greater good of society (Conte & Karr, 2001). Historical events have shown that this lofty proclamation of working together for the greater good has not always been the case. Catastrophic wars, depressions, monopolies, inflation, global competition, and many other significant events have demanded a greater role for government to protect the public and provide an environment to encourage economic growth and prosperity.

The government's role in the economy expanded significantly in the 1930s with the inception of the New Deal, which aimed to give relief to the people suffering from the Great Depression. This social contract was a dramatic change from the past; new programs and laws were established to help and protect the common citizenry during desperate times. Conte and Karr (2001) noted,

> ... [these] laws regulated sales of stock, recognized the right of workers to form unions, set rules for wages and hours, provided cash benefits for the unemployed and retirement income for the elderly, established farm subsidies, insured bank deposits, and created a massive regional development authority in the Tennessee Valley (Growth of Government Intervention section, p. 2).

Many programs and agencies established during this time, such as the Securities and Exchange Commission, the Federal Deposit Insurance Corporation (FDIC), and the Federal Housing Administration, are still in operation.

Regulatory Agencies

Today more than 100 federal regulatory agencies monitor commercial activities involved in many aspects of the economy, including trade, communications, nuclear energy, product safety, medicine, employment opportunities, transportation, and banking. These agencies provide both social and economic safeguards for those who cannot protect themselves. Social safeguards refer to regulations aimed at protecting the citizenry from undue harm in the participation of economic development. These regulations have addressed many issues, including workplace safety, environmental protection, and consumer advocacy. Economic safeguards are used to foster economic stability, sustain economic confidence, and stimulate economic growth. Strategies and regulations on price controls and insured bank deposits are examples of these safeguards that have aided and controlled economic activity.

Regulatory agency board members are appointed by the President and confirmed by the Senate. In theory, agencies work independently from government, which appropriates their funding. Political pressures from congressional representatives and past administrations, however, have been known to influence public policy.

Many business and industrial leaders have voiced concerns regarding the overregulation of industries by government, feeling it is intrusive and costly. Some citizens feel that the cost of regulations has severely diminished the ability of some industries to remain competitive. This is especially true in the global arena where competitors are not held to the same standards and do not incur the same costs. As noted by Factor (2007), "The cost of compliance with federal and state regulations continues to soar. The threat of new regulations directly hurts the stock market" (p. A13).

As seen in this aforementioned discussion, economic regulations are seen as a double-edged sword. On the one hand, they aim to protect the citizenry and stimulate economic growth; on the other hand, the costs of bureaucracy and compliance can work counter to the original intent by decreasing businesses' ability to compete.

Legal and Physical Infrastructure

Another critical role of government is to provide the legal and physical infrastructure that creates an environment where markets can function successfully, leading to economic growth in the form of better jobs, improved living standards, and greater investment opportunities. Our current economy has shifted from manufacturing to technology and services. Influenced by this shift, major investments in research and development, education, communications, and technological infrastructures, as well as policies and legislation that encourage open global competition, are seen as key elements in remaining competitive in the 21st century.

Economic Stability

Providing economic stability is a key role of government today. Stabilizing price fluctuations is a daunting task especially in light of global pressures that have become increasingly prevalent in all business and consumer activities. Global competition, our reliance on foreign fossil fuel resources, currency exchange volatility, and the cost of war have all contributed to the destabilization of prices. Volatility in the stock market and housing sector and the increasing cost of oil and consumer debt have posed many challenges for the U.S. government to keep the economy growing and stable. Recent economic events have directly influenced many citizens who have seen the loss of a home, a business, a job, or entire investments. As noted by Federal Reserve Chairman Bernanke (Crutsinger, 2008), "The outlook for the economy has worsened in recent months and the downside risks to growth have increased" (p. A1). It is the government's role to "act in a timely manner to support growth and provide adequate insurance against downside risks" (Crutsinger, 2008, p. A9).

The role of the U.S. government in the 21st century economy has developed far beyond the social contract of the New Deal. Worldwide competitive, technological, and economic pressures have compelled government to provide a new social contract that not only protects and supports, but also invests in educating citizens and strengthening institutions to keep the U.S. economy competitive. By maintaining a sound infrastructure, economic stability, and appropriate regulations to support competition, the U.S. government will help prepare the country for future challenges.

Teaching Strategies

A plethora of resources and ideas are available to aid in teaching and learning about the role of the U.S. government in the economy. Information on this topic can be accessed from *The Outline of the U.S. Economy* (Conte & Karr, 2001), which is a publication offered by the U.S. Department of State (http://usinfo.state.gov/products/pubs/oecon/). But theory and content alone will not engage students to fully understand the real implications and impact of U.S. government actions on the economy. The following discussion highlights several teaching and learning strategies that include interactive websites, videos and case studies, and debates and role-playing to provide relevance and spur student interest.

Interactive websites. Many interactive websites are available for classroom use. One of the best, offered by the National Council on Economic Education, is called EconEdLink (2008) (http://www.ncee.net/resources). On this site, teachers have access to creative online lesson plans that link competency development to the NCEE standards and to current events. The lesson plans also offer video links and additional resources to add relevancy and currency to every topic. Over 530 lessons are developed and available on economic literacy topics for all age groups. Instructors have easy access to any lesson by selecting the grade level, topic, and standards in the website's search engine. For example, a search for lesson plans at the 6-8 grade levels on the topic "The Role of Government" yields several lesson plans. One such lesson plan deals with innovation and investment in transportation. This topic is specifically geared toward NBEA Standard VII, Level 2 in the Economics content area, wherein students must explain the impact of taxation on consumers and producers and identify the impact of government regulations on business, society, and the individual in an economy (NBEA, 2007).

Another resource that can be accessed from EconEdLink is an interactive website especially geared to young children called KidsBank.com (http://www.kidsbank.com). This website explains the fundamentals of money and banking including savings, checking, interest, and electronic transfers using cartoon characters that children find fun and interesting. This site is an excellent resource to help students achieve NBEA Standard VII, Level 1, wherein student performance focuses on the basics of defining money, discussing how it is used, and differentiating between earned and unearned income (NBEA, 2007).

Budget Hero (http://marketplace.publicradio.org/features/budget_hero/) is an interactive game that has students balance the federal budget by analyzing needs and values of society. This is an ideal forum for students to achieve the same NBEA Standard VII, Levels 3 and 4, which focus on the student's ability to evaluate taxes, analyze the effect of national debt or surplus on the economy, and analyze the effect of the federal deficit on the economy (NBEA, 2007).

Videos and case studies. Videos and case studies can show students the impact of government actions and regulations on the economy. For example, a case about the Textile Workers Union battle to influence the creation of public policy regarding brown lung disease (McInnis, 2008), or the run on banks seen in the movie "It's a Wonderful Life," gives students a perspective on the issues that government has to address and the impact these issues have on people's lives. By looking at historical and current events, students can gain a greater understanding of how government spending and other economic policies affect businesses and individuals. These strategies can help address NBEA Standard VII, Level 3, wherein students are able to discuss the history of banking and how government programs affect the well-being of people and businesses (NBEA, 2007).

Debates and role-playing. Arranging classroom debates and role-playing scenarios are other ways to help students recognize the thought processes and choices that go into developing governmental policy and regulations. One interesting role-play activity is to have students act as advisors to the President in developing budget considerations for the agencies they represent. One student in the role-play could serve as the President, and a panel of several students could serve on an advisory board representing different governmental agencies. Students could be asked to explore the mission, needs, and values of their agencies in an effort to provide a rationale for requesting funding. The President would need to evaluate all funding options—given finite resources—and the requests for funding in such a manner that his or her decisions can best serve society as a whole. This type of exercise specifically relates to NBEA Standard VII, Level 4, where students are able to analyze the effect of government spending on the economy (NBEA, 2007). These examples are but a sampling from numerous available resources that can be used to make learning about the role of government in the economy an educational, stimulating, interactive, and enjoyable learning experience.

TOOLS OF ECONOMIC INFLUENCE

The tools used by the U.S. government to encourage and support a vibrant economy are limited and complex. Today's economic environment is exceptionally challenging because greater efficiencies are required, global interdependence is the norm, and advanced technologies are continually changing how work is done. The government is responsible for safeguarding economic activity in a free enterprise system by maintaining healthy levels of employment, stable prices, and an environment conducive to economic growth. To support this dynamic economic platform, two major tools are used: fiscal policy, which is the ability to tax and spend, and monetary policy, which is the ability to control the money supply.

Fiscal Policy

Fiscal policy refers to decisions made by government relating to taxation and government spending. This section addresses how fiscal policies are developed and describes the tools of taxing, spending, and borrowing that the U.S. government uses to support a vibrant economy. Developing fiscal policy is a process that starts each year when the U.S. President proposes a budget to Congress outlining spending and taxation priorities. How and where the government spends and how much revenue it generates directly influence economic activity. The biggest source of income for the federal government is from income taxes, which it uses to finance government agencies, national defense, and social programs. Another source of revenue comes from taxes on corporate profits. Most state and local governments generate revenue through property and sales taxes (Conte & Karr, 2001).

Because the development of taxation and spending policies are politically charged, elected officials oftentimes find it easier to spend than to raise taxes. However, to keep a country, state, or locality economically vibrant, a well-developed strategy must be devised. Excessive debt or excessive spending can have a devastating effect on the lives and livelihoods of people and the businesses that employ them. Too little spending with little or no responsible debt can stifle investment and the opportunity to remain competitive. Governments need funding for social programs, national defense, and services demanded by the electorate. In addition, strategically investing in and supporting the development of key resources that will provide a competitive position for the United States in the global economy now and in the future have become critical.

Taxing. The taxation tool gives the U.S. government the ability to raise or lower taxes to cover operating costs and invest in future initiatives that support and protect the common good. The challenge for the government is to find a balance where the level of taxation provides sufficient funding for the necessities for the common good and yet does not stifle individual investment and spending to support a robust economic activity. Another important aspect of reasonable taxation by a government is the fact that businesses and other investors invest in nations, states, and localities that have low tax rates. Investment in new factories and service industries creates jobs, the jobs provide individuals with income, and income spurs still more economic activity and investment, thus increasing the tax base. Excessive taxing can limit individual opportunity. Taxes reduce an individual's disposable income, thereby limiting personal purchases and investments. Excessively low taxes (meaning lower government revenue), on the other hand, can limit the government's ability to spend sufficiently to maintain the quality and extent of services and investments needed for its citizenry.

Many government "watchdog" groups, like the Heritage Foundation, believe that a more efficient government can reduce the costs of many federal programs, thus avoiding unnecessary tax increases. Clumsy government actions, waste, and inefficiencies, like the Defense Department's $100 million spent on airline tickets that were never used or the purchase of the infamous $130 toilet seats, have increased expenses and directly depressed the economy. Factor (2007), Chairman of the Free Enterprise Fund, notes that "by lowering government spending whether by eliminating wasteful earmarks, better competition for the purchases by government, significant entitlement reform or just leaving certain functions to the private sector will mean more money for the productive side of the economy" (p. A13).

Spending. The government can also influence the economy by its spending activities. Society depends on government to support a robust and growing infrastructure for economic activity, which includes investments in roadways, telecommunications, education, and research and development in many areas that will keep the nation competitive. This infrastructure is critical to economic growth. Government spending can also jumpstart a lagging economy by increasing the demand for goods and services. For example, federally funded public works projects, such as building roads and bridges, have stimulated the demand for goods and services related to construction and created jobs. Jobs, in turn, provide individuals with income, and the income is used to purchase products and services to fulfill their wants and needs, thus increasing the demand for goods and services. This cycle of earning and spending in an economy is explained in more detail in Chapter 3, "Economic Systems and Institutions."

Government spending, however, must be balanced with individual spending to maintain stability in the economic environment. English economist John M. Keynes observed that simultaneously strong government and consumer spending can push the demand for goods and services beyond what the economy can produce (Conte & Karr, 2001). This situation can cause inflation where prices and wages enter an ever-increasing cycle. The decision as to whether government spending or individual spending can best benefit the entire economy and maintain price stability is often debated throughout society.

The underlying question of debate is whether the money is best used by the government or the individual. In order to put more money into the hands of individuals, the government can reduce taxes to stimulate spending. This was the intent in 2008 when President George W. Bush and Congress decided that the economy needed more individual spending in the form of an economic stimulus package. Faced with the threat of a recession (negative growth in the economy), the President signed a $152 billion (addition to national debt) bill providing individuals and businesses with additional revenues to jumpstart economic activity ("Congressional Budget Office Cost Estimate," 2008). At the time this chapter was being written, it was yet to be determined how effective this strategy would be in spurring economic growth.

Borrowing. Another economic tool used by the government is borrowing. In 2008, the federal debt stood at well over $9 trillion. This money was borrowed to cover the cost of running government. In other words, the U.S. government is spending more money than it is receiving through taxes. The U.S. government currently spends well over $400 billion each year in interest alone to cover the cost of this debt. Who are our lenders? More often than not, these lenders include foreign governments like China, Japan, and Saudi Arabia. The opportunity cost is that money—if not used to pay interest to lenders—could be invested in the economic infrastructure, such as education, roads, social services, and research and development. This debt is also one of several elements influencing the devalued currency that is weakening the buying power of U.S. citizens.

Monetary Policy

The Federal Reserve (Fed) is an independent U.S. government agency responsible for monetary policy—the second tool the government has in influencing the economy. Monetary policies are actions taken by the Fed to influence the availability and cost of money and credit. The Federal Reserve System includes 12 regional Federal Reserve Banks and 25 Federal Reserve Branches (Conte & Karr, 2001). Its goal is to create financial (money supply) conditions that foster economic growth by providing stable pricing (low inflation) and offsetting shifts in consumer demand (e.g., keeping demand and supply at equilibrium) (Santomero, 2004). Creating these conditions is not easy in a dynamic, ever-changing economy.

The Fed uses three methods in an attempt to accomplish these goals: buying and selling government securities, specifying levels of currency reserves, and raising or lowering the discount rate. These tools allow the Fed to increase and decrease the supply of money in the economy as conditions demand. In simple terms, increasing the money supply will influence greater spending, buying, employment, and investment. Too much of a supply of money, however, may overheat the economy, causing prices to rise and the value of the dollar to plunge as too many dollars chase the same number of goods or services. On the other hand, decreasing the money supply will usually increase interest rates for borrowing, making money tight and reducing spending. The ultimate goal of the Fed, however, is to bring the economy into equilibrium: stable prices and continued economic growth.

Government securities. Buying and selling government securities (called open market operations) is one tool used by the Fed to control the supply of money and credit. Depending on economic conditions, the Federal Open Market Committee (FOMC) determines whether the money supply needs to be tightened or expanded. Normally, if inflationary pressures exist within the economy, money will be tightened. The opposite is true if the economy shows recessionary traits. To increase or decrease the availability of money, the Fed will buy and sell government securities. When the Fed buys government securities (paid for by check) and the checks are deposited in banks, the banks will have more reserves from which to lend or invest. Thus, more money is circulated in the economy. The opposite is true when securities are sold, which limits reserves by taking money out of the system and thus limits the ability of banks to lend and invest. In other words, it tightens the supply of money ("In Plain English," 2000).

Reserves. Another tool used by the Fed to control money supply is the ability to mandate the reserve level that banks must have in their vaults (cash) or at their Regional Banks (account deposits). A larger required bank reserve will limit the money supply, thus increasing the cost of credit (the interest rate) and discouraging borrowing. As a result, business and consumer spending will decline. This strategy is used to curtail an overheated economy where prices are rising too fast (inflation).

A smaller required bank reserve will expand the money supply, having the opposite effect. Smaller bank reserves will make more funds (credit) accessible to the general public. Lower interest rates (cost of borrowing) will encourage borrowing. As a result, business and consumer spending will rise. This method is often used to jumpstart a stagnant economy that needs to increase growth and development ("In Plain English," 2000).

Discount Rate. The discount rate is the final tool of monetary policy in the Fed's arsenal to maintain economic stability. The discount rate is the interest rate that commercial banks pay to borrow funds from Reserve Banks. By raising or lowering the discount rate (cost of the loan), the Fed can influence borrowing and the level of revenue that banks have available for making loans ("In Plain English," 2000). When the economy experienced a severe housing slump in 2007-2008 that slowed business growth, the Fed responded by cutting the discount rate several times to boost economic activity. On the other hand, in periods of inflation (increasing prices), the Fed has responded by increasing the discount rate, thus limiting available credit and cooling an overheated economy.

Even though these aforementioned tools enable the Fed to expand or limit the supply of money, its job in keeping the economy in balance is much more complex. Public impressions of the Fed's competence and confidence in their decisions can be as powerful as any action taken. As noted by Santomero (2004),

> The effectiveness of monetary policy hinges on public confidence—people's belief that the Fed has a commitment and capacity to maintain stable prices and foster maximum sustainable economic growth. Establishing this confidence is not easy, particularly in a world where shifts in public expectations can themselves create episodes of economic instability (p. 5).

Teaching Strategies

Creative planning can help students understand the differences between monetary and fiscal policy, the purpose and role of the Federal Reserve, and the tools used by government to maintain stability in the economy. In addition to the previously mentioned U.S. State Department publication on the U.S. economy, an excellent resource on all aspects of the Federal Reserve is the publication *In Plain English: Making Sense of the Federal Reserve* (available at http://www.stlouisfed.org/publications/pleng/). This publication gives a clear explanation of the Federal Reserve System, as well as the tools available to the Fed to affect monetary policies. This information can directly be geared to achieving NBEA Standard VII, Levels 3 and 4, in the Economics content areas, where students are able to identify monetary policies used by the Federal Reserve and critique the ability of monetary policies to influence economic activity (NBEA, 2007).

Interactive websites. Another Federal Reserve resource, *FED 101* (n.d.), (available at http://www.federalreserveeducation.org/fed101/), is an interactive resource that includes general facts, lesson plans, websites, videos, and games that make learning fun and interesting. One interesting feature on this site is a game called *Fed Clue*. This game takes students through a mission reviewing facts about monetary policy, monetary instruments, and monetary policy limitations and advantages. This learning activity also can assist students in meeting NBEA Standard VII, Level 3 (described above).

Current events videos. Bringing reality to the theories on monetary and fiscal policy can be done by using current events. C-SPAN Classroom (available at www.c-spanclassroom.org) offers free resources and video downloads to make classroom learning activities come alive (Manzo, 2006). Viewing current events can help students see first-hand the monetary and fiscal policy makers, the current issues addressed, and the impact of these policy decisions on the lives of individuals and business. Many of the higher-order performance standards identified in NBEA Standard VII, Levels 3 and 4 can be accomplished using this resource.

Team research projects. Team research projects on the effects of past monetary or fiscal policies and how they influenced the overall economy can give students perspective on the consequences of actions and decisions made by the Fed and the government. Presentations of their findings will allow the entire class to understand the ongoing implications and complexities of policy choices made throughout history.

CHALLENGES IN THE 21ST CENTURY
The current dynamic and challenging economic environment characterized by the worldwide expansion of markets makes economic policy decision-making increasingly complex. The following discussion explores the political, social, and global challenges affecting the U.S. economy now and in the future.

Political Challenges
The difficulty in a democracy, where policy makers are elected or appointed by other elected officials, is providing for the wants, needs, and desires of constituents while recognizing the need for maintaining a robust national economic infrastructure and defense system. Taking a local versus national perspective and setting policy that is conducive to saving versus spending are two challenges that government regulators face today.

Pressures from local constituents and special interest groups need to be balanced with the pressure to secure national interests that will keep the economy strong. Although elected officials would like to meet everyone's needs, in the reality of limited resources, trade-offs and compromises are essential.

The challenge of saving versus spending is also constant in a limited resource environment. However, as previously mentioned, an elected official finds it easier to spend rather than to take politically unpopular actions like saving or raising taxes. Saving and investment, although not immediately gratifying, are necessary for the long-term survival of a robust economy. Balancing spending to meet short-term needs and saving and investing to prepare for the future will always be a constant struggle.

Social Challenges
Providing protection for those most in need and increasing the wealth of all individuals to support a higher standard of living are social challenges that will continue in the 21st century. In an environment of limited resources, social programs oftentimes take a back seat to more pressing national needs. As Hacker (2004) noted, "Social protections for working Americans have changed remarkably little since the

mid-twentieth century—and when they have changed, they have usually been cut, not expanded" (p. 15). As a result, many middle-class families are finding it difficult to meet basic expenses. More citizens lack health insurance, and workplace benefits such as pensions have all but disappeared (Hacker, 2004). This situation has increasingly created a society of "haves" and "have nots." This is illustrated by Domhoff (2006):

> As of 2001, the top 1% of households (the upper class) owned 33.4% of all privately held wealth, and the next 19% (the managerial, professional, and small business stratum) had 51%, which means that just 20% of the people owned a remarkable 84%, leaving only 16% of the wealth for the bottom 80% (wage and salary workers) (¶ 5).

Providing a safety net for those citizens who struggle to meet essential needs will continue to be a challenge for government. So, too, will creating an economic environment that provides more citizens the ability to meet their personal responsibilities and increase their standard of living.

Creating an economic environment that can deliver high-quality jobs and prepare workers for these jobs will necessitate government investment in the future. Former U.S. Treasury Secretary Henry Paulson noted (2006),

> The most effective method for generating new, high-quality jobs and higher living standards is to develop the skills and the technologies that promote economic competitiveness. This means help people of all ages pursue first rate education and training opportunities (p. 3).

The need for quality educational opportunities for all citizens has long been recognized to remain competitive in the global economy. Efforts to fund schools and training initiatives, to offer better preparation for teachers, and to hold participants in the educational process accountable in achieving stated outcomes is an essential priority in preparation for our future.

Increasing pressures from the electorate will prevail for social programs that serve our aging population (e.g., healthcare and pensions) and provide opportunities and services (e.g., education and social security) for those in need. The ultimate challenge is to balance the costs of these needed services with available revenues.

Global Challenges

Influenced by advances in technology, communications, transportation, and open trade, globalization has opened markets worldwide and thereby increased competition. As a result, much of what happens in the U.S. economy has an effect on global markets, and, conversely, what happens in the global economy has a direct impact on the U.S. economy. Paulson (2006) recognized that "Globalization and interdependence are here to stay. No nation can turn back the clock" (p. 2). Surviving and thriving in this global environment will challenge our nation to provide an educated workforce, reap the efficiencies of advanced technologies, and invest in innovation. (Chapter 6 provides a more detailed look at global economic concepts.) Success in remaining competitive in the global economy will depend on meeting the challenges of greater investments in education, technology, and innovation.

Competence is the key to survival in the globalized economy. The best jobs will go to the best qualified workers, no matter where they live or work. This poses a tremendous challenge to U.S. workers who must be educated, trained, and retrained throughout their careers to remain competitive.

Technological advancements that provide better efficiency and effectiveness in business, government, and industry processes and products will provide a competitive advantage in the global economic environment. Investment in new technologies and the ability to use them in the best ways possible will support the ability to do things better, faster, and more cost-efficiently.

Investing in businesses, industries, and projects that will enable the United States to seize future opportunities, solve problems, and make contributions for a better society is imperative for U.S. economic competitiveness. Wise investments in industries of the future will enable the nation to remain an economic leader in the world economy. The economic future in the United States will greatly depend on our willingness to accept these challenges that globalization present.

Teaching Strategies

Strategies that allow students to explore choices, make decisions, and understand consequences of their decisions should be addressed when focusing on the political, social, and global challenges the U.S. economy faces in the 21st century. Keeping the economy strong is not only the responsibility of elected or appointed officials. Students should recognize that they have a personal responsibility to participate through their votes, education, workforce participation, and community service. The strategies described below help students make a personal connection with government actions in the economy and focus on NBEA Standard VII, Level 3, where students investigate the effects of government and economic conditions on personal financial planning (NBEA, 2007).

Guest presenters from business, banking, and community service organizations can give a good perspective on the issues they each face. Attending a city council budget meeting with students would also bring many of these challenges to light by showing the deliberate thought process that goes into meeting current needs and investing in the future. Structuring projects that have students research what other countries' governments are doing to give their economies a competitive edge will help emphasize the urgency of making smart choices in an expanding competitive environment.

SUMMARY

This chapter reviewed the role of the U.S. government in keeping the economy strong, stable, competitive, and vibrant in the 21st century. The chapter addressed the role and purpose of the U.S. government in reaching these objectives and the tools available to affect positive economic change. These tools include fiscal policy created by the President and Congress focused on taxes, spending, and debt, and monetary policy created by the Federal Reserve System that focus on government securities, reserves, and the discount rate. .

Making the right economic decisions at the right time has become increasingly difficult in a world filled with complexities and uncertainty. The chapter discussion on the challenges in the 21st century showed how politics, social protections, and globalization influence decision-making.

Throughout the chapter several teaching/learning strategies and resources on these topics are introduced and linked to the NBEA standards on "The Role of Government." These techniques and resources included publications, interactive websites, projects, and video links.

The role of government in keeping the U.S. economy strong and robust is extremely challenging and fraught with complexities. Understanding this role will make students more aware of how these actions affect their personal lives and how they as citizens can make effective decisions to support a productive economy.

REFERENCES

Bernanke, B. S. (2008, April 9). The importance of financial education and the national jump$tart coalition survey. Jump$tart Coalition for Financial Literacy. Retrieved July 17, 2008, from http://www.jumpstart.org/news.cfm

Congressional Budget Office Cost Estimate (2008). *H.R. 5140, Economic stimulus act.* Retrieved July 25, 2008, from http://www.cbo.gov/doc.cfm?index=8973

Conte, C., & Karr, A. R. (2001, February). Monetary and fiscal policy. *USA Economy.* Retrieved November 9, 2007, from http://usinfo.state.gov/products/pubs/oecon/chap7.htm/

Conte, C., & Karr, A. R. (2001, February). The role of government in the economy. *USA Economy.* Retrieved November 9, 2007, from http://usinfo.state.gov/products/pubs/oecon/chap6.htm/

Crutsinger, M. (2008, February 15). Fed chief: Economy 'sluggish.' *Monterey County Herald,* A1 & A9.

Domhoff, G. W. (2006). Wealth, income, and power. *Who rules America?* Retrieved July 20, 2008, from http://sociology.ucsc.edu/whorulesamerica/book.html

EconEdLink. National Council on Economic Education (NCEE). Retrieved February 14, 2008, from http://www.econedlink.org/

Factor, M. (2007, March 3). Fluctuations and fundamentals. *The Washington Times*, p. A13.

FED 101. (n.d.) Kansas City: Federal Reserve Bank of Kansas City. Retrieved November 9, 2007, from http://www.federalreserveeducation.org/Fed101/

Hacker, J. S. (2004, August 16). False positive. *The New Republic,* 14-17. *In plain English: Making sense of the Federal Reserve. (2000).* Public Affairs Department, Federal Reserve Bank of St. Louis. Retrieved November 9, 2007, from http://stlouis fed.org/publications/pleng/default.html

Manzo, K. (2006). C-SPAN offers current events aligned to states' standards. *Education Week, (26)*14, 16.

McInnis, D. (2008, July 18). The cotton dust storm returns. *The New York Times.* Retrieved July 18, 2008, from http://query.nytimes.com/gst/fullpage.html?res= 9902E2DF1139F93BA3575BC0A964948260&sec=health&spon=&pagewanted=all

National Business Education Association. (2007). *National standards for business education: What America's students should know and be able to do in business.* Reston, VA: Author.

National Council on Economic Education. (1997). *Voluntary national content standards in economics.* New York: Author.

Paulson, H.M. (2006, September 13). Remarks on the international economy. *Washington Transcript Service.* Retrieved February 15, 2008, from http://elibrary. bigchalk.com/

Santomero, A. M. (2004, April 1). Great Expectations: The role of beliefs in economics and monetary policy. *Business Review.* Retrieved February 15, 2008, from http:// elibrary.bigchalk.com/

Global Economic Concepts

Chia-An Chao

Aruna Chandra

Indiana State University

Terre Haute, Indiana

The world economy is becoming increasingly integrated. An abundance of evidence indicates growing interconnectedness among countries, from trade in goods and services to capital flow and human migration patterns. This chapter begins with a brief overview of recent trends and drivers of global economic integration, followed by a close examination of the impact of globalization, including discussions of key concepts such as the benefits of trade, the monetary market, trade barriers, and protectionism. Integrated throughout this chapter are instructional strategies and resources for teaching global economic concepts.

THE GLOBALIZATION PHENOMENON

Trade in natural resources and manufactured goods, along with the flow of capital, labor, and knowledge across national borders, have occurred for centuries. While commerce among nations continues to grow as it has in previous centuries, in the last few decades contentious issues—such as the outsourcing of jobs from industrialized nations to emerging economies such as India and China and the remarkable economic growth rates of the latter—have gained much attention. Before delving into these issues, however, this chapter begins with a brief overview of globalization, including its history, recent trends, and the forces behind the trends.

Brief History of Globalization and Recent Trends

Intercontinental trade can be traced as far back as the first century of the Roman Empire, when roads and sea routes, simple customs dues, and a single currency system established by the Romans facilitated goods exchange among trading partners in Western Europe, the Middle East, and North Africa. The scope of intercontinental trade was further expanded to include the Americas and Asia in the 15th century as a result of explorations led by explorers such as Columbus and Vasco da Gamma. O'Rourke and Williamson (2000) identified three eras of global commodity exchange and specialization. In the first era (from the 15th to the late 18th century), trading among countries was focused on the exchange of non-competing, luxury commodities that were locally unavailable or in limited supply (e.g., spices, silk, and sugar were imported into Europe, whereas Asian countries imported linens, woolens, and silver). In the second era (19th century), basic competing goods such as textiles and wheat were traded. In the third era of commodity exchange and specialization (beginning in the 20th century), both basic and highly differentiated manufactured products began to be traded. O'Rourke and Williamson (2000) contend that globalization began in the second era, when the trading of competing goods among nations affected domestic commodity prices and widespread resource reallocation, which, in turn, impacted the living standards and income distribution of the masses.

The trend toward globalization continues into the present day, including cross-border flows of financial capital and labor. The exceptions to this globalization trend were the two World Wars and the Great Depression when protectionism led to disruptions in international economic integration. However, recent developments in globalization have resulted in several different trends (Organization for Economic Co-operation and Development [OECD], 2007). First, the scale and rapid pace toward globalization in recent years are unprecedented. World trade constituted 42% of Gross Domestic Product (GDP) in the 1990s; in the 1960s, the share of world trade in GDP was only 26% (Arora & Vamvakidis, 2005). In addition, fueled by large foreign direct investment (FDI) and more integrated world capital markets, international capital flows exhibited a similar growth pattern. The FDI, which involves some degree of ownership of foreign assets such as plant and equipment, is used as a market entry strategy by large and mature multinational companies wanting to relocate all or part of their value chains in other locations to capitalize on comparative advantages available in local economies, such as low-cost labor or the availability of natural resources. The pace at which developing countries, such as China, India, Brazil, and Russia, emerged as key players in the world economy since the 1980s has no comparison in the history of globalization. The rapid economic development of these countries can be partially attributed to increasing FDI flows into these countries. Second, the increasing geographically fragmented production processes, particularly in high-tech industries, highlights the complexity of global economic collaboration in recent years. Production activities that used to be completed in one location are now divided among multiple locations to help reduce costs. Multinational corporations have become key players in the global value chain. Intra-firm trades account for about 40% of U.S. merchandise trade, and more than 50% of world imports in 2003 were intermediate goods such as tools and steel used in the production of other goods (OECD, 2007).

Finally, unlike trade in the 19th century when manufactured goods and capital flowed from "core" countries in Western Europe to developing countries in the periphery, the current phase of globalization exhibits a different trend: Production activities are carried out more often in emerging markets and the flow of capital between emerging economies and developed nations has become bi-directional (Bernanke, 2006). In 2007, developing countries had a current account surplus of $640 billion (IMF data cited in Kroszner, 2007). The net outflow of capital from key developing countries, such as China, Russia, and OPEC nations, to industrialized countries reveals a divergent pattern of growth and investment. Whereas high savings rates and relatively less robust financial systems exist in the developing countries, high consumption rates and perceived high rates of investment return exist in industrialized countries, resulting in a net flow of capital to the industrialized nations. Strategies for introducing high school and postsecondary students to these concepts are presented in the following section.

Teaching ideas. The University of California, Santa Cruz's UC Atlas of Inequality website (http://ucatlas.ucsc.edu/home.html) provides teaching resources and tools on various topics related to global integration and inequality, including economic globalization, income inequality, gender, and health. The site offers rollover world maps showing various topics of interest, such as trade flows among countries around the world, amounts of trade and per capita GDP, and changes in FDI from the 1960s to 2000. Data underlying these interactive maps can be downloaded and saved in Excel spreadsheets. The quantitative data in the forms of spatial displays and spreadsheets facilitate comprehension and further analyses of the data in a variety of ways. Besides these tools, the website offers teaching ideas on key topics, including one on FDI.

Using the FDI as a topic for student research, one teaching strategy is to have students develop an investigation that requires them to analyze an array of trade variables related to world economies. In this project, students could begin by scrolling over the maps to study the overall patterns of net inflows of FDI as a percentage of GDP to countries in various regions of the world and identify any dramatic shifts in patterns, such as FDI received by developed versus developing countries over the decades. Then, students can download the data, sort the data in Excel to identify the top five countries that had the highest net inflow of FDI, create a chart to compare changes over time, and offer explanations. Also, they can take advantage of the website's glossary to look up key terms such as globalization, purchasing power parity, and FDI, and they can query the online database to gather more information (e.g., economic, education, and population indicators) about certain countries or economic or geographic regions.

Drivers of Globalization
What factors contributed to the unprecedented pace and scale of globalization in terms of international trade, production activities, and financial flows? This section outlines the key drivers of globalization and provides an explanation for the rapid

expansion in global economic integration. Similar to past centuries, technological innovations and government policies are two key drivers of global economic integration. Improvements in shipbuilding, steam-powered engines, aviation, and telecommunication technologies in previous centuries significantly lowered transportation and transaction costs. In recent decades, information and computer technologies (ICT), such as enterprise resource planning (ERP) systems that integrate all back-office functions (accounting, inventory management, production, sales, etc.) in a single information system, have enabled businesses to run more efficiently and make better decisions with accurate, real-time information. With the advent of the Internet and mobile computing, businesses large and small are able to reach customers anytime and anywhere. Furthermore, with the adoption of supply-chain management (SCM) systems, businesses are better able to plan and coordinate their activities with their business partners and have more precise control over the entire production cycle from materials sourcing, pricing, and production planning to distribution and after-sale activities. While data showing a positive correlation between ICT investments and economic performance have been inconclusive due to issues with productivity measurement, the positive impact of ICT on company- and industry-level productivity is well documented (e.g., Cline & Guynes, 2001; Li & Ye, 1999).

Along with better visibility and control of the production cycle, more businesses are slicing up their production processes and relocating them to different countries to reduce costs, take advantage of growth opportunities abroad, and gain access to strategic assets such as skilled labor and technological expertise (OECD, 2007). The trend toward *offshoring* (offshore outsourcing) affects not only production activities, but also professional services such as information processing, research, and consulting, which are increasingly internationalized. While opponents of offshoring attribute it as the cause of de-industrialization (the declining number of manufacturing jobs in developed nations), some economists point to the higher productivity in the manufacturing sector (as compared to the service sector) and trade specialization as the primary reasons for de-industrialization (OECD, 2007; Rowthorn & Ramaswamy, 1997).

While technological advancements have significantly minimized the effect of natural trade barriers and lowered transportation and information costs, reduction of artificial trade barriers such as tariffs and import restrictions by countries around the world has also facilitated international trade (Mussa, 2000). Prior to the end of World War II, countries erected artificial trade barriers to protect domestic producers of goods and services and to generate revenue for the state. Since then, the world has seen a general decline in tariff rates and gradual integration of industrialized countries into trade blocs, i.e., countries seeking various levels of political and economic union with attendant reduction or elimination of trade barriers amongst them. Notable examples of these economic unions are the European Union (EU) and the North American Free Trade Agreement (NAFTA), where trade barrier reduction has been even greater. The EU, a 27-member political and economic community, was formed to reduce barriers to trade and investment, thereby benefiting from comparative advantage-based specialization, greater resource use efficiencies, and broader markets. The combined GDP of the EU in 2007 was $14,953 trillion USD (IMF, 2007). NAFTA, established in 1994, is made up of Canada, Mexico, and the United States. It is the largest trade bloc in the world with a combined GDP of $15,857 trillion USD in 2007 (IMF, 2007). Even though trade blocs have been instrumental in increasing regional trade, the level of protectionism among developing countries is still high relative to the developed countries; however, as more developing countries have adopted open trade policies, such as those in the former Soviet bloc, there has been a significant reduction in trade barriers in those countries as well.

Besides government policies, world economic bodies such as the World Trade Organization (WTO) play an important role in facilitating trade by reducing barriers to trade and investment. For example, India has reduced its average tariffs from 59% to 28% partly as a result of joining the WTO. The WTO was established in 1995 as a successor to the General Agreement on Tariffs and Trade (GATT) in order to promote global trade in goods and services. The WTO currently has 151 members and has been successful in reducing tariff and other barriers to trade amongst its members through several rounds of trade talks. Most notably, after eight years of protracted negotiations, the Uruguay Round (which ended in 1993) successfully reduced tariff and non-tariff barriers to trade and services. The most recent round of talks, termed the Doha Development Round, was far more ambitious in its reach and was termed the "development round" to emphasize market openness for developing countries. However, it has reached deadlock due to disagreement between developed and developing countries on farm subsidies. The United States and the European Union could not agree on the size of the tariff reductions on farm goods, and big emerging economies like Brazil and India were unwilling to concede much since they believed that developed countries needed to make more significant concessions in reducing barriers to agricultural trade. A deadlocked Doha Round has resulted in plural bilateral trade deals between countries in what Jagdish Bhagwati (2003) calls a "spaghetti bowl" of "preferential" trade agreements, which may not fully advance a fair and nondiscriminatory, multilateral global trading system as envisaged by the WTO.

Regional trade agreements, such as NAFTA, or bilateral agreements, such as those the United States has signed with Chile or South Korea, could therefore result in locking out the poorer countries rather than helping them in their development efforts. Such preferential or "discriminatory" trade agreements have exploded lately, with over 300 agreements signed in the past decade (Wolf, 2007). Given the multiple benefits of global economic integration via trade and investment, preferential trade agreements may, in fact, harm developing countries by fragmenting the global economy, increasing trade complexity, and excluding those countries in dire need of trade by diverting trade from the more efficient to the less efficient countries.

Another issue raised by critics of the WTO relates to the question of global trade in terms of "free" versus "fair" trade. While the proponents of a barrier-free, multilateral trading system are in favor of reducing tariff and non-tariff barriers to trade and services, fair trade advocates promote the concept of "fairness" to groups of countries that have asymmetric power balances relative to the rich world, i.e., paying fair wages to workers in local communities, adopting environmentally sustainable policies, and paying fair market prices to producers in less developed countries to create a more even playing field between producers in less developed countries and consumers in developed countries. Products such as coffee are certified by the Fair Trade Council to ensure an advantage to producers who respect fair trade rules (Shah, 2007). In addition to calls for fair trade, anti-globalization protests in developed nations such as the United States and European Union have been on the increase. The issues raised by these protestors and their calls for national protectionism is addressed below, after a brief discussion of teaching strategies.

Teaching ideas. The University of California, Santa Cruz's UC Atlas of Inequality website (http://ucatlas.ucsc.edu/trade/subtheme_trade_blocs.php) is also a good resource for helping students gain a better understanding of the four trade blocs (NAFTA, EU, ASEAN – Association of South East Asian Nations, and MECORSUR – Mercado Común del Sur or Southern Common Market, a regional trade agreement among Brazil, Argentina, Uruguay and Paraguay). A variety of information on each trade bloc, such as export composition and percentage of GDP, is available on the website. One teaching idea for high school students would be to assign groups of students the task of investigating the four trade blocs to learn their history, key missions, impacts, and the arguments for and against them. Also, students can collaborate across teams to compare and contrast the trade blocs. The business teacher can then facilitate a debate on whether trade blocs advance or hinder economic cooperation and development on a global scale.

IMPACT OF GLOBALIZATION

What are the benefits and downsides of globalization? Who are the winners and losers? This section examines the impact of an integrated global economy including its pros and cons, the controversial issue of offshoring and employment, and the complex relationship between currency exchange rates and the domestic economy in interconnected financial markets.

Mutual Benefits of Economic Integration

Nations trade with each other in order to increase their standard of living through access to goods and services they would not have in a world without trade. Trade allows nations to specialize in producing what they do best and buy the rest from other countries. Adam Smith, in *Wealth of Nations* (1776/1991), argued for the benefits of free trade by pointing out the drawbacks of the mercantilist view of trade to the wealth of nations. Smith argued that each country would benefit by producing the goods that it had an absolute advantage in producing (i.e., producing them at the lowest cost using the fewest resources), and exporting them to other countries while importing the rest. The absolute advantage principle frames trade in somewhat black-and-white terms, neglecting the relative advantages of both countries engaged in trade. David Ricardo (1817/2006) argued it would be beneficial for countries to trade even though one country has an absolute advantage in the production of both products. In this theory, the opportunity cost of production (how much production of one good needs to be reduced in order to increase production of another good by one more unit) is more important than the absolute costs of production.

In a world of perfect free trade, there would be no barriers to trade, and consumers would be able to purchase the best products for the lowest prices from the countries that are the most efficient producers of goods or services. This situation would foster competition among domestic producers since they would have to compete on the basis of cost and quality with producers from around the world, thus making them more competitive in the long run. In addition, these very same producers would benefit from the ability to import intermediate goods from other countries at lower costs, thus allowing them to earn higher profits. Consumers, in turn, would benefit from lower cost and higher quality products, which would increase their standards of living. Some exceptions to this argument are low-grade or even hazardous products made by overseas manufacturers, such as toys coated in lead paint and contaminated pet foods from China. Also, the lower product costs described in this scenario are the result of producer competitiveness, not the artificially lower prices of exports as is the case with dumping. Hence, in a more open trading environment, inflation would be kept under control, thus benefiting all trading partners. Arora and Vamvakidis (2005) studied the economic spillover effects of economic integration and found that growth rates and income levels of a country's trading partners have a positive influence on its domestic economy since positive economic conditions abroad often lead to increases in demand for exports to those countries as well as growing foreign investment to the home country.

Impacts of Globalization on Employment

Using each country's increases in trade as shares of GDP from 1980 to 2000, Dollar and Kraay (2001) identified the top third of developing countries that have significantly opened up to international trade. Dollar and Kraay studied these countries' income distribution and poverty rates and found that benefits of economic growth from trade are widely shared. In addition, they found a corresponding decrease in income distribution inequality in most of these countries. Furthermore, they found poverty rates in these countries had decreased along with an attendant decrease in the per capita income gap between rich countries and the newly globalizing developing countries.

While globalization benefits the U.S. economy to the tune of $1 trillion a year, it is argued that most of these profits go to well-educated, highly skilled workers at the upper end of the pay scale or to corporate profits. In the past, low-skilled, blue-collar workers in the manufacturing sector saw their wages squeezed by competition from developing countries, such as China, which has turned into the factory of the world. Offshoring is beneficial to some economies since it benefits and enhances firm competitiveness and allows some developing nations to specialize in labor-intensive jobs where they have a comparative advantage. However, with the spread of information technology and lower costs of telecommunications, more service and white-collar jobs are being offshored to overseas locations, such as India and the Philippines, which offer good value at competitive prices. According to Forrester Research (McCarthy, 2004), 3.3 million jobs will be offshored by 2015. Some economists, like Alan Blinder, argue that this number may increase further in the near future, with estimates indicating that nearly 30% of jobs may be offshored (Blinder, 2006). In the new wave of offshoring, the offshored jobs are higher skilled jobs, such as computer programming, radiology, legal, or accounting work, as opposed to call center or medical transcription work as in the last wave. As developing countries migrate up the information technology value chain by upgrading their workforce skills, this trend could depress wages even for some of the higher skilled professional jobs in developed countries and reduce labor's bargaining power tremendously (Chandra, Fealey, & Rau, 2006).

Teaching ideas. Protecting U.S. jobs from being offshored is a highly debated topic. A meaningful and timely learning activity for high school and postsecondary students would be to assign students the task of searching the Bureau of Labor Statistics (BLS) website for changes in manufacturing, information technology, and other types of jobs that have been known to be offshored. Next, students could be asked to study Part I and III of the three-part debate on offshore outsourcing published by the Yale Center for the Study of Globalization (available at http://www.yaleglobal.yale.edu). In Part I of the debate, Dossani and Kenney (2004) state, "It is now possible that during the next decade, the winds of globalization will sweep through the formerly cosseted ranks of white-collar workers" (p. 8). Students can discuss whether they agree with this statement, based on data they gathered from the BLS website. According to Dapice (2004) in Part III of the outsourcing debate, "If technology still accounts for most displaced workers, then the anger directed at trade and outsourcing is misplaced, and measures to restrict trade or outsourcing would raise costs without much helping those workers" (p. 4). The teacher can lead a discussion on the role of technology in the reduction of trade barriers and its role as an enabler of job outsourcing. In addition, students can look for articles from credible sources such as *BusinessWeek* and Forrester Research to support or refute this assertion.

In a world of interconnected trade and capital flows, the value of a nation's currency can impact trade through its balance of payments with other countries. The impact of a stronger or weaker currency, in this case the U.S. dollar, is discussed next in the context of interconnected global financial markets.

Impact of International Financial Markets on the U.S. Dollar

The international monetary system provides a framework of rules and regulations for cross-border trade and investment. Each sovereign nation has its own financial market system consisting of stock exchanges, banks, and other public and private financial institutions. Globally interconnected and interdependent financial markets enable capital flows to the country that has relatively high interest rates, low inflation, and good long-term prospects for economic growth. The U.S. dollar was perceived as a safe-haven currency due to the United States' strong economic fundamentals. However, in 2008 a gaping current account deficit of 8% of GDP in the United States, coupled with turmoil in the U.S. subprime housing mortgage sector and subsequent credit crisis, resulted in significantly slower growth and the threat of recession.

Growing trade deficits in the United States, coupled with lower interest rates, weak exports, and strong imports, resulted in a weaker U.S. currency. A trade deficit or current account deficit arises when a nation's imports exceed its exports. For instance, when the United States runs a current account trade deficit with a trading partner like China or other Asian countries, it means the United States is importing more goods from these countries than it is exporting to them. So, what do these countries do with the U.S. dollars they get in return for their exports? They use the dollars to purchase assets, such as U.S. government treasury securities, which, in effect, amounts to foreign financing of U.S. debt. U.S. consumers have a low savings rate and thus depend on investments from abroad to finance government and consumer expenditures. Developing countries have high rates of savings coupled with developing financial markets, so their excess savings help finance U.S. debt. This situation will last as long as these countries perceive the U.S. dollar as a safe haven for their assets. Large, persistent current account deficits relative to GDP can suffocate a nation's economic growth due to heavy capital outflows required to service the debt through interest payments and dividends to foreign bond and stockholders. In turn, this may mean that the United States could no longer depend on foreign inflows of capital to finance its current account deficit, which could lead to a credit crunch and subsequent higher interest rates on consumer as well as government debt.

Although a weaker U.S. dollar could reduce the current account deficit by making imports more expensive and exports less expensive to foreign buyers, it also means U.S. consumers have to pay more for imported goods. Rising consumer prices could lead to price inflation. Producers exporting their goods would become more price-competitive in the international marketplace, but those that import intermediate or finished goods could see an increase in prices.

A weaker dollar not only affects the U.S. trade and current account balance with other countries, but also it has a direct impact on other countries' economies due to high volumes of U.S. dollars in their foreign reserves and the linked exchange rate systems, where some countries have fixed or pegged exchange rate systems and others use floating exchange rates. An historical overview of different exchange rate systems and their impacts on central bank domestic monetary policy is provided in the following section.

Impact of Exchange Rate Systems on Domestic Monetary Policy

After World War II, a system called the Bretton Woods Accord was devised to ensure stability in international monetary and financial markets. The international agreement pegged the value of the U.S. dollar to gold at a fixed rate and created the International Monetary Fund (IMF) and World Bank. The IMF's role was to monitor and stabilize currencies and to lend money to developing countries at times of economic and financial crisis. The World Bank, on the other hand, was set up to provide loans to developing countries and to reduce poverty. Ballooning U.S. government deficits caused by financing the Vietnam War and government spending in the late 1960s, along with an ever-increasing trade deficit, led to the collapse of the fixed exchange rate between the U.S. dollar and gold. With the collapse of the Bretton Woods Accord, major currencies were traded freely on world markets with the forces of demand and supply setting the exchange rates. This setting of exchange rates is known as the *floating* exchange rate system. This system provides governments greater freedom to set monetary policy to suit domestic needs; i.e., the central bank in a country can raise or lower interest rates in response to domestic economic conditions. For example, the United States and the European Union are two large trade blocs that allow their currencies to float freely in response to market signals. However, as the U.S. dollar has weakened progressively and significantly against other major currencies such as the euro, exports from the euro zone have become less competitive, thereby raising political concerns. In addition, capital flows into U.S. government securities could dry up in light of lower interest rates further weakening the dollar. If the dollar's decline becomes chaotic at some point in the future, the U.S. Federal Reserve could come under pressure to raise interest rates to support a falling dollar at a time when a faltering domestic economy is in desperate need of interest rate cuts (Guha, 2007).

Some developing countries maintain a fixed exchange rate system by pegging their currencies to the value of the U.S. dollar, the euro, or to a mixed basket of currencies that include major currencies such as the dollar, euro, pound sterling, and yen. For example, Saudi Arabia has its currency, the riyal, pegged to the U.S. dollar, whereas Kuwait pegs its currency to a mixed basket of currencies. China makes use of a managed float system by maintaining its currency, the renminbi, within a trading band. A fixed or managed system of currency exchange provides greater stability and control with the central bank buying and selling currencies to manage the fixed or managed float.

Increasingly interconnected global financial markets and growing international trade have created both positive and negative impacts on developing and developed nations. Globalization trends, drivers, impacts, and key global economic concepts, including the role of trade, protectionism, and monetary markets discussed in this chapter, aim to illustrate the complexity of global economic integration and illuminate the relationship among the key concepts. The growing interconnectedness among nations also underscores the importance of global economic knowledge and understanding in business and economic education.

Teaching ideas. Given that many global economic concepts are interrelated, business educators of all levels are advised to adopt a holistic instructional approach employing project-based learning with clear performance requirements and rubrics for assessing multiple dimensions of student comprehension of subjects. For example, middle school business educators may assign students to study countries that are trading partners (e.g., United States, China, and Japan) and to gather information on each country, including major resources, exports and imports, currency and exchange rates, trade balances, and major economic decisions and policy changes in recent years. Upon completing their research, students could be required to give a presentation that explains the absolute and comparative advantages of each country, or analyze factors such as currency appreciation or depreciation in a given period, and discuss the exchange rate system and its relationship to its balance of payments with its trading partners.

ADDITIONAL RESOURCES FOR TEACHING GLOBAL ECONOMIC CONCEPTS

To many people, globalization means offshoring, increased competition, and unfair trade practices (Easton, 2008; OECD, 2007). As discussed in this chapter, globalization is a complex phenomenon and has both positive and negative effects. The challenge for business educators is to help students develop a balanced perspective on issues related to globalization to prepare them for future careers in a global community. In addition to the teaching ideas presented earlier in this chapter, the following teaching resources and ideas may help achieve this objective.

The National Council on Economic Education (NCEE) website (http://store.ncee. net/international.html) has many packaged instructional materials. Several focus primarily on global economic concepts, such as *Thinking Globally: Effective Lessons for Teaching about the Interdependent World Economy, Focus: Globalization,* and *Focus: International Economics* (for grades 9–12). The *Wide World of Trade* and *Beyond Economic Growth* can be used with grades 6–8 or 6–12. Each instructional package (some on CD-ROM) contains lesson plans, handouts, visuals, background readings, and learning activities ranging from role-playing exercises, debates, simulations, data-gathering and analysis projects, and other hands-on group and individual activities.

Besides packaged instructional resources, NCEE provides an annotated list of websites (http://www.ncee.net/thinkingglobally/documents/tg_websites.pdf)—such as those of the CIA Factbook, the Heritage Foundation, the U.S. Census Bureau, the World Bank, and many others—where teachers and college students can find a variety of current information about the United States and other countries to supplement their teaching and learning materials. For example, the U.S. trade balance, imports, and exports with its trading partners can be found on the U.S. Census Bureau website, and development indicators for over 150 countries around the world are available on the World Bank website.

Another website, Indianaglobalbusiness.com, was developed through a grant from the Lilly Foundation as a companion site to international business classes taught at Indiana State University (ISU). It serves as a pilot experiment in designing a dedicated, course-specific website to showcase student-developed content and to provide current information on international business topics. The "Teaching Resources" section has outlines of student group projects for teacher use. Student-developed content includes voice-narrated PowerPoint presentations as well as a "News Briefs" section with brief reports on international business topics of current interest. Interviews with distinguished ISU alumni and other international business executives are also included.

SUMMARY

To provide business educators an update on globalization and drivers behind the increasingly integrated global economy, this chapter began with a brief overview of the globalization phenomenon. The key drivers of globalization are (1) technological innovations that minimize or eliminate natural trade barriers of transportation and information costs, and (2) government policies that lower artificial trade barriers such as tariffs and import restrictions. Regional trade blocs (e.g., EU, NAFTA) and world economic bodies such as the WTO also play important and sometimes controversial roles in facilitating economic co-operation among nations.

The focus of the chapter then shifted to the impact of globalization, including various benefits of free trade for consumers, producers, and nations. Changes and disruptions in employment due to globalization were discussed, including the impacts of outsourcing manufacturing and service jobs from developed to developing countries. The final section of the chapter focused on the intricate relationship between currency exchange rates, monetary policy, and the domestic economy in interconnected financial markets. This section also provided an overview of the implications of a weaker U.S. currency. Also included throughout this chapter were various online and print resources and suggestions for business educators for teaching key global economic concepts and ideas and for providing students with activities that actively engage them in understanding those concepts.

REFERENCES

Arora, V., & Vamvakidis, A. (2005). Economic spillovers: Exploring the impact trading partners have on each other's growth. *Finance and Development, 42*(3). Retrieved January 31, 2008, from http://www.imf.org/external/pubs/ft/fandd/2005/09/arora.htm

Bernanke, B. S. (2006, August 25). Global economic integration: What's new and what's not. Speech at the Federal Reserve Bank of Kansas City's Thirtieth Annual Economic Symposium, Jackson Hole, WY. Retrieved January 18, 2008, from http://www.federalreserve.gov/newsevents/speech/bernanke20060825.htm

Bhagwati, J. (2003). *Free trade today.* Princeton, NJ: Princeton University Press.

Blinder, A. S. (2006). Offshoring: The next industrial revolution? *Foreign Affairs,* March/April. Retrieved January 18, 2008, from http://www.foreignaffairs.org/20060301faessay85209/alan-s-blinder/offshoring-the-next-industrial-revolution.html

Chandra, A., Fealey, T., & Rau, P. (2006). National barriers to global competitiveness: The case of the IT Industry in India. *Competitiveness Review, 16*(1), 12-19.

Cline, M. K., & Guynes, C. S. (2001). A study of the impact of information technology investment on firm performance. *The Journal of Computer Information Systems, 41*(3), 15-20.

Dapice, D. (2004, March 1). Outsourcing debate - Part III: The losers in globalization must be helped. Yale Global Online. Retrieved April 28, 2008, from http://yaleglobal.yale.edu/display.article?id=3442

Dollar, D., & Kraay, A. (2001). Trade, growth, and poverty. *Finance and Development, 38*(3). Retrieved January 31, 2008, from http://www.imf.org/external/pubs/ft/fandd/2001/09/dollar.htm

Dossani, R., & Kenney, M. (2004, February 25). Outsourcing debate - Part I: American white-collar work going abroad means the US must re-train its workforce. *Yale Global Online.* Retrieved April 28, 2008, from http://yaleglobal.yale.edu/display.article?id=3406

Easton, N. (2008, January 18). Free trade fear on the rise. *CNNMoney-Fortune Magazine.* Retrieved January 21, 2008, from http://money.cnn.com/2008/01/18/news/economy/worldgoaway.fortune/index.htm

Guha, K. (2007, November 11). The world's currency could become America's problem. *Financial Times,* November 11, p. 7.

International Monetary Fund. (2007). World Economic Outlook Database. Data for 2007. Retrieved April 28, 2008, from http://www.imf.org/external/pubs/ft/weo/2008/01/weodata/index.aspx

Kroszner, R. S. (2007, May 15). International capital flows and the emerging-market economies. Speech at the Central de la Republica Argentina (BCRA) Seminar, Central Bank of Argentina, Buenos Aires, Argentina. Retrieved January 18, 2008, from http://www.federalreserve.gov/newsevents/speech/kroszner20070515.htm

Li, M., & Ye, L. R. (1999). Information technology and firm performance: Linking with environmental, strategic and managerial contexts. *Information & Management, 35*(1) 43-51.

McCarthy, J. C. (2004, May 14). Near-term growth of offshoring accelerating: Resizing U.S. service jobs going offshore. Retrieved April 27, 2008, from http://www.forrester.com/Research/Document/Excerpt/0,7211,34426,00.html

Mussa, M. (2000, August 25). Factors driving global economic integration. Speech at the Federal Reserve Bank of Kansas City's "Global Opportunities and Challenges" Symposium, Jackson Hole, WY. Retrieved January 18, 2008, from http://www.imf.org/external/np/speeches/2000/082500.htm

Organisation for Economic Co-operation and Development. (2007). Staying Competitive in the global economy: Moving up the value chain. Paris, France: OECD Publishing.

O'Rourke, K. H., & Williamson, J. G. (2000, April). *When did globalization begin?* NBER Working Paper Series. National Bureau of Economic Research (NBER Working Paper Series: Working Paper 7632). Cambridge, MA. Retrieved January 28, 2008, from http://faculty.lebow.drexel.edu/SyropoulosC/w7632.pdf

Ricardo, D. (2006). *The Principles of Political Economy and Taxation.* New York: Dover Books. (Original work published 1817)

Rowthorn, R., & Ramaswamy, R. (1997). Deindustrialization–Its causes and implications. *Economic Issues, 10.* Retrieved April 10, 2008, from http://www.imf.org/external/pubs/ft/issues10/index.htm

Shah, A. (2007). Free trade and globalization. Retrieved February 14, 2008, from http://www.globalissues.org/TradeRelated/FreeTrade.asp

Smith, A. (1991). *Wealth of Nations.* New York: Prometheus Books. (Original work published 1776)

Wolf, M. (2007, April 3). A Korean-American strand enters trade's spaghetti bowl. *Financial Times.*

Aggregate Supply and Aggregate Demand

Stephen L. Jackstadt
University of Alaska
Anchorage, Alaska

A proper understanding of aggregate supply and demand is essential to understanding macroeconomic concepts such as inflation, fiscal policy, and the effects of the business cycle. An understanding of this concept provides an analytical framework for students to master Standard IX in the economic content area of the National Business Education Association's (NBEA) standards: "Analyze how the U.S. economy functions as a whole and describe selected macroeconomic measures of economic activity" (NBEA, 2007, p. 66), as well as one of the National Council on Economic Education's (NCEE) 20 *Voluntary National Content Standards in Economics*, namely that:

> A nation's overall levels of income, employment, and prices are determined by the interaction of spending and production decisions made by all households, firms, government agencies, and others in the economy and that federal government budgetary policy and the Federal Reserve System's monetary policy influence the overall levels of employment, output, and prices (NCEE, 1997, p. 35).

This chapter defines aggregate supply and aggregate demand as total production of the economy (gross domestic product) and total spending on that production, and identifies the forces that lead to changes in aggregate supply and aggregate demand, thereby causing recessions, economic booms, inflation, and deflation. Virtually all of the curriculum materials needed to teach the classroom lessons at the end of each section of this chapter can be found on the CD entitled *Virtual Economics: An*

Interactive Center for Economic Education (2005), published by the National Council on Economic Education (www.ncee.net). The CD contains lesson plans, copies of classroom handouts, and audio and video clips.

AGGREGATE SUPPLY

The term "aggregate" is synonymous with "total." Aggregate supply may be defined as the total of all the goods and services produced by an economy in a specified period of time, and it is measured by the gross domestic product (GDP), the dollar value of all *final* goods and services produced in the nation in a single year (Miller, 2008).

GDP includes only final goods, such as loaves of bread and automobiles, in order to avoid double counting. If everything produced by the citizens and businesses of a country, including so-called intermediate goods, were counted, wheat might be counted when it is produced by a wheat farmer, then again when it is included in a loaf of bread sold at a bakery.

Two Ways to Measure GDP

When one person buys a good or service, the money he or she spends becomes someone else's income. This idea is often represented by the circular flow diagrams found in most high school and college economics textbooks (Lopus, Morton, Reinke, Shug, & Wentworth, 2005). Figure 1 illustrates the flows between households and firms in a highly simplified model of the economy. Business firms make income payments to households in return for land, labor, capital, and entrepreneurship resources. Households, in turn, use these payments to buy the goods and services that the firms produce. Since the total of all expenditures on goods and services produced in the United States equals all the income received by the people who produce it, GDP can be measured by using either the expenditure approach or the income approach.

Figure 1

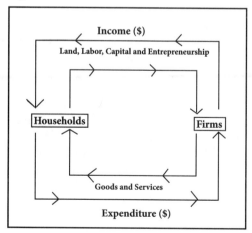

With the *expenditure approach*, GDP is measured by totaling the money spent in four categories: (1) consumption spending, (2) investment spending, (3) government purchases, and (4) net exports or spending by foreigners. Consumption spending is spending by people (consumers) on everyday things like automobiles, cans of soda, and haircuts. Consumer purchases account for about 70% of the U.S. GDP.

Investment spending includes spending by businesses on things like machinery, tools, and factory buildings (so-called "fixed investment"), spending on new housing ("residential investment"), and additions to existing inventories ("inventory investment"). Additions to existing inventories are counted as an investment, since inventories are an asset to a business. The more inventory businesses purchase, the more they can sell to consumers in the future (Sexton, 2008). In recent years, investment expenditures have accounted for about 15% of GDP.

Government purchases include all spending by all levels of government on goods and services. Purchases of jet fighters by the U.S. Air Force, purchases of computers by the U.S. Department of Agriculture, and the wages paid to police officers in New York City are all part of government spending. Government purchases account for a little less than 20% of the U.S. GDP.

Since people and businesses in other countries purchase goods and services produced in the United States, exports are counted as part of U.S. aggregate demand. Examples of U.S. exports to the rest of the world include grain, commercial airplanes, and scientific instruments. The things that U.S. consumers buy from abroad, such as oil and consumer electronics, however, are not part of U.S. output, so they are subtracted from total spending. Thus "net exports" are calculated as exports minus imports. Every year since 1982, the United States has bought more from foreigners than they have from us, so net exports have recently been negative by an amount equal to 5% of GDP.

To test their understanding of the expenditure approach to GDP, students can list what they have purchased in the past week (or day), with their responses recorded on the board. They might say sodas, DVDs, clothing, or a haircut. After they estimate the approximate prices of each good or service, they or the teacher can total the prices and point out that the dollar total represents their contribution to this year's expenditures in the consumption component of GDP (out of a total of $8.5 trillion in 2007). Of course, if they bought an imported item, it does not count. For example, if a student bought a latte for $3.00, 50¢ may be attributable to the imported Colombian coffee. In this case, only $2.50 would ultimately count toward the U.S. GDP since the coffee would have been subtracted in the calculation of net exports.

Using the *incomes approach* to calculating GDP, there are four categories of payments to individuals who provide productive resources to the economy: (1) wages and salaries, (2) profits, (3) interest, and (4) rents. Wages and salaries is the most important category since around 70% of U.S. incomes are received in this form. The next most sizeable component of income is profits. This category includes corporate profits made by firms like FedEx, Disney, and Coca-Cola, and the profits of smaller businesses such as a local dry cleaner or restaurant. Profits constitute about 20% of U.S.

incomes. The remaining components of income are interest on savings and other investments, and the rental income of property owners (Miller, 2008).

GDP as a Measure of Welfare

Gross Domestic Product represents a valuable way to keep track of a country's economic output over time and provides a means for comparing the size of one nation's economy with others. The GDP's use as a measure of economic welfare, however, is limited. First of all, GDP omits the value of non-market transactions such as the output of homemakers. If a family pays a professional yard maintenance service to tend its lawn, for example, that expenditure counts as part of GDP. If a member of the family cuts the lawn, however, the lawn still gets cut but the labor of the family member is not added to the GDP. When a woman marries her chauffer, as the old saying goes (or when a man marries his maid), the GDP falls!

Sales of used goods are omitted from GDP as well. When someone sells his or her 1995 Chevrolet, the buyer may be very pleased and the seller may have more money to spend, but the GDP does not change. The car was counted when it was produced in 1995. The same is true of the activity at a garage sale. Buyers go away with treasures they may find at remarkably low prices, and sellers can exchange unwanted goods for cash, but GDP is unaffected.

Obviously, illegal activities and cash transactions that are not reported for tax reasons are also excluded from GDP. The so-called *underground economy* includes gambling, drug dealing, and prostitution, as well as flea market deals, payments to babysitters that go unreported, and money earned by contractors who work "off the books." Economists' estimates of the size of the U.S. underground economy vary from less than 4% to more than 20% of GDP (Sexton, 2008).

GDP can also miss improvements in the quality of many of the goods produced today. For example, the quality of cell phones, computers, and medical care have all improved over the past decade, but much of this improvement has not shown up in measured GDP. GDP also makes no adjustment for economic "bads" such as pollution, congestion, noise, property losses resulting from natural or other disasters, and other things that have adverse affects on our lives.

Lastly, the value of leisure is left out of GDP calculations. Since the early 1900s the average workweek in the U.S. has declined from about 53 hours to about 35 hours. In addition, U.S. workers enjoy longer paid vacations and leave time (McConnell & Brue, 2008). This increase in leisure has increased the overall well-being of workers but does not show up in GDP calculations. While most measures of human well-being are related to GDP levels—for example, infant mortality declines as GDP rises—GDP also cannot and does not count all meaningful economic transactions or all sources of economic gains.

Determinants of Aggregate Supply

The ability of a nation to produce goods and services depends on four things: (1) the quantity of its land, labor, capital, and entrepreneurial resources; (2) its productivity; (3) input prices; and (4) the legal and institutional environment of the country.

The sheer quantity of a country's productive resources (land, labor, capital, and entrepreneurial ability) will help determine its ability to supply goods and services. An economy with a large population and lots of natural resources and machines will be able to produce more than an economy with less population, fewer natural resources, and fewer machines. The United States and China, for example, each produce more than either Switzerland or The Seychelles. As a country grows in population and adds more machines, factories, and other buildings to its capital stock, it will also be able to increase its aggregate supply. When the United States had a population of 181 million in 1960, its GDP adjusted for inflation was $2.5 trillion. In 2007, with a population of over 300 million (and a larger, more advanced capital base), its GDP, adjusted for inflation, was over $12 trillion.

Even without more resources, however, an economy can increase aggregate supply if *productivity* increases. Productivity, the amount of goods and services that can be produced by a given amount of resources in a specific period of time, is often described in terms of labor or output per worker (Clayton, 2008). Better education, improved technology, or smarter business practices can all increase productivity.

Input prices, i.e., the prices paid for the things that go into producing goods and services, affect aggregate supply by encouraging or discouraging production. Lower wages for carpenters and lower prices for lumber will make construction less expensive and increase the supply of houses. Lower prices for flour make it cheaper to make pizza and increase the number of pizzas produced at any given price. Of course, houses and pizzas are individual goods, but lower prices for key inputs like labor or raw materials make it less costly to produce most goods and services and increase aggregate supply.

Conversely, higher input prices make final goods and services more costly to produce and discourage increases in supply. In the 1970s, then-record-high world oil prices increased the cost of gasoline, fertilizer, plastic, and many other products. This situation led to a decrease in aggregate supply not only in the United States, but also in other countries and ushered in a decade of "stagflation," defined as stagnating economic growth accompanied by inflation.

Lastly, the legal and institutional environment of a country has a strong influence on its ability to produce output. Laws that protect property rights and promote competition among businesses, for example, promote productive activity. Costly government regulations that increase production costs, on the other hand, decrease production.

Well-functioning social institutions, including financial and court systems, are essential for productive economies. The Heritage Foundation and the Wall Street Journal publish an annual *Index of Economic Freedom* that focuses on institutions that help promote economic growth, including business freedom (how easy it is to start a business), financial freedom (the openness of a country's banking system), and freedom from corruption (Index of Economic Freedom, 2007).

Classroom Lesson: Gross Domestic Product (GDP) and How to Measure It

To evaluate your students' grasp of how GDP is measured, conduct Lesson 33 from Unit 6 of *Capstone*, "Gross Domestic Product (GDP) and How to Measure It" (Lopus et al., 2005, pp. 215-219). This activity will require two or three class sessions. The lesson is available on the NCEE's *Virtual Economics* CD (*Virtual Economics*, 2005).

AGGREGATE DEMAND

Aggregate demand is the total amount of spending on all final goods and services produced by the economy in a specified period of time. It is the quantity of the nation's GDP that consumers, business firms, governments, and foreigners are willing to purchase. It is equal to GDP minus inventories. The components of aggregate demand are consumption, investment (minus inventories), government purchases, and net exports.

Computing aggregate demand is nearly identical to computing GDP using the expenditure approach, except for the treatment of inventories. Inventories, since they represent production, are counted in GDP, but if they are not purchased, they are excluded from aggregate demand. If goods are not being purchased, GDP (aggregate supply) will be less than aggregate demand. On the other hand, aggregate demand can exceed aggregate supply if consumers, businesses, governments, and foreigners want to buy more than is being supplied.

Anything that changes the amount of total spending in the economy will affect aggregate demand (Sexton, 2008). An increase in consumer confidence, a tax cut, or a stock market boom that increases consumers' wealth will increase aggregate demand. An increase in interest rates that makes it more expensive for businesses to borrow in order to build more factories or buy more machines, or a reduction in government spending will decrease aggregate demand.

Classroom Lesson: Which Side Are You On?

After introducing the basics of aggregate supply and aggregate demand to middle or high school students, the teacher divides the class into two or more teams for a 20-question quiz show called "Which Side Are You On?" In this game, students score points by correctly determining whether one of 20 items that the teacher identifies is part of aggregate supply or aggregate demand. For example, "A shoe salesman" is in the category of aggregate supply, as is "A coal mine." "A woman buys a hamburger for her little boy" and "The government purchases a new submarine" are part of aggregate demand. Complete directions for playing this simple (and fun) game are in *Focus: High School Economics*, pages 232-233 and page 241 (Watts, McCorkle, Meszaros, & Schug, 2001). The lesson may also be accessed via the National Council on Economic Education's *Virtual Economics* CD (Virtual Economics, 2005).

MACROECONOMIC EQUILIBRIUM AND THE BUSINESS CYCLE

Macroeconomic equilibrium exists when aggregate supply is equal to aggregate demand; all the final goods and services offered for sale in the economy are purchased. If aggregate demand falls short of aggregate supply, however, goods will be left unsold on the shelves of retail stores, and businesses that produce services like haircuts and legal advice will find that they are losing customers. If businesses already have goods that they cannot sell, they may lower their prices to attract more customers and reduce their orders of goods from the factories that produce those goods. In turn, factories will cut output and lay off workers. If barber shops, lawyers' offices, and other service providers lose business, people in the service sector will be laid off.

Recessions and Unemployment

If aggregate demand falls enough, a recession may occur. A recession is a decline in real GDP lasting six months or more (Clayton, 2008). Recessions are usually accompanied by increases in the unemployment rate, which is the percentage of the civilian labor force that is without jobs but is actively looking for work. Not all citizens are part of the labor force. Students, retired people, and homemakers, for example, are not counted as part of the labor force. In 2006 the U.S. population totaled 300 million people, but only 230 million were in the labor force.

High unemployment is a problem not only because it reduces the amount of goods and services available to society, but also because it can create loss of self-respect, plummeting morale, family breakup, and sociopolitical unrest (McConnell & Brue, 2008). The unemployment caused by a decrease in aggregate demand relative to aggregate supply is called *cyclical unemployment*, since it is related to a downturn in the business cycle.

Business cycles are alternating increases and decreases in business activity over months or years. The most damaging and disastrous downturn in U.S. history was the Great Depression of the 1930s. From 1929 to 1933, real GDP fell by 30%, and the unemployment rate went from 3.2% to 25.2%. More recent recessions have been much milder and associated with much smaller increases in unemployment, although the recession that began in 2008 may turn out to be quite severe. As the consumption, fixed investment, and export components of aggregate demand fell during 2008 and the first part of 2009, GDP declined and the unemployment rate went up. During the last quarter of 2008, GDP fell at an annual rate of 3.8% and unemployment rose from 6.2 to 7.2%, as over 1.5 million U.S. workers lost their jobs (U.S. Department of Labor, 2009).

Demand-Pull Inflation

If, on the other hand, aggregate demand increases faster than aggregate supply, businesses will find that they cannot keep goods on their shelves. They will increase their orders to factories and factories will increase output, offer their employees overtime, and try to hire more workers. Service providers will find that they have more customers, and they will hire more workers as well. The unemployment rate will fall, GDP will increase, and the economy will expand.

If consumers, businesses, government, and foreigners try to buy more than the economy can produce, however, shortages will result and prices will be "pulled" up by excessive demand (Clayton, 2008). Inflation, defined as an increase in the general level of prices of final goods and services in the economy, is the dark side of economic booms caused by increases in aggregate demand.

The main measure of the price level in the United States is the Consumer Price Index (CPI). It compares prices for a fixed "basket" of over 300 goods and services commonly purchased in one year by consumers, such as hamburger, haircuts, and automobiles, to prices of the same goods and services in some earlier base period. The result is a measure of prices in any given year that can be compared with prices in the base period (currently set as equal to 100 for 1982-1984). In 2007 the value of the CPI was 210.0, indicating that the price level in 2007 was over twice what it was in 1982-1984, the base period.

Changes in Aggregate Supply

If aggregate supply increases rapidly due to a dramatic decline in oil prices such as occurred during the mid-1980s, or a productivity boom occurs as in the mid-1990s, the economy will grow rapidly, but price increases will stay low. The low-inflation economic expansions of the 1980s and 1990s are viewed by many economists as having been driven largely by the supply side of the macroeconomy.

A decrease in aggregate supply, however, caused by rising input prices, a slump in productivity, or laws that dramatically increase production costs can put a squeeze on profits, reduce the amount of output that firms are willing to supply at the existing price level, and result in *cost-push inflation* (McConnell & Brue, 2008).

As costs increase, the price level for the economy as a whole rises and the economy slows down. The period of *stagflation* (stagnating GDP and employment accompanied by inflation) suffered by the United States and other industrialized countries during the 1970s was due largely to big increases in oil prices brought about by the Oil Producing and Exporting Countries (OPEC) cartel oil embargo and the Iranian revolution. Anything that changes aggregate supply relative to aggregate demand will affect the levels of output and employment in the economy.

Classroom Lesson: Economic Ups and Downs
"Economic Ups and Downs," a lesson in *Focus: High School Economics* (Watts et al., 2001), can help middle and high school students understand the business cycle. In this lesson students use economic data to determine the relationships between GDP, inflation, and unemployment to understand how economic expansions and contractions can affect their own career goals.

USING AGGREGATE SUPPLY AND DEMAND CURVES
In recent years the most widely accepted innovation in teaching introductory macroeconomics has been the use of aggregate supply and aggregate demand curves to illustrate key macroeconomic concepts and policy issues (Lopus, et al., 2005). The *Virtual Economics* CD (Virtual Economics, 2005) includes an excellent introduction to aggregate supply and demand curves with animated audio-visual clips.

The Aggregate Supply Curve
The aggregate supply curve (AS) shows the amount of real GDP that will be produced at various price levels. As shown in Figure 2, the AS curve slopes up and to the right because if the prices of final goods and services go up and wages and other costs of production do not, overall profits will rise and induce producers to supply more to the marketplace—they offer more real GDP as the price level increases. The opposite is true if the price level falls (Miller, 2008).

Figure 2

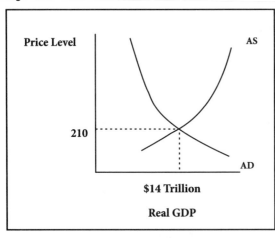

The Aggregate Demand Curve
The aggregate demand curve (AD) shows the amount of final goods and services that will be purchased by consumers, businesses, government, and foreigners at various price levels. The AD curve slopes down and to the right for two reasons. First, as the price level falls, consumers and others in the economy will find that their purchasing power has gone up. As a result, they will be able to buy more of everything. Of course as the prices rise, their purchasing power will decline, causing them to cut back on their purchases.

Second, as the price level falls in the United States, its goods become relatively cheaper for foreigners. They will buy more U.S. goods and services and thus contribute to an increase in the GDP. If U.S. prices rise, however, foreigners cut back on their purchases of Chevrolets, for example, and may cancel their planned trip to Disney World.

Putting Aggregate Supply and Aggregate Demand Together: Macroeconomic Equilibrium

Equilibrium level prices and real GDP are determined at the intersection of the AS and AD curves where everything supplied is equal to the amount that consumers, businesses, government, and foreigners want to buy. In Figure 2, the equilibrium price level is 210 and the equilibrium real GDP is $14 trillion. In macroeconomic equilibrium, there are no unsold inventories of goods, nor are any goods on "backorder" and temporarily unavailable, and prices are stable.

However, if something happens to cause one of the curves to shift, such as a stock market crash that reduces consumers' wealth and shakes their confidence, the economy will be thrown out of the existing equilibrium; prices, aggregate demand, and aggregate supply will adjust, and a new equilibrium will result. Figure 3 shows the effects of a decrease in AD. Such a decrease could be caused by anything that reduces spending by consumers, businesses, government, or foreigners. The drop in AD will result in unsold inventories. To reduce inventory levels, businesses will cut prices and reduce output. The price level will fall and output will decrease.

Figure 3

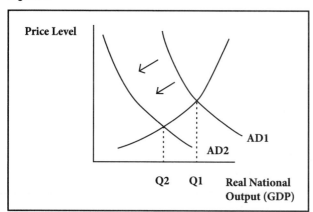

As can be shown using AS and AD curves, increases in AD will cause output and prices to rise. Increases in AS will increase output and put downward pressure on the price level, while decreases in AS will reduce output and cause the price level to rise.

Classroom Lesson: Aggregate Demand and Aggregate Supply

Instructors at all levels can secure their students' grasp of AD and AS curves by having them go through the comprehensive *Capstone* lesson on "Aggregate Demand and Aggregate Supply" (Lopus, et al., 2005). This lesson, which is also available on the *Virtual Economics* CD (Virtual Economics, 2005), lets students apply their understanding of these concepts in four different but related activities that take 150 minutes in total. In the first two activities, students identify different components of AD and AS and the factors that shift AD and AS. In the last two activities, students use AD and AS analysis to predict the effect of events and government monetary and fiscal policies on inflation, unemployment, and economic growth. (Governmental fiscal and monetary policy is discussed in Chapter 5 of this yearbook.)

SUMMARY

As stated in NBEA's *National Standards for Business Education* (2007), today's students "must understand how the American economic system operates as well as their own role in the system" (p. 60). Understanding macroeconomics, including aggregate supply and demand, is a matter of cultural literacy, self-interest, and civic responsibility (DeLong & Olney, 2006). A basic understanding of macroeconomics is essential in following economic events and understanding news reports, participating in public debates and discussions, and simply talking about economic issues with friends. In addition, the macroeconomy affects us all personally. Bouts of unexpected inflation hurt savers and lessen the burden of debt for borrowers, and swings in the business cycle can either help or hurt people looking for jobs. Lastly, as voters and as members of political parties or other civic organizations, an understanding of macroeconomics can help us distinguish good economic policies from bad. The more citizens know about the causes of recessions, unemployment, and inflation, the better chance we have of pursuing public policies that will raise our living standards.

REFERENCES

Clayton, G. (2008). *Economics: Principles and practices.* New York: McGraw-Hill Companies, Inc.

DeLong, J. & Olney, M. (2006). *Macroeconomics (2nd ed.).* New York: McGraw-Hill Companies.

Gwartney, J., Stroup, R., Sobel, R., & MacPherson, D. (2006). *Economics: Private and public choice (11th ed.).* Mason, OH: Thomson Higher Education.

Index of economic freedom. (2007). Heritage Foundation and the Wall Street Journal. Retrieved December 19, 2007, from http://www.heritage.org/research/features/index/index.cfm

Lopus, J., Morton, J., Reinke, R., Schug, M., & Wentworth, D. (2005). *Capstone: Exemplary lessons for high school economics.* New York: National Council on Economic Education.

McConnell, C. & Brue, S. (2008). *Economics: Principles, problems, and policies (17th ed.).* New York: McGraw-Hill Companies, Inc.

Miller, R. (2008). *Economics: Today and tomorrow.* New York: McGraw-Hill.

National Business Education Association. (2007). *National standards for business education: What America's students should know and be able to do in business.* Reston, VA: Author.

National Council on Economic Education. (1997). *Voluntary national content standards in economics.* New York: Author.

96

Chapter 7

Saunders, P., & Gilliard, J. (Eds.). (1995). *A framework for teaching basic economic concepts.* New York: National Council on Economic Education.

Sexton, R. (2008). *Exploring economics (4th ed.).* Mason, OH: Thomson Higher Education.

U.S. Department of Labor, Bureau of Labor Statistics. (2009, January). Employment Situation Summary. Retrieved February 6, 2009, from http://www.bls.gov/news.release/empsit.nr0.htm

Virtual economics: An interactive center for economic education (Version 3) (2005). [Computer Software]. New York: National Council on Economic Education.

Watts, M., McCorkle, S., Meszaros, B., & Schug, M. (2001). *Focus: High school economics (2nd ed.).* New York: National Council on Economic Education.

Personal Decision-Making

Heidi Perreault
Missouri State University
Springfield, Missouri

Teenagers make financial decisions daily. Most of these decisions relate to purchasing personal items. Teenagers spent an estimated $189 billion in 2006, and that figure is expected to grow to $208 billion by 2011 ("Technical Savvy," 2007). The most popular items purchased by teens are clothing, food, personal care products, and entertainment ("Teens Market in the U.S.," 2007). Teens strive to be financially responsible and 50% indicate they want to save money; however, many admit that they do not contribute to saving accounts because they routinely spend all their money ("Teen Market Profile," 2004).

Opting to spend today instead of saving for tomorrow is a financial issue faced by adults as well as teens. Marks and Scherer (2005) reported that individuals of all ages in the United States no longer contribute to savings accounts. The personal savings rate for the nation fell to less than 1% in 2005. While personal savings rates have been declining, personal debt has been increasing. The percentage of debt to disposable income has risen to over 125%. In comparison, during the 1950s, the percentage of debt to disposable income was about 40% (Bennett, 2006). According to Marks and Scherer (2005), many consumers are unable to gain control of their finances because they are too easily influenced by promotions and the desire for immediate gratification. Their undisciplined buying decisions result in a lack of funds available for savings and an increase in personal debt.

Education is the foundation for wise financial decision-making. Individuals who exhibit poor personal financial habits in their teens will continue to use the same habits as adults unless some sort of intervention is provided (Varcoe, Martin, Devitto, & Go, 2005). This chapter examines personal financial decision-making and provides instructional strategies to support informed financial practices and planning.

OVERVIEW OF PURCHASING DECISIONS

Everyone has needs and wants. From a budget perspective, needs must be purchased; wanted items do not need to be purchased. The problem for undisciplined consumers is that they do not separate the two concepts. Wants are routinely purchased as if they were needs. Couch (n.d.) noted that young consumers do not necessarily have a clear concept of the difference between needs and wants and blamed parents for this lack of understanding. Many parents often are not good financial management role models, and they fail to provide their children with basic financial management guidance. These parents typically do not discuss the difference between needs and wants with their children, nor do they include children in discussions relating to family or personal financial planning (Varcoe et al., 2005). Lack of planning can result in family purchasing decisions focused only on the immediate benefit that can be derived from a purchase. The following section provides an overview of factors that may influence young people to buy more than they can afford, and lists teaching strategies for helping students gain control of their purchasing habits.

Purchasing Influences

Both adult and teen purchasing habits are influenced by business marketing strategies. Marketing strategies often are designed to highlight the immediate benefit that consumers can gain from purchases, to stimulate desire for products or services, or to encourage immediate buying decisions. Wise consumers understand that advertising strategies are designed to call attention to items and to promote sales. Advertising, however, can be useful to consumers as it provides product information and can help consumers compare product features and costs. Some strategies, however, are designed to encourage consumers to purchase additional items that they may not have intended to buy, such as when a sandwich shop offers a discount when a large drink and bag of chips are purchased with a sandwich, or a clothing merchant offers a buy-one-get-one-half-off promotion. To avoid overbuying, shoppers need to make thoughtful purchasing decisions by evaluating the actual marginal benefits that may be realized with the purchase of additional items versus the money sacrificed to obtain those marginal benefits.

In addition to being swayed by marketing strategies, the ease with which young people can make purchases today sometimes contributes to poor decision-making. Purchasing opportunities are constantly available and encouraged by retailers. Easy access to cash from ATMs and the wide availability of credit cards compound the problems associated with poor buying habits. ATMs can contribute to impulsive buying by making it easy for consumers to obtain cash for unnecessary purchases. Instead of making a thoughtful decision regarding desired items, the items can be immediately purchased with cash obtained from an ATM located just outside the store. Credit cards make the purchasing process even easier. Consumer do not need to locate an ATM and do not need to have a balance of cash on hand from which to withdraw funds. A purchase can be made without regard to the current availability of funds or how the funds used will ultimately be repaid.

Credit cards are regularly issued to young consumers. Most students will have multiple credit cards by the time they enter college (O'Malley, n.d.). Fewer than half of college students with credit cards are able to pay their balances in full each billing cycle; many students make only the minimum payment allowed each billing period (Jones, 2005). Students reported feelings of anxiety related to their credit card debt, and anxiety levels increased when debt went over $500 ("Undergraduate Students," 2005). Anxiety levels associated with debt can negatively influence a student's likelihood of success. About 30% of the students in one study indicated that credit card debt was a main influence on their decisions to leave college or to take a job which prevented them from concentrating on their studies (Tan, 2003).

Purchasing Decisions
When considering a purchase, informed consumers first determine if the purchase is actually needed. Needs are necessities whereas wants are things desired but not needed. After determining if a potential purchase is a need or a want, the next step is to assess the opportunity cost and trade-off associated with the potential purchase. An opportunity cost is something of equal value that is no longer available because a financial decision has been made to purchase something else. Opportunity cost does not have to be viewed in monetary terms. In the example of the students needing to take a job to pay credit card bills, the opportunity cost resulting from the credit card purchases is the time no longer available for studying. The opportunity cost can be viewed as the alternative to the purchasing decision. If the students had not made excessive purchases, taking a job would be unnecessary and they would still have time available for their studies.

A trade-off represents what the purchaser gives or forgoes in exchange for the purchased item. If cash is used, the trade-off for making the purchase is having less cash available for future purchases. If the purchaser had enough money for two moderately priced items but chose instead to purchase one high-priced item, the trade-off would be getting only the one item instead of two. To make informed decisions, individuals need to consider the opportunity cost and trade-off associated with purchases with respect to their personal budgets and long-term financial goals. The lack of attention paid to opportunity cost and trade-off is not due to their complexity; they are not complex concepts. Young children can grasp the concepts. The problem is a lack of knowledge about these concepts or failure to use that knowledge.

Purchasing Instructional Activities

Mundrake and Brown (2001) stressed the importance of providing basic financial decision-making instruction early in the education system. Many parents look to schools to provide their children with financial literacy skills because they do not feel they are effective in providing financial guidance to their children (American Savings Education Council, 2001). By learning some of the following techniques for making wise purchasing decisions, students will be better able to manage their finances and begin building a foundation for financial success.

Purchasing choices. Elementary students can understand basic economic principles associated with purchasing decisions. After receiving instruction about the differences between needs and wants, the Indiana Council for Economic Education (2001) suggests having students draw pictures about their purchasing choices and label them as needs or wants. Based on their purchasing choices, students then write short paragraphs about which alternatives (opportunity costs) were available to them. Evaluation of student learning with these activities should be focused on whether students can differentiate between needs and wants and provide logical examples of opportunity costs.

An activity for older students is to have them examine their own spending weaknesses. The objective is to have the students develop a plan for controlling their personal purchasing habits by identifying where, why, and when they make most of their unplanned purchases. The first step is to determine when and where poor decisions occur. Poor buying decisions may occur when the student is on the Internet during the late evening, on Saturday mornings at a shopping mall, or when shopping with friends. After identifying potential problem times, places, or scenarios, the challenge for each student is to develop a plan for avoiding those situations. For example, students who identified late evening buying on the Internet as one of their weaknesses could set their own rules for Internet use after 9:00 p.m. One rule might be to avoid all shopping sites in the evening, or another could be to record desired items and wait until the morning to decide whether or not to purchase them.

The rationale for having students examine their own purchasing habits is to empower them to take control of their spending decisions. Establishing a plan and taking steps to control poor purchasing habits are key aspects to managing personal financial decision-making. Learning assessment for this activity should focus on the student's ability to identify poor decision-making habits and to establish a realistic plan to correct problematic buying behaviors.

Marketing awareness. Interesting and engaging activities to help elementary through junior high students understand how marketing techniques influence their purchasing decisions are available through a PBS online site called *Don't Buy It* (listed in the "Resources for Teachers" section). These activities help students identify and understand marketing strategies so they are less likely to be overly influenced by these types of strategies. One of the suggested activities is to have students create their own advertisements. Students then provide feedback to one another about the advertisements created, select the ones they think would most likely influence others to purchase an item, and explain those influences. Assessment of the success of student learning would focus on how well each student can identify basic marketing enticements and explain how such advertisements are intended to influence consumer behavior.

High school students can do more detailed examinations of marketing strategies. They can provide input on the goals of marketing from both a business and consumer viewpoint. One activity that can be enjoyable and meaningful to students is to have them locate what they feel are the most effective marketing strategies they see over a period of one week. In groups, they share details about the strategies and identify targeted consumers. To make the activity more relevant for teenagers, students can be instructed to select only strategies they feel are designed to influence teen buying. The purpose of the activity is to help students identify the intentions of various marketing strategies so they will be less influenced by them. Ideally, the activity would be followed by a discussion of how and why consumers should make quality purchasing decisions. Evaluation of student learning should be focused on how well students can differentiate between product information and the marketing strategies designed to make people buy. In addition, students should be able to explain the importance of making informed, planned purchasing decisions backed by logical planning.

Managing credit. Students of all ages are familiar with credit cards, but they may not know the true cost of credit card debt. A good resource for learning about the true cost of credit, *EconEdLink,* is provided at the end of this chapter. With this resource, students use an online credit calculator to compute how much they will actually pay if they select to make only the minimum payment due on credit card outstanding balances. The same resource offers a lesson on credit reporting that explains how a credit report is generated and how a credit report is used by financial organizations to evaluate borrowers' credit worthiness and extend credit.

With instructor facilitation, students should research and discuss the advantages and risks associated with credit cards. While credit cards can be an excellent way to build a credit history, they can be dangerous if used carelessly. Equipped with this information, students could create a consumer advice website that provides other students with information on proper credit card usage. Assessment of the website project could include evaluation of basic web design components, English usage, and the economic concepts relating to credit card usage.

A local speaker from a savings and loan or bank can be recruited to provide students with information on lending and the importance of a strong credit rating. The speaker should be asked to explain the likelihood of being approved for a loan given various levels of credit worthiness, and to compare the total cost of a loan for individuals who have a strong credit rating and a sizable down payment with the total cost to individuals who do not have strong credit worthiness. The purpose of the speaker is to make students aware of the importance of managing credit.

OVERVIEW OF FINANCIAL PLANNING DECISIONS

Karp (2007) suggests starting the financial planning decision-making process by setting realistic financial goals and then designing a plan to meet the goals. For example, a goal might be to have a certain amount of money available for a down payment on a car by the end of a year. The plan for reaching that goal of a needed down payment might be to put a fixed amount of money into a savings account each week. By focusing on a goal and sticking to a plan, a consumer is better able to resist the temptation to purchase unneeded items.

Consumers are responsible for developing their own financial plans. However, as financial options become more complex, it is wise to look to others for guidance and information. Most banks offer some financial planning guidance, particularly relating to investing funds. Information on pension plans and other financial benefits supported through the workplace can be obtained through an employer's human resources department. Benefits may include investment options and health and life insurance plans. Many consumers choose to work with financial advisors to get advice or to learn more about financial planning options. A financial advisor will assist individuals and families in setting realistic goals and developing plans for meeting those goals. A fee is charged for this assistance. Although an advisor will provide information on financial options and guidance on developing financial plans, consumers must make the decisions relating to their own personal financial goals and accept the responsibility to take the steps needed to achieve those goals.

Personal Information Management

An area related to financial management needing continuous consumer attention is protecting personal information. Over 8 million U.S. citizens are victims of identity theft each year ("FTC Releases," 2007). Identity theft occurs whenever a person uses another individual's personal identifying information without permission. Personal identifying information examples are social security numbers, names, and credit card numbers. Thieves get the information by rummaging through trash for personal information, stealing wallets, and getting individuals to share personal information by pretending to be a representative of the individual's bank or credit card company. Today, much of this theft is done through bogus e-mail messages claiming to originate from banks or credit card companies. Diligence is also needed to protect personal information when using debit or credit cards. Card numbers should be guarded and a PIN never shared.

Students' understanding of their liability if a debit or credit card is stolen or used without their authorization is important. Liability for unauthorized use of a debit or credit card can range from $50 to $500. Reporting a lost card or unauthorized use to the credit or debit card company within two business days typically reduces the potential loss to $50. The financial institution issuing the debit or credit card must disclose liability limit information and provide details on the consumer's responsibility for reporting unauthorized use in its written agreement with each cardholder. Card users must read and understand their credit card agreements. Although their policies and procedures may vary, institutions must follow the guidelines set by the government. Regulations pertaining to debit cards are covered by the Electronic Fund Transfer Act, while credit card liability and error resolution procedures are covered by the Fair Credit Billing Act ("Facts for Consumers," 2003).

When making online purchases, extra care is needed. Passwords should never be shared and students need to be aware that e-mail scams trying to obtain passwords abound. Individuals are responsible for securing their own passwords. Consumers need to be alert to online scams and only make purchases from reputable companies. Although online shoppers indicate they are concerned about the safety of making online purchases, only about 60% of shoppers actually check the security policy on the sites where they shop (Mello, 2005). Credit card information should be shared only with sites that provide assurances that transactions are secure and that personal information will be protected and not shared. Reputable retailers will detail their privacy policies and security information on their websites. Each privacy policy will indicate if a shopper's personal information is to be shared with other business organizations and should provide an option for customers to indicate if they do not want any of their personal information shared. Vendor online security policies typically will include an explanation of how the organization protects financial transactions, such as if the vendor uses encryption technology. Encryption technology scrambles text and numeric information being sent from the buyer's computer, and unscrambles the data when it reaches the company's secure server. The purpose is to prevent sensitive financial and personal information from being intercepted in transit by third parties. Should encrypted information be intercepted, it is unreadable without the encryption code.

Financial Planning Teaching Activities

Real-life examples are an excellent way to introduce financial planning to students ("Focus on Finance," 2006). Activities should require students to make the same type of decisions as they can expect to make in life. If students are not familiar with making structured decisions, a lesson on how to make quality decisions would be appropriate. The decision-making process includes identifying the problem, gathering information on alternative solutions, considering the consequences of each alternative, selecting the best course of action, and evaluating the results. Resources for teaching structured decision-making are provided in *EconEdLink*. Lesson plans requiring decisions on real-life financial issues will engage students in using their decision-making skills as they learn financial planning concepts.

Savings plan. One fundamental financial planning concept is to develop a savings plan. No matter what their ages, students will benefit from discussions relating to the opportunity cost and trade-off associated with decisions about savings versus spending. If a purchase is made, one identifiable opportunity cost is the interest that could have been earned on the same amount of money had it been saved instead of spent. The trade-off is not having that money for future purchases. Adams (2000) suggested having students create personal spending and savings plans early in the school year. The teacher then collects and seals the plans in an envelope. Later in the year, the students open their envelopes and evaluate their progress relating to their plans. Student evaluation is not based on whether they met their plans' objectives, but how well they explain why they did or did not follow their plans. A follow-up activity is to have students make adjustments as needed to their original plans. These activities hold students responsible for designing their own plans, meeting their objectives, and for determining if their plans are wise and realistic for their situations.

Following a savings plan may require a student to modify spending habits. Students should be encouraged to think about spending habits in relation to long-term goals. Good resources to teach planning for savings (with lesson plans and handouts) are available through the Federal Reserve Bank of Dallas program called *Building Wealth* (listed under "Resources for Teachers"). A print version and an online, interactive tutorial are available. Students are challenged to provide their own definitions of wealth and to set personal financial goals. In order to meet their goals, students have to determine what changes may be required in their current spending habits. Evaluation of student learning would include having students describe their decision-making processes and the logical steps in their respective plans of action to reach their personal financial goals.

Financial management. Another financial planning activity that is appropriate for students of all ages involves using a budget to guide personal spending. Whether a student's income comes from an allowance or a job, a budget can be used to set spending limits and establish savings goals. Developing a budget provides an opportunity for the student to use spreadsheet technology, mathematics, and decision-making skills. The objective is to have students set financial goals that will guide a spending plan. Using the budget, they can do a series of "what if" scenarios to examine the consequences to their financial plan if they made unplanned purchases or incurred unanticipated expenses. Evaluation of student learning should focus on the student's ability to develop a budget to fit a set goal and to explain why goals and plans are needed for financial success.

Older students can be expected to make similar judgments but on a more complex level. They might be asked to list and justify two strategies for meeting goals, explain how they will monitor and make adjustments to plans, indicate how budgets support financial planning, devise strategies for establishing or improving a credit history, or outline the consequences of excessive debt. Activities may have multiple evaluative criteria. For the criteria relating to decision-making, the assessment should focus on the process the student followed to make a selection or judgment.

A quality instructional resource to consider for planning activities is the *NEFE* (National Endowment for Financial Education) *High School Financial Planning Program* listed "Resources for Teachers" below. The focus is on individual student planning by making all activities relevant to students. Students create budgets to fit their situation and make plans based on personal goals.

To depict the importance of financial decision-making for families, students can work in small groups and develop a series of budget scenarios for young families with different incomes. Based on the scenarios, students can set realistic savings goals for each family and create a spending plan based on each family's income. The teacher can insert special events into the scenarios such as a sale on desirable but nonessential items, a financial loss such as a fire or traffic accident, or the birth of a child. The objective is to have students determine the opportunity costs when funds are used for immediate purchases instead of saved for investments, emergencies, or down payments on major purchases such as a car.

The family financial planning activity can be expanded by having the students create hypothetical financial statements and charts as a means to examine the many factors involved in managing household finances. Discussions should be part of the teaching strategy in order to emphasize personal responsibility and the careful decision-making that must be part of a wise financial management plan. Working in teams will provide students with opportunities to discuss options and to make compromises since team members are likely to have different spending priorities. This activity can simulate a real family setting where one member's immediate goal may be to build a savings account balance while another member's goal may be to allocate the funds for a down payment on a major purchase. Neither goal is wrong; they are just different. Family members need to make compromises and work together to build financial security. This activity will help develop these skills.

An engaging program requiring real-life decision making skills is *LifeSmart* (listed in "Resources for Teachers"). *LifeSmart* provides a competitive and challenging game environment that incorporates financial information and consumer responsibility issues. Students work in teams and compete against other teams across the nation. Learning assessment should involve students in justifying their actions and indicating what information they used as the basis for their decisions.

A big decision that high school students must make that is directly related to financial planning is whether to attend college or go directly into the workforce. Students can do the research to obtain information on expected salaries for different careers, some of which may require a degree and some of which may not. They can determine potential incomes in various jobs and compute the opportunity costs of the competing opportunities. Students can then select a career based on their personal financial goals and interests. Based on that career decision, a financial plan can be devised. The plan must be realistic and flexible enough to allow for unexpected events over a five-year period.

Investing is also an important financial concept requiring considerable research and careful decision-making. Two resources provide excellent investment-related guidance materials for high school students. The NEFE High School Financial Planning Program engages students in creating personal investment plans. The Stock Market Game provides a series of lessons to prepare students for an interactive simulation where student teams are given $100,000 to invest and the goal is to build equity in the stock market. All transactions are recorded by each team so the teacher will have a record of group decisions. Learning assessment should include having students identify their investment options, predict investment growth, identify and describe potential risks, justify the choices they made, and provide an assessment of alternative choices that were available.

COLLABORATION WITH ACADEMIC AREAS

The educational standards associated with financial decision-making are appropriate for multiple academic areas. The National Standards for Business Education note that all citizens and consumers need to be prepared to make decisions relating to personal finance (NBEA, 2007). Collaboration between business education and other academic areas to support financial awareness is suggested. Collaboration can include joint teaching activities or coordinating activities so the financial concepts covered in the business education classroom are being complemented by the lessons being presented in other academic areas. One of the resources listed in the next section designed for teachers from multiple disciplines is *The Mint*. *The Mint* provides activities with lesson objectives and guidelines on basic financial decision-making topics, such as opportunity cost, and more advanced financial concepts, such as investments and credit risk.

National standards for social studies include economic concepts such as scarcity, trade-off, and opportunity cost (National Council for the Social Studies, 1994). While the business classroom may focus on trade-off and opportunity cost from a personal finance viewpoint, the social studies classroom can cover the same concepts from a community or national perspective in lessons involving micro- and macroeconomics. Teachers in both areas can coordinate with each other to have similar concepts introduced at the same time so that activities completed in the business classroom complement the activities being completed in the social studies classroom.

Mathematics is another academic area with national standards (National Council of Teachers of Mathematics, 2000) that can be aligned with financial planning. One of the national standards for mathematics is to have students solve realistic problems outside the contexts of mathematics. Creating a budget and developing savings plans will allow students to practice financial goal setting while using mathematics applied to real-life situations. One of the resources listed in the following section, *It all adds up,* focuses on math and financial planning. Learning activities are aligned with standards for mathematics and include getting credit, buying a car, budgeting, and funding college. Teachers in either the math or business discipline can use these suggested activities. The ideal situation would be for the math and business teachers to coordinate so that the financial planning concepts taught in the business classroom also apply in lessons taught in the mathematics classroom. Many of the resources listed in the next section are appropriate for business or non-business courses.

RESOURCES FOR TEACHERS

The resources in this section are provided by reputable organizations at no charge or at very little cost. Each of them includes interesting and engaging activities that focus on developing savvy purchasing and financial planning skills, and require students to make decisions that mirror potential real-world decisions. Activities appropriate for introducing personal financial decision-making to students of all ages are offered. Instructional materials include lesson plans and handouts.

1. *Building Wealth*: http://www.dallasfed.org/ca/wealth/index.cfm. Either a print or an interactive version is provided to help young adults develop plans for financially secure futures. Controlling debt, investing, and budgeting are stressed.

2. *Don't Buy It*: http://pbskids.org/dontbuyit. This interactive website is for younger students. Activities are designed to have students think critically about advertising strategies so they will be able to make informed purchasing decisions.

3. *EconEdLink*: http://www.econedlink.org/. This site, hosted by the National Council on Economic Education, provides a multitude of lesson plans with handouts and online resources for students and teachers to use.

4. *It All Adds Up*: http://www.italladdsup.org. Lesson plans with math and economic financial awareness are provided. Budgeting, obtaining and using credit, saving, and funding college are included. Lessons are very appropriate for high school students.

5. *LifeSmarts*: http://www.lifesmarts.org. High school students work in teams and compete against other teams in a game show format. Learning topics with this resource include personal finance and consumer responsibility.

6. National Council on Economic Education: http://www.ncee.net/programs. The Council provides links to a series of programs and materials designed for grade levels from kindergarten through high school. A listing of CD-ROM and Internet-based teaching materials is also provided.

7. *NEFE High School Financial Planning Program*: http://hsfpp.nefe.org/home. NEFE provides a series of lesson plans at no charge to teachers. Student workbooks and assessment strategies are available. Topics include budgeting, investing, and using credit wisely.

8. *The Mint*: http://themint.org. The Mint provides lesson plans for teaching money management to students in middle and high school. Lessons focus on making decisions relating to personal finances.

9. *The Stock Market Game*: http://www.smg2000.org/. Students research investment opportunities, work in teams to evaluate investments, and use virtual cash to make investments in the stock market.

SUMMARY

Making informed financial decisions is a life-long process (Jones, 2004). Since parents are not always providing their children with the foundation upon which to make prudent purchasing decisions, educators can provide their students with that information. Opportunities to discuss the differences between wants and needs, to identify marketing ploys, to develop savings plans, and to create sound personal budgets provide students with fundamental financial decision-making skills and set the stage for more advanced financial decision-making concepts to be learned throughout life. Armed with the skills to create and monitor personal purchasing habits and establish essential savings plans, students can begin making quality financial decisions that can influence their financial well-being throughout their lives.

High school students should be provided with real-life projects. Activities such as developing personal money management plans, investment portfolios, and completing the loan application process are excellent for learning about financial issues (Policies Commission, n.d.). Activities should require students to use their academic as well as business skills. They should be challenged by the activities and given opportunities to do research, evaluate alternatives, and make financial decisions based on their personal goals. An important aspect to include in all assessment criteria is evaluating the decision-making process itself. Whether the exercises have students creating budgets or examining investment options, evaluation should include student reflection on the process used to make judgments. Students should be able to explain their reasoning, justify their strategies, and describe the benefits and potential disadvantages of their decisions.

Individuals need to be adequately prepared with the knowledge and skills necessary to make quality decisions and to plan for their own financial futures (Adams, 2000). Having students learn prudent personal decision-making while engaged in realistic situations will help prepare them for the challenging financial decisions that they will be making throughout their lifetimes.

REFERENCES

Adams, E. (2000). Consumer finance: A teaching framework including strategies, activities, and resources. *Instructional Strategies, 16*(3), 1-6.

American Savings Education Council. (2001). Parents, youth & money. Washington, DC: Author.

Bennett, J. (2006, August 8). Why consumer debt is rising. *Newsweek*. Retrieved September 20, 2007, from http://www.msnbc.msn.com/id/14251360/site/newsweek/page/0/

Couch, C. (n.d.). 4 fiscal lessons you need to teach your kids. Bankrate.Com. Retrieved October 24, 2007, from http://www.bankrate.com/brm/news/pf/20070807_financial_lessons_for_kids_a1.asp.

Facts for Consumers. (2003). Federal Trade Commission. Retrieved September 26, 2007, from http://www.ftc.gov/bcp/conline/pubs/online/payments.shtm

Focus on Finance. (2006, March). *Keying In 16*(4). The Newsletter of the National Business Education Association.

FTC Releases Survey of Identity Theft in the U.S. (2007, November 27). News Release. Retrieved November 28, 2007, from http://www.ftc.gov/opa/2007/11/idtheft.shtm

Indiana Council for Economic Education. (2001). KidsEcon Posters. Retrieved October 17, 2007, from http://www.kidseconposters.com

Jones, J. (2005). College students' knowledge and use of credit. *Financial Counseling and Planning, 16*(2), 9-16.

Jones, M. (2004). Impulse buying: Keeping impulse purchases under control. Retrieved August 23, 2007, from http://www.betterbudgeting.com/articles/money/impulsebuying.htm

Karp, G. (2007). Time, distance can quell impulse buying. *Chicago Tribune Online*. Retrieved August 27, 2007, from http://www.chicagotribune.com/business/yourmoney/sns-yourmoney-0325spending,0,515

Marks, A. & Scherer, R. (2005, August 3). Spendthrift nation. *Christian Science Monitor*. Retrieved September 20, 2007, from http://www.csmonitor.com/2005/0803/p01s02-usec.html

Mello, J. (2005, November 11). Less than half of consumers feel safe shopping online. *E-Commerce Times*. Retrieved September 26, 2007, from http://www.ecommercetimes.com/story/47272.html

Mundrake, G., & Brown, B. (2001). A case for personal financial education. *Business Education Forum, 58*(1), 22-25.

National Business Education Association. (2007). *National standards for business education: What America's students should know and be able to do in business.* Reston, VA: Author.

National Council for the Social Studies. (1994). *Curriculum standards for social studies.* Silver Spring, MD: Author.

National Council of Teachers of Mathematics. (2000). *Principles & standards for school mathematics.* Reston, VA: Author.

O'Malley, M. (n.d.). Educating undergraduates on using credit cards. Retrieved September 19, 2007, from http://www.nelliemae.com/library/cc_use.html

Policies Commission for Business and Economic Education. (n.d.). *This we believe about the role of business education in financial education: Policy statement #69.* Retrieved November 27, 2007, from http://www.nbea.org/curfpolicy.html

Tan, D. (2003). Oklahoma college students credit card study. University of Oklahoma, Center for Student Affairs Research. Retrieved September 26, 2007, from http://www.ou.edu/education/csar/credit_card/credit_card_report.pdf

Technical savvy and purchasing power to drive teen market beyond $200 billion by 2011, despite decline in teen population. (2007, June 26). Press Release. Retrieved September 25, 2007, from http://www.packagedfacts.com/about/release.asp?id=922

Teen market profile (2004). Magazine Publishers of America. Retrieved September 18, 2007, from http://www.magazine.org/content/files/teenprofile04.pdf

Teens market in the U.S. (2007). Report Buyer. Retrieved September 20, 2007, from http://www.reportbuyer.com/consumer_goods_retail/demographics/teens_market_u_s_.html

Undergraduate students and credit cards in 2004. (2005). Nellie Mae. Braintree Hill, MA: Author.

Varcoe, K., Martin, A., Devitto, Z., & Go, C. (2005). Using a financial education curriculum for teens. *Financial Counseling and Planning, 16*(1): 63-71.

Earning and Reporting Income

David J. Hyslop
D.J. Kern-Blystone
Bowling Green State University
Bowling Green, Ohio

There is a direct relationship between the educational background of an individual and that person's lifetime earning potential. The purpose of this chapter is to help provide business teachers with a foundation upon which they can understand key concepts about earning and reporting income and to help them develop experiential learning activities for their students. The chapter begins with a discussion of the relationship between learning and earning and is followed by an examination of income categories other than wages. The chapter then discusses career selection and planning income potential within career fields, occupational interest considerations, and enhancements to wages. Next, the chapter discusses the evaluation of income needs and concludes with a discussion of earner-taxpayer considerations. Each section includes a subsection containing teaching ideas and resources.

RELATIONSHIP BETWEEN LEARNING AND EARNING

As students begin to investigate their career options, they find that the key to meeting their employment goals is graduation from high school and completion of some level of postsecondary education or training. Research shows that ethnicity (White, Black, Hispanic, Asian/Pacific Islander) and gender have no significance in relation to income potential when an employee has less than a high school education (Day & Newburger, 2002). Day and Newburger report from the U.S. Census Bureau (2002) that approximately 84% of the American population 25 years of age and older has a high school diploma, with 26% of that group having earned a baccalaureate degree. Further, census reports indicate that high school dropouts working full-time for 40 years will earn (in 1999 dollars) approximately $750,000 in their lifetimes. This increases to approximately $1.2 million for the average high school graduate; for those with a bachelor's degree, average lifetime earnings increase still more to approximately $2.1 million. Students in high school and those in postsecondary education need to understand the important difference that college graduation makes in their potential earnings and subsequent prospective life style. Porter (2002) reports a positive benefit in standard of living as measured by personal and professional opportunities, quality of life for family members, consumer spending and savings power, and opportunities for recreation when an individual earns a college degree. Students need to realize that the education milestones of high school and college graduation are key elements when working toward advanced opportunities on a career path and increased earnings potential.

Paying careful attention to national and global economic situations can help students select occupations with good earnings potential for their futures. As students consider career options, they also need to research economic trends related to their fields of interest. Students will find that the Bureau of Labor Statistics predicts a decline in goods-producing industries such as construction, manufacturing, agriculture, forestry, fishing and hunting, and mining. Conversely, researchers predict job growth in education and health services, professional and business services, leisure and hospitality, non-government services, information services, financial services, trade, transportation and utilities services, and government services (Bureau of Labor Statistics, 2007). Business educators also need to stay abreast of these employment trends in order to mentor their students in career exploration activities.

Teaching and Assessing Learning and Earning Concepts

As a method for students to discover potential career paths, business educators should use projects that engage students in research. An inquiry-based project is best suited for students to answer the fundamental question, "What occupational area will best suit me in my life?" Personally meaningful employment information can be obtained by students when engaged in research about careers of interest to them versus just being instructed that career research should be done with a given set of resources.

Middle school students may begin this process by participating in a self-assessment of interests, aptitudes, and abilities. The business teacher will need to work with the guidance and/or career education staff to use instruments approved by their school. Once students have determined patterns of interest, they can find a multitude of resources in school and in local libraries and possibly from local citizens employed in their preferred career areas. An excellent opportunity to develop communication and research skills is for students to interview someone employed in their chosen fields or to read about their chosen fields in resource materials such as the *Occupational*

Outlook Handbook (http://www.bls.gov/OCO/) and compile written and/or oral presentations. Using assessment rubrics from colleagues in the English or language arts department will help build continuity between disciplines and reinforce related standards and benchmarks across curriculum areas.

Secondary and postsecondary teachers may use their classrooms as a center for active learning to promote deep and meaningful education in the topic of learning and earning. In his book *Active Learning*, Mel Silberman (1996) discussed the need for socialization as a part of the learning process and promoted the use of collaborative learning with adolescents and young adults. This approach encourages teachers to become guides in the learning process as students discover answers to questions posed by the instructor. When the answers are outside the realm of classroom resources, this collaborative approach can be extended by bringing community partners to the school to further help students with their inquiry. Such outside business partners may visit the classroom via electronic means (through the use of Skype, blogging, and/or email or messaging) or with face-to-face discussions in the school or through field trips to the workplace. Teachers may also use the Internet as a resource in this process to help students examine the interconnectedness of global economies and job opportunities as influenced by global supply and demand. The Bureau of Labor Statistics website (http://www.bls.gov/jobs/) has numerous links to undertake such an investigation.

NON-WAGE INCOME SOURCES

Non-wage income refers to revenue derived from savings or other income produced by investing wages. From the time young people begin earning money with initial jobs (such as yard care, babysitting, and housework), they often start to formulate plans for future earnings and how to spend their income. However, the opportunity to earn money from their wages in a wise manner is not always a part of the student's early planning. Reviewing non-wage earning potential with students gives the educator an opportunity to teach students to extend their earning power.

As students look at various occupations and the earnings potential of various jobs, they should also be taught to compare and contrast the advantages and opportunity costs of moving a portion of their potential income into investments and other areas for generating non-wage earnings (National Business Education Association, 2007). This analysis could include income sources from retirement plans, interest from savings programs, self-employment income, capital gains on investments, partnerships or corporate income, and dividends. These sources have been identified as the six key areas for non-wage income earnings in the United States (U.S. General Accounting Office, 1996). Sources for non-wage income may also include employer 401(k) plans, company stock options, Roth IRAs, and/or direct deposit savings opportunities. Students may have jobs while in school but whether currently employed or not, they need to appreciate the importance of successful planning with regard to non-wage earnings opportunities.

Teaching and Assessing Non-Wage Income Concepts

Teaching this topic can be enhanced by using a project approach. Students could research non-wage income sources and complete an analysis of the benefits of each source they select in terms of future income that might be generated in addition to wages from employment. Potential sources could include retirement plans (401(k), 403(b), government and private source pensions, IRAs), interest from savings programs, self-employment income, capital gains, partnerships or corporate income, and dividends. Projects with simple scenarios can give students the opportunity to research the most common sources available to them given hypothetical employment scenarios. The goal for such an activity is for the students to determine which of the sources would suit their individual situations and income goals. Students may develop a plan to use one or more of these sources at the beginning of a job and tailor the mix of these sources as they advance through their hypothetical employment life cycle.

For example, at the middle school level, each student would be given a specific amount of money to be invested for income growth. Teachers could use the example of allowances, yard care or babysitting income, and/or gifts as the original sources of income. Teachers may focus on savings opportunities with banks and mutual funds or dividend income from investment in shares of stock. At the high school or postsecondary levels, students may begin with a hypothetical amount of money that was "earned" through employment. The students who are unemployed may select an employer for purposes of this activity and determine a reasonable annual income by researching the *Occupational Outlook Handbook* (discussed in "Analysis of Income Potential" below). If students are employed, they can use their own paycheck data to assess the potential income that they might generate through simple savings accounts at banks or credit unions. At this level, students may investigate retirement plans, investing in their employment company and other business ventures, and starting their own company as they examine the potential for generating income from all of the major sources listed above. They might also project potential retirement income or potential income from stock option programs available from their employers. They could also study the impact of government taxation laws, such as deductions for income tax and costs and benefits of Medicare and Social Security.

Assessment of this learning would include several items—

- A check-sheet of all areas required for exploration in the project, which includes examples of income earned in the last five years by investors in those areas examined;

- Written and/or verbal reflection on each area investigated for its potential for income and the relationship or lack of relationship to the student's personal goals for the future;

- A plan developed by the student for use over the next several years to generate non-wage income;

- A discussion with classmates to compare information gathered and assess the quality of the research.

Teachers may also use prepared lesson plans to help facilitate the learning in this area. As an example, *EconEdLink,* provided by the National Council on Economic Education (http://www.econedlink.org), has several lesson plans for student activities. Teaching strategies, student materials, and assessment tools are provided. "The Benefits of Investing Early" (http://www.econedlink.org/lessons/index.cfm?lesson=MM 603&page=teacher) has a lesson plan and student resources (http://www.econedlink. org/lessons/index.cfm?lesson=MM603) that demonstrate the concept of compound interest. Students can challenge themselves to investigate their own capacity to save, and by so doing, see how they can maximize their non-wage earning potential throughout their lives. The lesson plan is linked to economic concept standards and provides an assessment of the learning.

CAREER SELECTION AND PLANNING
The National Business Education Association standards (2007) specify that student career development exploration should include analysis focused on self awareness, career research, workplace expectations, career strategies, school-to-career transitions, and lifelong learning:

- Self-awareness involve identifying work and non-work preferences and abilities;

- Career research focus on investigating a career field (i.e. business management);

- Workplace expectations include job conditions as well as expectations for employees while on the job;

- Career strategies involve exploring the steps and paths that might lead from an entry-level position to the peak career desired;

- School-to-career transitions involve a review of the preparation needed at various levels of education (middle school, high school, and postsecondary) to secure the position desired; and

- Life-long learning includes analysis of what is needed to remain in a specific career and/or to be prepared to take another path in the field as it evolves.

Teaching and Assessing Career Selection and Planning Concepts
Individual career exploration lessons could begin with a review of personal interests as discussed earlier in the chapter. Then a teacher can use a common career self-test assessment (such as the Kuder test, The Career Key, Work Preference Inventory, or Job Diagnosis) to give individual feedback related to the 16 career clusters identified by the U.S. Department of Education report on secondary taxonomies (U.S. Office of Vocational and Adult Education, n.d.). All states have information about specific career

fields and the employment opportunities within their state. Teachers should review their respective state department of education websites, particularly in the subcategory of career and technical education, to find many sources of information about the 16 career clusters offered within their schools.

Business teachers will also find extensive information about career options and the required academic qualifications for each career field at the National Tech Prep Network website (http://www.cord.org) or their state Tech Prep website. Information about the career clusters, career and job trend data, earnings data, education require-ments, and ideas for field experiences is available in each. An issue of the NBEA news-letter contained an article entitled "Emerging Careers" (*Keying In*, 2007) is another resource for students.

The *EconEdLink* site (http://www.EconEdLink.org) and the National Endowment for Financial Education (http://www.nefe.org) provide teaching materials that can be tailored to the needs of each student. By utilizing the resources from these two organi-zations, students can explore their own interests and begin to see the relationship between their interests and career planning. They can become aware of the link between education and success in a career and realize that education for proper preparation for a career will help them realize the lifestyle choices they have targeted as goals. For example, teachers will find two topics on the EconEdLink site with lessons and student material links for these two topics: "Education: Weigh Your Options" and "College: Where Am I Going to Go?" NEFE offers specific career investigation information through its web portal (http://hsfpp.nefe.org/home/) with free teacher and student materials. Teacher resources are simple to order by registering with NEFE. The materials offered encompass an identification of personal skills, job skills required, benefits of education, employee benefits comparison, job trends, and other factors to consider when selecting a career.

Effective teaching, especially in business education, is enriched using contextual learning. This approach promotes the use of authentic or "real world" project-based and/or problem-based learning strategies that can be tailored to meet the learning styles of all students. For example, a specific problem (like "What career is best for me?") could be posed by the teacher, used by students in their investigation, and summarized for sharing with others.

The steps students could complete as part of this project would include the following:

- Students select a career field based upon previous research completed using the Tech Prep resources as well as their personal career inventory self-assessment described above. The target job within that field would reflect the learning about the relationship of education and employment opportunities (using EconEdLink and/or NEFE lessons described above);

- Students identify the following sources for current research in the career field:

  Community people who currently are employed in the field selected for interview research

  Internet cites with current information on the job fields, careers information (such as NEFE), and education programs (postsecondary websites)

  Library resources for career field information;

- Students compile their career information to match a list of requirements as determined by the business educator;

- Students write a report, create a poster, and or develop a presentation for a class career fair to share with their peers.

The use of this contextual teaching and learning exercise would have several significant benefits in this area. Projects would extend the learning to in- and out-of-school settings to explore realistic problems, the experiences would mimic personal and family roles and responsibilities in career selection and planning, and students would be able to develop and advance their critical thinking skills. A project that incorporates a self-analysis of this information and requires a final report will then offer the student the opportunity to make all of the information relevant and useful on a personal level. To add authenticity to the assignment, the students' works could be offered as a collection of resources for the school library to be used by their peers.

The National Business Education Association 2008 Yearbook, *Effective Methods of Teaching Business Education*, offers a number of suggestions for business educators to use as assessments of student performance (NBEA, 2008). The tools suggested include checklists for performance of specific tasks and rubrics to clearly identify expected outcomes and measure performance. Examples include case studies, teacher-made tests, portfolios, demonstrations, and presentations. The contextual project outlined above may incorporate any of these in the process of the learning.

ANALYSIS OF INCOME POTENTIAL

An important consideration in selecting an employment position or planning a career in a particular field is to examine the financial aspects of employment by evaluating the income potential of various jobs in the field. Information on wages and salaries within most occupations is readily available through data collected by state and federal government agencies. For example, data collected by the Bureau of Labor Statistics of the U.S. Department of Labor are provided in annual wage bulletins (Bureau of Labor Statistics, *Occupational Outlook Handbook*, 2007) for over 800 specific occupations nationwide. Information may be obtained by logging onto the website (http://www.bls.gov) and searching under the heading "Wages by Area and Occupation." Data collected reflect compensation levels on a geographic basis, thus showing differences in various sectors of the country and by population distribution. The *Occupational Outlook Handbook* provides comprehensive data on employment trends, wage and salaries levels, industry employment changes, and employment projections. This publication, available from the U.S. Bureau of Labor Statistics, is published annually with quarterly updates.

Entry income levels and potential increases based on education, time on the job, and performance can be viewed as one component in career analysis. When examining the earning potential of positions within a career field, students should include some other components in their decision-making process.

For example, the continued shift of jobs from goods-producing sectors to the service-producing sectors will impact the demand and income levels of jobs within each career area. The Department of Labor predicts that approximately 18.7 million of the 18.9 million new jobs generated by 2014 will be in the service sector, with three out of every 10 of those jobs in health care, social assistance, and private educational services. As demand for these types of employees increases (with significantly increasing employment opportunities), the pay levels for these positions will increase at a rate greater than for those positions with less demand. This potential greater income can impact a student's career decision.

Similarly, pay levels will vary across geographical areas within the United States. Current data show that of the 78 metropolitan areas surveyed, the areas of northern California, the New York-New Jersey corridor, and the Boston area had the highest ranking of pay levels across the United States (BLS, 2007) In addition, data provided by the Bureau of Labor Statistics reflect a consistent correlation between educational levels and income.

Teaching and Assessing Income Analysis Concepts

A relevant learning activity for students to help them understand the relationship between income levels, education, job growth, and geographic differences in income potential involves students collecting current income data about careers in a career cluster. Interviews with individuals currently holding positions in the selected career field will help students further expand their understanding of the relationships between education and compensation factors.

In a gallery-style presentation (using sheets of paper hung on walls or poster boards set up on desks/tables) in which students visually share their findings, participants could view data on sheets or posters as well as listen to presentations about student findings and their analysis of future earning probability. With the teacher acting as facilitator, this activity could take place as follows:

- Students use the career choice determined through prior class work;

- They then brainstorm questions to determine appropriate facts to be collected;

- They research potential interviewees who would possess the information required, and find their contact information (phone, mail or email addresses);

- They contact their interview subjects with questions;

- They compile the information they gathered and organize it into a poster, PowerPoint presentation, research paper, podcast, etc. (determined by the teacher);

- They present their project findings to their peers, teacher, and other interested parties.

The teacher would use a rubric for assessment that includes multiple sections: quality of material collected with relevance to project directive, questions development, identification of sources for gathering information, report components (using school English/Language Arts rubric if available for consistency in whole school learning), and presentation components (again, with the English department rubric for guidelines).

EVALUATION OF INCOME NEEDS AND EXPECTATIONS

This section examines other aspects students need to understand related to earning income. It includes information on gross and net income, disposable and discretionary income, and fringe benefits. These are essential concepts for students to develop an understanding of compensation available within a given occupation.

Disposable and Discretionary Income

Decisions about a career can also center on students' income needs based on their current and projected spending patterns and financial obligations. The term "disposable income" is defined as an individual's total income less all deductions such as federal, state, or local taxes, insurance, and deductions for savings and other obligations. This amount, commonly referred to as "take-home" pay, is the amount available to meet an individual's financial obligations and additional savings expectations. The higher the current expenses one has, the greater the disposable income needed to meet these recurring financial obligations. If too many or too much of an individual's monthly financial obligations are fixed, thereby representing an excessively large portion of an individual's disposable income, the individual will have little remaining disposable income for other expenses and for meeting savings goals. For example, if an individual has an excessively large mortgage payment (a fixed expense) that totals 50 percent or more of monthly disposable income, the amount remaining to cover other fixed and variable expenses and to meet savings goals could be so minimal as to create a financial hardship and possibly lead to default or indebtedness.

Once a student has mastered the concept of disposable income, the teacher can introduce the concept of discretionary income. Discretionary income is the amount of income left after essential commitments, such as housing and food, have been paid. This income category denotes the amount available for expenditures that can be freely spent on leisure pursuits selected by individuals to meet their personal tastes and lifestyles. Discretionary income can vary significantly from one individual to another, based on spending patterns, lifestyle considerations, and the psychological factors that are relevant in determining personal happiness. Some discretionary income spending decisions include what clothes to buy, what type of neighborhood to live in, how much to spend on dining outside the home, and what to spend on entertainment and other leisure activities such as vacations.

Fringe Benefits

Another important aspect in determining income potential involves analyzing the dollar value of fringe benefits provided by employers. Fringe benefits are other types of remuneration that are not normally part of the paycheck amount. Some of the most significant fringe benefits include life insurance coverage, retirement benefits, medical coverage, employee discounts, sick pay, and vacation days. These benefits can be substantial. In today's organizations, significant differences in the types and amount of fringe benefits provided by potential employers require investigation by the job applicant when making job or career choices. Students need to compare the fringe benefits available from various potential employers during the job interview process and not just focus on the pay offered. For example, while teachers may not be earning high incomes in their profession, individuals entering the teaching profession receive very competitive incomes compared to other college graduates with bachelor's degrees when health insurance, medical coverage, retirement benefits, job security, and free time are taken into account,.

Teaching and Assessing Evaluation of Income Needs

A project-based learning approach can help all students develop the skills necessary to effectively evaluate their income needs and expectations. Middle school students may work on a hypothetical job situation of their or their teacher's choice while high school or postsecondary students would be able to use their career field choice as a basis for the investigation. Students should start by researching and examining data on opportunities for generating initial income levels suitable for their living standards of choice, and estimating career growth opportunities and future earnings potential in chosen job classifications. The *Occupational Outlook Handbook* is a good resource to begin this research. Next, students should examine cost-of-living data available from local, state, and/or national sources to compare and contrast the ability to make a living in a geographic area of choice and try to forecast future employment for the career field in the chosen locale. The student then develops a personal budget, including accurate estimates of all fixed and variable personal expenses. The students' needs and wants should be compared to the data related to income potential in order to determine the feasibility of living comfortably within the income in the position targeted. Next, they can gather information about the fringe benefits typically given to employees in the chosen career, estimate a dollar value for them, and estimate the effect these benefits have on their budget and standard of living. A capstone exercise to this project could be to have students prepare a written and oral presentation for their classmates. Teachers could use a project plan similar to those outlined previously in the section on "Teaching and Assessment for Career Selection and Planning" or "Teaching and Assessment for Analysis of Income Potential." A reflection paper may allow them to bring all elements of these projects together for integrated learning.

EARNINGS AND RESPONSIBILITIES AS A TAXPAYER

As a taxpayer, knowing information on all elements impacting compensation is critical in planning expenditures and managing financial resources effectively. As part of earning income, students should also understand their responsibilities and obligations regarding the reporting of income and estimating their tax liabilities. The primary source of information upon which to understand tax liabilities is the information published by the Internal Revenue Service on its website (http://www.irs.gov). This website provides individuals with numerous forms and publications, including examples of W-2 and W-4 forms, and instructions for preparing tax returns (Publication 17).

Students should know, for example, that upon employment, individuals are required to complete an Internal Revenue Form (W-4) that identifies the exemptions that can be claimed to determine federal income tax withholding. Information from this form then determines the level of federal income tax withheld from an employee's pay each designated pay period. At the end of the calendar year, the employer notifies the employee and the Internal Revenue Service of the earnings subject to tax and the federal income tax withheld; this is accomplished through the issuance of a W-2 form.

In addition to federal income tax obligations, individuals will also assume responsibility for tax liability from other taxing units including states, counties, and cities. The W-2 form provided to individuals from an employer also reports the total amount of tax withheld for these tax entities. Learning the reporting responsibilities for determining tax withholding and all tax liabilities and reporting instructions can be obtained from various publications provided by the IRS and available on the IRS website.

Another obligation that should be understood by students is the requirement to report income for which federal tax has not been withheld. This income could include cash reimbursements in the form of tips and other direct cash receipts for services rendered. Self-employed individuals who may not pay themselves while taking out withholding deductions have a different liability for tax reporting. If such income reaches a prescribed level, then taxpayers are required to submit a quarterly tax estimate form along with quarterly payments to the IRS. While federal tax reporting requirements are complex and ever-changing, students must be made aware that paying taxes on their income is one of the legal inevitabilities of life.

Teaching and Assessing Responsibilities of a Taxpayer

To build knowledge of taxpayer responsibilities, students can be provided with a variety of publications and forms giving information on requirements for all individuals earning income. A teacher can use these resources for creating cases depicting a variety of situations with different earning levels, withholding information, and other factors determining tax liabilities. For example, the IRS provides sample W-2 and W-4 forms, and explains how each is completed to determine tax liabilities and withholding. One of the most basic and helpful classroom activities is to have students—especially employed students—complete tax-reporting forms (usually IRS Form 1040EZ or Form 1040A) at tax time. Many local tax services, banks, or credit unions will make a guest speaker available who will come to the classroom to assist students in completion of their federal income tax reporting forms. Students can bring their own W-2 Wage and Tax Statement forms received from their employers to complete their tax reporting. Teachers can easily download blank W-2 forms and 1040EZ forms from the IRS website and fill in wage and withholding information on the W-2s to give to students who are not currently employed so that they also can complete tax calculations.

While the teacher may elect to assess each completed tax reporting form and assign a grade for this activity, a simple "complete" or "did not complete" grading evaluation should suffice. Students who have jobs and are going to send in their completed forms are not likely to take the activity lightly; they will get it right.

SUMMARY

Financial success rests on having a sound background and understanding of strategies for earning income and making good spending decisions. Students in the 21st century have an opportunity to assess their earning potential through an examination of their personal career interests and lifestyle expectations and the development of a plan for achieving their earning goals in order to realize their lifestyle goals. As students become more familiar with their career goals and their earnings potential, they also should learn how to assess their total earnings by estimating non-wage income sources and the valuation of fringe benefits. When students earn money, they also need to be aware of their responsibilities as taxpayers and how taxation affects their financial goals.

REFERENCES

Bureau of Labor Statistics. (2007). Tomorrow's jobs. *Occupational Outlook Handbook*, 2006-07 Edition. Washington, DC: U.S. Department of labor. Retrieved June 4, 2008, from http://www.collegecareerlifeplanning.com/Documents/6%20Teacher%20 Resources/c%20Career%20Tools%20K-12/Tomorrow's%20Jobs%2006-07.doc

Day, J., & Newburger, E. (2002). The big payoff: Educational attainment and synthetic estimates of work-life earnings. *Current Population Reports*. Washington D.C.: U.S.

Census. Retrieved December 14, 2007, from: http://www.census.gov/prod/2002pubs/p23-210.pdf

Emerging Careers. *Keying In (18)* 1, September 2007. Reston, VA: National Business Education Association.

National Business Education Association. (2007). *National standards for business education: What America's students should know and be able to do in business.* Reston, VA: Author.

National Business Education Association. (2008). *Effective methods of teaching business education, 2nd Ed.* NBEA Yearbook, No. 46, M. Radar, ed. Reston, VA: Author.

National Council on Economic Education. (2005). The benefits of investing early. EconEdLink, Retrieved December 1, 2007, from http://www.econedlink.org/lessons/index.cfm?lesson=MM603&page=teacher (teacher materials); http://www.econedlink.org/lessons/index.cfm?lesson=MM603 (student material)

National Council on Economic Education. (2004) College: Where am I going to go? EconEdLink. Retrieved September 3, 2008, from http://www.econedlink.org/lessons/index.cfm?lesson=EM463&page=teacher

National Council on Economic Education. (2004) Education: Weigh your options. EconEdLink. Retrieved September 3, 2008, from http://www.econedlink.org/lessons/index.cfm?lesson=EM660&page=teacher

National Endowment for Financial Education. (n.d.). NEFE High School Financial Planning Program: Instructor's Log-in. Retrieved September 3, 2008, from (http://hsfpp.nefe.org/home/)

National Endowment for Financial Education. (n.d.). NEFE High School Financial Planning Program: Unit 7, Your Career: Doing What Matters Most. Retrieved September 3, 2008, from http://hsfpp.nefe.org/students/channels.cfm?chid=60&tid=1&deptid=15

National Tech Prep Network. Retrieved September 3, 2008, from http://www.cord.org

Porter, K. (2002). The value of a college degree. ERIC Clearinghouse on Higher Education Washington DC. Retrieved December 14, 2007, from http://www.ericdigests.org/2003-3/value.htm

Silberman, M. (1996). *Active learning: 101 strategies to teach any subject.* Needham Heights, MA: Allyn and Bacon.

U.S. General Accounting Office. (1996). *Report to the Chairman, Subcommittee on Oversight, Committee on Ways and Means, House of Representatives: Tax administration. Tax compliance of nonwage earners.* Retrieved December 1, 2007, from http://www.gao.gov/archive/1996/gg96165.pdf

U.S. Office of Vocational and Adult Education. (n.d.) America's Career Resource Network (ACRN). Retrieved December 14, 2007, from http://www.ed.gov/about/offices/list/ovae/pi/cte/acrn.html

Managing Finances and Budgeting

Teresa Yohon
Colorado State University
Fort Collins, Colorado

Cyril Kesten
University of Regina
Regina, Saskatchewan, Canada

Every period in U.S. history has had its financial challenges. From depression to growth, from inflation to stagflation, each period had economic tests that affected individuals' abilities to manage their money. Our current economic environment of housing foreclosures, tighter credit markets, and strong international monetary growth has played havoc with people making financial decisions. This chapter covers the importance of learning about managing finances and budgeting, the standards applicable in these areas, and the content that should be covered during instruction. To support instruction, best teaching methods, resources, and academic integration ideas are presented for each topic.

THE IMPORTANCE OF MANAGING FINANCES AND BUDGETING

The key to successful money management is to live within one's means. Stanley and Danko (1996), in *The Millionaire Next Door: The Surprising Secrets of America's Wealthy*, tell us that if we have a steady income, spend less than we earn, save and invest on a regular basis, and stay away from unnecessary debt, we can achieve stability and security in our financial life. This section presents research findings that describe the level of understanding of high school and college students regarding personal finance, money management, and budgeting.

Students' Money Management and Budgeting Skills

Visa (2005) surveyed 1,000 parents of high school students about their children's money management and budgeting skills. Approximately 70% of parents indicated that their children had not received any formal instruction in money management and 76% said their high-school children did not have a budget. These parents also indicated that they believe that schools should play a part in teaching teenagers how to manage their finances. In Capital One's (2006) annual back-to-school survey, 49% of teens reported that they were eager to learn about money management, but less than 15% took a class in personal finance.

College students also need to develop budgeting skills. In a poll conducted by Harris Interactive and Keybank (2006), 32% of freshmen college students admitted they were not prepared for managing their money on campus. Their biggest mistakes were overspending on food and entertainment and charging too much on their credit cards. A survey by Sallie Mae (2007) found that more than 50% of college students accumulated more than $5,000 in credit card debt while in college. According to the Student Monitor's Lifestyle and Media Spring 2006 Financial Service Study, 62% of college students expect to have a student loan debt of approximately $27,000 and expect to take about eight years to pay it off.

Money Management and Budgeting Skills beyond College Years

Money management is a life-long challenge. Nearly two-thirds of U.S. citizens acknowledge they do not save enough and over one-third stated they often (11%) or sometimes (25%) spend more than they can afford (Pew Research Center, 2006). According to a survey by Consumer Action and Capital One (2005), 36% of U.S. citizens report that they do not develop a budget to manage their expenses.

As U.S. citizens live beyond their means, consumer and credit card debts increase. In a report to the U.S. Department of Treasury, ACA International (2007) stated, "Outstanding credit card debt has doubled in the past decade and now exceeds one trillion dollars. Total consumer debt, including home mortgages, exceeds $9 trillion" (p. 5). Additionally, much of the increase in consumer debt was accumulated by consumers with the lowest level of disposable income.

The need for money management instruction is further emphasized by the increase in non-business bankruptcies and in housing foreclosures. According to the American Bankruptcy Institute (n.d.), 287,570 non-business bankruptcies were filed in 1980. In 2005, the number of filings was 2,039,214, an increase of over 700%. Many of these bankruptcies were filed by people under the age of 35 who had allowed their debt to get out of hand. Added to bankruptcy problems, the 75% increase in housing foreclosures from 2006 to 2007 shows the need for understanding credit and budgeting for loans and future contingencies (RealtyTrac, 2008).

MONEY MANAGEMENT AND BUDGETING STANDARDS

Teaching personal or consumer finance is becoming more prominent in the United States. The National Council on Economic Education's 2007 report card (McNeil, 2007) concerning the state of economics and personal finance education in the United States found the number of states requiring a personal finance course increased to seven, up from only one state in 2000.

Three national educational organizations provide academic standards in money management and budgeting: the National Business Education Association (NBEA), the Jump$tart Coalition for Personal Financial Literacy, and the National Council on Economic Education. Their respective standards in money management and budgeting are embedded in broader sets of personal finance standards.

National Business Education Association (NBEA) Standards

The standards for managing finances and budgeting contained in the Economics and Personal Finance content areas of the NBEA (2007) standards focus on developing and evaluating a spending/savings plan. Several levels of performance expectations are prescribed that apply to various grade levels of learner, from elementary through postsecondary. These performance expectations range from simple comprehension of sources of money for personal spending to more complex analytical tasks, such as describing how income and spending patterns change throughout the life cycle for the typical person and family.

Jump$tart Coalition for Personal Financial Literacy Standards

Jump$tart Coalition's standards addressing budgeting and managing finances are:

- Take responsibility for personal financial decisions (Standard: Financial Responsibility and Decision Making, Standard 1)

- Make financial decisions by systematically considering alternatives and consequences (Financial Responsibility and Decision Making, Standard 4)

- Develop a plan for spending and saving (Planning and Money Management, Standard 1)

- Develop a system for keeping and using financial records (Planning and Money Management, Standard 2)

- Develop a personal financial plan (Planning and Money Management, Standard 6)

- Discuss how saving contributes to financial well-being (Saving and Investing, Standard 1) (Jump$tart, 2007, pp. 4-5)

National Council on Economic Education Standards

The National Council on Economic Education (2008) identifies 20 standards for economics. The following economic standards are critical for budgeting and managing finances:

- Standard 1: Scarcity

- Standard 11: Role of Money

- Standard 12: Role of Interest Rate

MANAGING FINANCES AND BUDGETING IN THE CURRICULUM

Personal finance curriculum topics can be organized into three levels: basic, intermediate, and advanced. The basic level includes skills in planning and protecting one's financial future, budgeting, selecting banking options, understanding employment taxes, and protecting one's credit score. For a secure financial future, students also need intermediate and advanced personal finance skills. Intermediate skills include acquiring a variety of investment strategies, understanding taxes, and knowing how to get and manage a loan. Advanced skills include retirement and estate planning, home financing, and business financing.

The first two basic personal finance topics, i.e., planning and protecting a financial future and budgeting, are covered in this chapter. Best teaching practices, teaching resources and assessment tools, and academic integration ideas for each topic are also covered. Because of the broad importance of these topics, they are appropriate for both the secondary and postsecondary levels.

General Teaching Strategies

In teaching budgeting and money management, several key economic concepts should be reinforced. These concepts include scarcity, trade-offs, opportunity costs, and wants versus needs. Money management and budgeting should be taught using realistic examples and the students' own experiences. Attitude towards the stewardship of money resources is as important as the technical skills involved. To build positive attitudes toward money management, instructional strategies used to portray these attitudes and skills should be as compelling as possible. General guidelines for appropriate instructional strategies are as follows:

- Authentic budgeting and financial situations are used in the instructional process;

- Both students and teachers are actively involved in the learning process;

- Real data are used to build budgets and plans;

- Current information from financial resources is used to make budgeting decisions;

- Collaborative work and decision-making are used.

PLANNING AND PROTECTING AN INDIVIDUAL'S FINANCIAL FUTURE

To protect one's financial future, a financial plan is built. A financial plan evaluates personal money status by looking at current assets and liabilities, identifies wants or needs (i.e., financial goals), and develops a strategy to accomplish those goals. This section will discuss the importance of a financial plan, the cost of postsecondary education, financial plan development, changes in financial plans based on age, and evaluation of personal finances.

Importance of a financial plan. A financial plan is a crucial step in securing financial security. If a financial plan is not used, some students will not be able to pay for college, buy a car, support their future family, or build for their retirement. A financial plan can minimize:

- the effects of inflation (inflation decreases the value of money so money needs to grow faster than the inflation rate);

- taxes (taxes can be reduced by using tax-free investments or tax-deferred investments such as an Individual Retirement Account or IRA);

- surprises that wreck a person's financial health (an emergency cash fund allows for unexpected expenses such as new brakes for the car or an emergency trip back home).

Financial goals. There are three types of financial goals: short-term, medium-term, and long-term. Short-term goals are goals that are achievable in a few weeks or months, such as saving for prom or birthday gifts. Medium-term goals require several years of planning, such as paying for postsecondary education or purchasing a house. Long-term goals, such as planning for retirement, may take 20+ years to accomplish.

A fundamental concept in planning for medium- and long-term goals is the magic of compound interest. Compound interest is the students' partner in the saving process. Online compound interest calculators show students what they have to save each month or week to reach a financial goal. (See Table 1 for online calculators.)

Cost of postsecondary education. Planning for college requires a long-term view. According to the U.S. Department of Education's *eJournal USA* (2005), most four-year colleges cost at least $10,000 per year in tuition, and many more are in the $20,000 to $30,000 range. This cost does not include the expenditures for housing, transportation, textbooks, Internet access, parking, and living expenses. Students should be aware of the cost of postsecondary education, the difference in cost between private and public universities and schools, and the affordable option of community colleges. The choice of what type of postsecondary education institution to attend is based on the student's career choice. In developing a financial plan for a postsecondary education, start with career choice.

Develop a financial plan. A financial plan summarizes one's financial goals and explains financial strategies to be used. Financial strategies include savings and investment plans. Money management skills are necessary at every stage of a person's life. Needs and wants change over time, such as a teenager's desire to buy a car as compared to parents' desire to save money for their children's education; however, the mechanisms for prioritizing and decision-making are the same. Planning for longer-term goals such as a child's college education or retirement requires a commitment to saving as early as possible. Students should take advantage of compound interest, a concept mentioned earlier in this chapter. Financial considerations for each life stage are summarized below.

Teens. Teenagers tend to focus on short-term financial goals. However, they must be taught how to save for long-term goals such as purchasing a house, a new car, or a college education. Teaching the Rule of 72 (the rule that estimates the number of years required to double one's money at a given interest rate) helps teenagers see the value of saving early. Short-term or medium-term financial goals include planning for college expenses, a first apartment (including down payments for utilities), a new car or bicycle, a cell phone, and insurance (health, car, and renter's insurance). Even though teenagers may be covered by their parents' insurance, they need to recognize the costs involved. Also, they need to identify insurance options available to them as students on a college campus.

Twenties. People in their 20s are paying off college expenses and saving for "big ticket" items such as new furniture, a car, and electronics. However, this age range is also a time to save for long-term goals. They should not pass up the opportunity to contribute to voluntary tax-deferred retirement plans (such as Individual Retirement Accounts, or IRAs), participate in employer-sponsored retirement plans, and open investment accounts. Even saving $1,000 in an IRA each year will bring huge dividends at retirement age.

Intermediate financial goals, such as buying a house or saving for college for their own children, also place a strain on people in this age group. Choices need to be made between saving for intermediate financial goals and purchasing a brand new car or a home stereo system. Individuals in this age group also need to provide for an emergency fund so that if something goes wrong (e.g., their car breaks down or the refrigerator stops), money is there to pay for the necessary repairs. Providing for an emergency fund is better financially for an individual than putting the emergency purchase on a credit card and paying if off perhaps over a year or more while incurring exorbitant interest charges.

Thirties and Forties. People in this age range often have purchased their first home. If children are present, saving for their college education is important. Personal incomes at this time of life are normally increasing, so more disposable income is available to save for long-term goals such as retirement. However, affording short-term goals, such as children's extracurricular activities or memorable family vacations, also require cash.

Fifties. The 50s are peak earning years; however, large money outflows also occur. More money may be spent on children's college education and to fulfill personal goals such as a new car, a two-week cruise, or a vacation home. An important focus in this age range is long-term planning for retirement. If people find themselves at this time of life without prior savings, then 20% to 40% of income should be saved for retirement. A rule of thumb is that a person needs about 70% of pre-retirement income for retirement. *The Guide to Planning Your Financial Future* (Morris, Sieget, & Morris, 1995) states that if 10% of one's income is saved for retirement starting at the age of 30, enough money will be saved when it is time to retire.

Sixties. If a person has saved consistently, income from investments and pensions will likely be available for retirement. By this time, the family home should be paid for and all children should be out of college. Financial goals shift to leisure activities, home maintenance, and health care costs.

The economic concept of inflation plays an important role in whether these retirement years will be financially secure or not. Inflation is the increase in the cost of goods and services over time. Pensions and government payments (such as Social Security) increase based on a cost-of-living formula. In other words, payments increase a certain percentage each year based on a cost-of-living increase. Interest income on investments, such as stocks, bonds, and mutual funds, increase or decrease based on a combination of factors, such as the health of the stock market, the prime interest rate, and the stability of the economy. If the increases in pension payments, Social Security and Medicare payments, and dividend and interest income from investments do not keep pace with inflation, then the purchasing power of retirement income decreases in relation to increasing costs to live. Many retirees go back to work to supplement their pension and investment income because they failed to plan for inflation and its effect on the purchasing power of their retirement income.

Evaluation of personal finances. Part of money management is determining how much a person is worth. Students need to identify their assets (what they own) and their liabilities (what they owe). Assets such as cash, money in checking and saving accounts, or mutual funds are easy to identify from the monthly statements that accompany such accounts. However, students need help identifying the value of tangible assets or assets that are physical in nature, such as furniture or a car. For example, a car's value is hard to determine without using Kelly's Blue Book (www.kbb.com) or another reliable car appraisal source. Other items such as furniture, electronics, and clothing depreciate over time, so they are not worth as much today as when purchased.

Liabilities are typically also easy to identify. Liabilities include balances owed on installment loans, credit card balances, and money borrowed from relatives. Liabilities can also be classified as either short-term (the liability can be paid off within a year, e.g., a cell phone bill) or long-term (the liability takes longer than a year to pay off, e.g., a car loan).

Determining an individual's net worth involves subtracting total liabilities from total assets. Net worth is the value of total assets that are owned without any debt. The depreciated or appreciated value of some assets heavily influences net worth. For example, in a housing market crisis where home values are going down, a negative net worth on a house may occur, i.e., the market value of a home is below what is owed to the mortgage company on the house.

Table 1 provides suggested best teaching practices, online resources and assessment tools, and academic integration ideas for teaching students how to manage finances. Other resources, including websites and books, are listed at the end of the chapter.

BUDGETING
A realistic household or personal budget is the key to financial stability and long-term wealth. Students need to build budgets for their current stage in life and simulate building budgets based on future stages in life and different geographic locations. Family members need to help students gather realistic costs for maintaining a home and necessities to maintain a specific targeted lifestyle, including utility expenses, car costs, insurance, home mortgage expenses, and other costs of living. Learning about the budgeting process includes learning new terminology, understanding income resources and expenditures, developing a record-keeping method that includes keeping receipts, and evaluating a budget over time.

Learning new terminology. With any new skill, additional terms need to be learned. Important terms are income, expenses, variable expenses, fixed expenses, occasional expenses, and discretionary income. Income is money earned through employment, personal investments, or other income-generating means. (See Chapter 9 for a discussion of earning and reporting income.) Expenses are payments for goods or services that are purchased with one's income. Expenses can be outlays of money for tangible products such as food, clothing, or housing, or intangibles such as insurance or attorney fees.

Variable expenses are expenses that change from month to month while fixed expenses do not. Variable expense examples include utility payments, car operational expenses such as gas and repairs, and payment of a cell phone bill. Rent, mortgage payments, and car payments are fixed expenses because they normally do not change from month to month. Occasional expenses are expenses that occur once or twice a year such as homeowners' insurance, property taxes, and college tuition.

Table 1. *Planning and Protecting an Individual's Financial Future*

Topic	Best Teaching Practices	Resources and Assessment Tools	Academic Integration (Oral communication, reading, math, or writing)
Financial goals	Value clarification (Goal Setting)	Lessons on Financial Goals and Budgeting http://money.cnn.com/magazines/money mag/money101/lesson1/index.htm Goal Setting Worksheet http://www.cfp-ca.org/pdf/Focus_On_ Your_Finances_Establish_Your_Goals.pdf	• Write short-term and long-term financial goals. • Develop 3 strategies for accomplishing each goal.
Under-standing the impor-tance of a financial plan	Guest speakers Quizzes that determine financial mindset Book reviews of financial planning books	Determining Financial Fitness http://www.personalfinancebudgeting. com/financial-fitness-quiz.php What does it take to be a millionaire? http://partners.leadfusion.com/tools/ kiplinger/savings01/tool.fcs http://www.youngmoney.com/calculators/ savings_calculators/millionaire_calculator Test Your Financial Skills http://www.japersonalfinance.com/gsjapf/ sim/sim_intro2.htm Online compound interest calculators http://www.moneychimp.com/calculator/ compound_interest_calculator.htm http://www.easycalculation.com/ compound-interest.php http://www.coolmath.com/calculators/index.html http://www.youngmoney.com/calculators/savings _calculators/compound_interest_calculator	• Research the financial strategies that can be used in a financial plan. • Write a book review on a financial planning book. Present summary to the class. • After taking a financial fitness quiz, write a reflection on fitness status and a list of ways to improve.
Estimating cost of a post-secondary education	WebQuests Worksheets calculating costs	You're Going to College http://www.italladdsup.org/mod3/ Education: Weighing Your Options http://www.econedlink.org/lessons/index.cfm? lesson=EM660&page=teacher College: Where am I Going to Go? http://www.econedlink.org/lessons/index.cfm? lesson=EM463&page=teacher College worksheets http://www.moneyinstructor.com/wsp/wspcollege. asp#WORKSHEET http://apps.collegeboard.com/fincalc/college_cost.jsp http://www.finaid.org/calculators/costprojector.phtml	• After completing several of the suggested college cost calculators, write a summary of knowledge learned and develop a plan (along with parental help) to finance a postsecondary education (trade school, community college, or university.)
Changing focus of financial plan based on age	WebQuests Family interviews about spending based on life cycle	Timing is Everything (Lesson 2) (Concept: Saving early for retirement) http://www.e-connections.org/lesson2/lesson2.htm Assessment: http://www.e-connections.org/ lesson2/assessment.htm Rule of 72 Calculator http://www.moneychimp.com/features/rule72.htm or http://www.japersonalfinance.com/gsjapf/activities/ page3.jsp?key=Activity5Page1 Retirement planner (online calculator) http://moneycentral.msn.com/retire/planner.aspx	• Interview 3 family members at different life stages. List and compare how they spend their money (by category and percentage). • Develop a retirement plan. *(cont.)*

Table 1. *Planning and Protecting an Individual's Financial Future* (cont.)			
Topic	Best Teaching Practices	Resources and Assessment Tools	Academic Integration (Oral communication, reading, math, or writing)
Developing a financial plan	Complete a financial plan Interview others about their plans	What is a personal financial plan? http://www.ameriprise.com/amp/individual/planning-advice/financial-plan.asp Fundamentals of Personal Financial Planning http://ocw.uci.edu/courses/AR0102092/	• Develop a financial plan from today to age 30. Include financial goals.
Evaluating personal finances	Worksheet to determine financial worth Guest speakers	Net worth statement http://www.personalfinancebudgeting.com/budget_worksheet/NetWorthStatement.pdf	• Develop a net worth statement using a spreadsheet. • Interview a certified financial planner. Summarize and present information to the class.

Understanding income resources and expenditures. Teaching a budget process begins with students learning about their own income resources and how they spend their money or make expenditures. Income resources should be identified first. A teenager or young adult typically lists income from a job and/or an allowance from their parents. Their expenditures (or expenses) generally fall into the following categories: food, clothing, entertainment, communication (cell phone and Internet), and personal items. Once students have identified their expenditures, the expenditures should be organized into categories so students can analyze how they spend their money. Questions to be answered include: Was money saved? Was the money spent in areas of their financial goals? Was money overspent in one area? Could expenses be reduced or eliminated?

Developing a budget. Once students have listed and analyzed their income and expenditures, they can develop a budget. A budget should be developed for a period of time of from six months to a year. To develop a budget, students should first identify their financial goals (discussed previously). Financial goals will help students determine if income generation needs to be increased and how much money should be allocated to each expenditure and expense category.

An important concept that students should grasp is that of *paying yourself first*: a person should first determine how much money to save for contingencies and future needs before deciding on other expenditures. Once students have established a savings goal and can defend it, they should estimate their expenditures in each expense category. Expense categories should be clearly labeled. Labels like food, rent, car expenses, utilities, entertainment, and communications are easy to understand. Including a miscellaneous expense category with an allocation of a small amount of money allows for unexpected purchases such as a special meal or other unplanned entertainment. Students should identify which expense categories are fixed, which are variable, and which are occasional. Variable expenses, such as utilities, require additional planning since they may be higher some months than others. Occasional expenses such as insurance require saving money in prior months.

The final phase of the budget process is to have students subtract expenses and planned savings from their total income to determine if their budgets are balanced, i.e., that they have enough income to cover all expenditures. If the budget is not in balance, students need to either cut expenses or increase income. If income exceeds expenses, students have discretionary income or income that is not allocated to pay for a recurring expense. Discretionary income should also be managed by deciding how much to save for unexpected situations (such as new brakes on a car or an expensive textbook) and how much to spend.

Record-keeping methods. Students should experience various budget record-keeping methods. Pencil-paper budgets and electronic budgets using a spreadsheet should be developed. Learning to keep receipts from important purchases should be part of the record-keeping process. Income records to keep include pay stubs and statements of interest income on checking or savings accounts. Receipts for meals and small purchases (such as shampoo or a new toy for the dog) typically do not need to be saved. However receipts for items that may be returned, expensive items (such as an iPod or a Blue Ray player), or items with a warranty should be kept.

Evaluating a budget. Once a budget is established and has been used, it should be evaluated. A budget evaluation checks if bills are paid, savings are made, expenses are controlled, and financial goals are met. Although the budget will cover a 6- or 12-month period, it is important to keep records on a monthly basis and to evaluate financial positions regularly.

Table 2 provides suggested best teaching practices, online resources and assessment tools, and academic integration ideas for teaching students how to develop budgets. Other resources, including websites and books, are listed at the end of the chapter.

ADDITIONAL RESOURCES
Because research shows that many students graduate high school without personal finance skills, many educational groups and businesses have developed free, interactive money management and budgeting resources for teachers. Besides the resources discussed above in this chapter, the following resources are available:

- BankRate.com (http://www.bankrate.com)

Table 2. *Budgeting*

Topic	Best Teaching Practices	Resources and Assessment Tools	Academic Integration (Oral communication, reading, math, or writing)
Defining terms (income, expenses, variable expenses, fixed expenses, etc.)	Concept attainment via worksheets	Steps to Building a Budget http://www.personalfinancebudgeting.com/steps-to-building-a-budget.php How important is a budget? http://www.bankrate.com/brm/news/Financial_Literacy/Jan07_budgeting_online_poll_a1.asp?caret=4b Fixed versus Variable Expenses http://www.moneyinstructor.com/wsp/wsp0052.asp	• With a team, develop a list of three expenses that could be variable or fixed. Defend expenses chosen. • Ask family members what their variable and fixed expenses are. Prepare a report.
Understanding income resources and expenditures	Case studies Investigative reports Journalizing	8 Steps to Save Money (includes determining expenditures) http://www.personalfinancebudgeting.com/p1_save_money.php Solving the Spending Mystery (includes spending calculator) http://www.personalfinancebudgeting.com/solving_spending_mystery.php How much am I spending? (Itemizing living expenses) http://finance.yahoo.com/calculator/banking-budgeting/bud-02	• Journalize all income and expenses for a week or two. Write a report.
Developing a budget	WebQuests Learning Activity Packages	Budgeting Your Financial Resources (includes developing a budget based on career) http://www.themint.org/teachers/budgeting-your-financial-resources.html Monthly spending plan worksheet http://www.personalfinancebudgeting.com/budget_worksheet/monthlyspendingplan.pdf Steps to Building a Budget (includes budgeting terms) http://www.personalfinancebudgeting.com/steps-to-building-a-budget.php Budget Lessons and Online budget forms http://money.cnn.com/magazines/moneymag/money101/lesson2/index.htm http://cgi.money.cnn.com/tools/budget101/budget_101.jsp Budgeting Calculator http://www.bankrate.com/brm/calc/Worksheet.asp Online Budget Form http://www.kiplinger.com/tools/budget/ Budget Worksheets http://www.moneyinstructor.com/wsp/budgetworksheets.asp Develop Personal Budgeting Habits http://personalbudgeting.suite101.com/article.cfm/develop_personal_ budgeting_habits	• Create budgeting materials to share with middle school students. Present the budgeting information to a middle school class. • Develop a budget. Include "what if" situations and how the budget would change. • Develop a budget for a different life stage (such as age 30 or 40.) • Compare 2 budgets, looking for best budgeting practices.

(cont.)

Topic	Best Teaching Practices	Resources and Assessment Tools	Academic Integration (Oral communication, reading, math, or writing)
Table 2. _Budgeting_ (cont.)			
Using a budget record-keeping systems	Case studies Extended projects	Create your Budget on Paper http://personal-budget-creation.suite101.com/article.cfm/budget_planning Create your Budget using a Spreadsheet http://personal-budget-creation.suite101.com/article.cfm/ budget_templates_for_spreadsheets Create Your Budget using Financial Software http://personalbudgeting.suite101.com/article.cfm/how_to_choose_financial_software	• Research types of financial software. • Determine criteria for the best software and present it to the class.
Keeping receipts	Simulations	Keeping a Money Diary http://www.themint.org/kids/keeping-a-money-diary.html 9 Steps to Get Organized for Financial Success http://www.personalfinancebudgeting.com/organized_financial_success.php	• Write a brochure informing people what receipts to keep and why.
Evaluating a budget	Simulation Case studies	Simulation: Cottage Budget Lesson http://www.moneyinstructor.com/lesson/cottagebudget.asp	• In a team, develop a budget that has one or more problems. Exchange budgets with another group. Analyze the budget and make suggestions for improvements.

- Brooks, Y. (2002). *Financial planning for teens: Teen success series Volume 1*. Lincoln, NE: Writers Club Press.
- CNNMoney.com (http://money.cnn.com)
- EconEdLink (Underwritten by the Verizon Foundation) (www.econedlink.org)
- Federal Reserve Education Resources (www.FederalReserveEducation.org)
- Foundation for Teaching Economics (http://www.fte.org/teachers/)
- Gardner, D., Gardner, T., & Maranjian, S. (2002). *The Motley Fool investment guide for teens: 8 steps to having more money than your parents ever dreamed of*. New York: Simon & Schuster.
- Get Rich Slowly (http://www.getrichslowly.org/)
- It All Adds Up (underwritten by American Express Foundation) (www.italladdsup.org)
- JA/Goldman Sachs Foundation – Personal Finance Center (http://www.japersonalfinance.com/)

- Kiplinger.com (http://www.kiplinger.com)
- Learning, Earning and Investing (Underwritten by the Moody's Foundation) (www.lei.ncee.net)
- Moneyinstructor.com (http://www.moneyinstructor.com)
- National Council on Economic Education (www.ncee.net)
- National Endowment for Financial Education (http://www.nefe.org/)
- Personal Finance Budgeting (http://www.personalfinancebudgeting.com/)
- Practical Money Skills for Life (http://www.practicalmoneyskills.com)
- Smart Money (http://www.smartmoney.com/pf/)
- Stahl, M. Z. (2005). Early *to rise: A young adult's guide to saving, investing and financial decisions that can shape your life, 2nd Edition.* Aberdeen, WA: Silver Lake Publishing.
- Suite101.com (http://personalbudgeting.suite101.com/)
- Young Money (http://www.youngmoney.com/)

SUMMARY

Developing budgeting and money management skills are important for students. The National Business Education Association, Jump$tart Coalition, and the National Council on Economic Education have articulated specific standards to target for teaching these skills. Important budgeting concepts to be taught are to understand income resources and expenditures, develop a budget, choose an effective record-keeping method, and evaluate a budget. Money management skills are also important. Concepts to be learned are the importance of a financial plan, how to develop a financial plan for various stages of life, and evaluation of one's personal finances. The chapter tables provide ideas of how to teach each concept and ways to integrate academics into the content. Through the use of these chapter resources and the general teaching strategies of using authentic financial situations and an active learning process, students will gain needed money management skills.

REFERENCES

ACA International. (2007, November). *Comments of ACA International on interagency proposed guidance on garnishment of exempt federal benefit funds.* Retrieved March 1, 2008, from http://www.acainternational.org/images/0/acaintragencygarnishment comment.pdf

American Bankruptcy Institute. (n.d.). *Annual business and non-business filings by year (1980-2006).* Retrieved February 25, 2008, from http://www.abiworld.org/AM/ AMTemplate.cfm?Section=Home&TEMPLATE=/CM/ContentDisplay.cfm& CONTENTID=46621

Capital One. (2006). *Capital One's annual back to school survey finds teens eager to learn about money, but parents continue to overlook important learning opportunities.* Retrieved February 28, 2008, from http://findarticles.com/p/articles/mi_m0EIN/is_2006_July_17/ai_n16535413

Consumer Action and Capital One. (2005). *National survey shows Americans need to get financially fit; Capital One and Consumer Action find majority of Americans lack basic understanding of credit scores and the fundamentals of personal finance.* Retrieved February 28, 2008, from http://phx.corporate-ir.net/phoenix.zhtml?c=70667&p=irol-newsArticle2&ID=752906&highlight

eJournal USA. (2005, November). *The cost of college in the United States.* Retrieved March 1, 2008, from http://usinfo.state.gov/journals/itsv/1105/ijse/costs.htm#fees

Harris Interactive and Keybank. (2006). *One-third of college upperclassmen admit being financially unprepared as freshmen.* Retrieved February 28, 2008, from http://www.harrisinteractive.com/news/allnewsbydate.asp?NewsID=1108

Jump$tart Coalition for Personal Financial Literacy. (2007). *National stqndards in K-12 personal finance education.* Washington, DC: Author.

McNeil, M. (2007, June 20). Report finds lack of economic instruction. *Education Week, 26*(42). Retrieved March 2, 2008, from http://www.edweek.org/ew/articles/2007/06/20/42economics.h26.html?qs=lack+of+economics+instruction

Morris, K. M., Sieget, A. M., & Morris, V. B. (1995). *Guide to planning your financial future.* New York: Lightbulb Press, Inc., & Dow Jones & Co.

National Business Education Association. (2007). *National standards for business education: What America's students need to know and be able to do in business.* Reston, VA: Author.

National Council on Economic Education. (2008). *National standards.* New York, NY: Author. Retrieved May 28, 2008, from http://www.ncee.net/ea/standards/

Pew Research Center. (2006). *We try hard. We fall short. Americans assess their saving habits.* Retrieved February 29, 2008, from http://pewresearch.org/pubs/325/we-try-hard-we-fall-short-americans-assess-their-saving-habits

RealtyTrac. (2008). *U.S. foreclosure activity increases 75 percent in 2007.* Retrieved March 2, 2008, from http://www.realtytrac.com/ContentManagement/pressrelease.aspx?ChannelID=9&ItemID=3988&accnt=64847

Sallie Mae. (2007). *Sallie Mae launches new 'Be Debt Smart' campaign to educate students, parents and graduates on managing debt and understanding credit.* Retrieved February 28, 2008, from http://www.salliemae.com/about/news_info/newsreleases/021407_bedebtsmart.htm

Stanley, T. J., & Danko, W. D. (1996). *The millionaire next door: The surprising secrets of America's wealthy.* New York: Simon & Schuster, Inc.

Student Monitor. (2006). *Lifestyle & media spring 2006 financial services study.* Retrieved January 28, 2008, from http://www.studentmonitor.com

Visa. (2005). *Visa USA 2005 national back to school survey.* Retrieved February 28, 2008, from http://www.practicalmoneyskills.com/english/presscenter/releases/080905_results.php

Saving and Investing

Beryl C. McEwen
Thaddeus McEwen
North Carolina A&T State University
Greensboro, North Carolina

By age five, most children are able to understand what it means to save money. If encouraged, they will put away coins and bills, saving them until they are ready to make special purchases. As they grow older, they are better able to understand why it is so important to save for the future and the opportunities that exist for saving and investing money to meet future needs. If started early and reinforced at the various levels of the education system, children can mature into adults who are knowledgeable about how to save and invest and who have developed good money management habits. The critical importance of including instruction about saving and investing in the public school curriculum is highlighted by the variety of national curricula that emphasize personal financial planning, including saving and investing. This chapter draws attention to various curricula, discusses the U.S. saving and investing rates and their impacts on future U.S. spending, and discusses the importance of saving and investing and how individuals can make good saving and investing decisions.

CURRICULUM STANDARDS

Various organizations have developed curriculum standards to help promote students' financial literacy and provide them sound money management skills. Among them are the Jump$tart standards, which primarily focus on personal financial literacy; the National Business Education Association (NBEA) standards, which include economics and personal finance standards; the standards developed by the National Council on Economic Education (NCEE), two of which focus on saving and investing; and the National

Endowment for Financial Education (NEFE) High School Financial Planning Program®
National Academic Standards, in which Units 3 and 5 focus on saving and investing.

Jump$tart's Financial Literacy Standards

Jump$tart's *National Standards in K-12 Personal Finance Education*, now in its third edition (2007), was created and is maintained by the Jump$tart Coalition for Personal Financial Literacy. The content area focused on Saving and Investing includes such performance standards as (1) discussing how saving contributes to financial well-being, (2) explaining how investing builds wealth and helps meet financial goals, (3) evaluating investment alternatives, (4) describing how to buy and sell investments, (5) explaining how taxes affect the rate of return on investments, and (6) investigating how agencies that regulate financial markets protect investors.

National Business Education Association (NBEA) Standards

The NBEA, in 2007, published the third edition of the *National Standards for Business Education*. The standards indicate what K–14 students should know and be able to do in business. These standards cover 11 content areas in business education, including economics and personal finance. Each content area includes achievement standards and performance expectations. The economics and personal finance standards cover such topics as (1) developing and evaluating a spending/savings plan, (2) evaluating savings and investment options to meet short- and long-term goals, (3) evaluating services provided by financial deposit institutions to transfer funds, and (4) analyzing choices available to consumers for protection against risk and financial loss.

National Council on Economic Education (NCEE) Standards

The NCEE standards were developed in collaboration with the National Association of Economic Educators and the Foundation for Teaching Economics. Each of the 20 standards includes a rationale for its inclusion and benchmarks that indicate attainment levels for various grades. The most relevant standards for teaching saving and investing are standards 11, Role of Money, and 12, Role of Interest Rates. These two standards cover money, saving, investing, and interest rates.

National Endowment for Financial Education (NEFE) Standards

Like the standards discussed earlier, the 2007 NEFE Standards focus on broad areas of financial planning. Two standards focus directly on saving and investing: Standard 3, Investing: Making Money Work for You, and Standard 5, Your Money: Keeping it Safe and Secure. Each of these standards is broken down into learning objectives that are cross-referenced to a study guide. Exercises, assignments, and unit assessments are also provided.

U. S. SAVINGS AND INVESTING RATES

The *personal savings rate* for the United States is calculated by subtracting total spending from total after-tax (disposable) income. During the 1990s, U.S. consumers spent about 95 cents of every after-tax dollar earned and saved 5 cents— a 5% savings rate. However, the rate declined to 1.8% by 2004, and entered the negative range— minus 0.4% saved—by 2005. The savings rate has been in the negative range ever since (Abate, 2006). This negative savings rate means that, as a nation, U.S. consumers are spending more than our aggregated after-tax incomes. About 70% of the U.S. population lives from one paycheck to the next, with many borrowing to supplement their income. The next section of the chapter presents the effects of the U.S. saving and investing rates on the economy and the importance of establishing early saving and investing habits.

Micro and Macro Effects of the U.S. Saving and Investing Rates
Microeconomics is concerned with the behavior of individual consumers, house-holds or firms, i.e., the small scale; *macroeconomics* looks at the big picture, focusing on the nation as a whole. The failure of most U.S. citizens to save and invest for their future activities will result in a variety of *microeconomic* and *macroeconomic* challenges, including the following:

1. Retirement. An 18-year-old who saves $5 weekly ($20 monthly) can have more than $200,000 by the time he or she retires at age 65. Yet, a 2003 study by Merrill Lynch found that the average retirement savings per household is about $40,000 and 25% of U.S. workers have no retirement accounts. More than 50% of employees surveyed did not even know how much money they will need during retirement. The microeconomic effect is that many retirees will live near the poverty line and will need to work during their retirement years. If individuals and households are not able to meet their health care and other retirement needs, the national economy will be forced to respond through Medicaid and other social programs.

2. College education. Approximately 39% of parents are not actively saving for their children's education (Dorval & Hubbell, 2002). Some parents expect that they will pay for their children's education as they attend college, some do not expect their children to attend college, and others expect their children to pay their own way through college. Many of these children will need government assistance through Federal Pell Grant and other programs—a macroeconomic effect.

3. Declining savings rate. The U.S. personal savings rate, negative since 2005, means that U.S. households consumed more than their combined household after-tax (disposable) income. At that point, they started using up their savings or borrowed money in order to spend even more. This situation leads some to wonder whether the United States has become a spendthrift nation. This recent and persistent downturn in the personal savings by U.S. citizens could lead to dependence of the U.S. economy on foreign investments (Guidolin & La Jeunesse, 2007).

Establishing Early Saving and Investing Habits
Teens (13- to17-year-olds) are increasingly more active as consumers. The Mintel International Group (2004) reported that teen spending was approximately $175 billion

in 2003 and was expected to be approximately $190 billion in 2006, yet teens have little or no money management skills. Establishing early saving and investing habits is very important to maintaining an acceptable standard of living in later years. Financial education should include learning activities for students at all grade levels. The following examples, adapted from Renick (2007), are suitable for younger students—Pre-K through the elementary grades:

1. **Communicate**. Talk to students about money. One of the biggest mistakes that parents and teachers make is not talking to students about money.

2. **Separate and count coins**. Older children may also be able to keep a running total of the money they count each week.

3. **Slogans.** Create slogans for students, such as "saving makes me strong"; "from every dollar, save a dime"; "change adds up"; and "money likes to grow and grow." Use them frequently, and explain them when necessary.

4. **Piggy banks and saving jars**. Students or classes might have a piggy bank, preferably a transparent one that allows them to see their money grow, as this visualization can be a motivator for continued savings.

Students will more likely be motivated to save, and to develop the habit of saving, if they are achieving current saving goals, so help them to set and achieve realistic goals. High school and college students should also be helped to understand that starting to save for major goals, such as retirement, means that goals can be achieved at a potential cost of only pennies a day. Starting early will help them to truly benefit from the magic of *compound interest*—earning interest on the interest that one's saving has made. Over time, it can mean a great deal more money saved for retirement, as illustrated at the CreditunionsRock.com website (www.creditunionsrock.com/whysaveearly.php).

Teaching Applications, Discussion Questions, and Assessment

Below are activities for various grade levels to emphasize the advantages of saving early.

4th Grade	8th Grade	12th Grade
Describe the advantages and disadvantages of saving for a short-term goal. Describe ways that people can cut expenses to save more of their incomes.	Give examples of how saving money can improve financial well-being. Describe the advantages and disadvantages of saving for short- and medium-term goals. Explain the value of an emergency fund. Explain why saving is a prerequisite to investing.	Describe the advantages and disadvantages of saving for short-, medium-, and long-term goals. Identify and compare saving strategies, including "paying yourself first," using payroll deduction, and comparison shopping to spend less. Develop a definition of wealth based on personal values, priorities, and goals.

Source: Adapted from the NCEE 2007 standards

The following are examples of review questions:

1. Why should saving and investing begin at the earliest possible age?

2. Explain the difference between saving and investing.

3. How much money would an 18-year-old have accumulated in total by age 65 if he or she made just one contribution of $4,000 to an IRA at his or her 18th birthday, with an average return of 8% per year?

The Importance of Saving and Investing

Financial literacy is also important because of the problems that can arise from lack of adequate knowledge of saving and investing. They include (1) making bad saving and investing choices, (2) starting too late and not having enough money for retirement and other major life goals, (3) acquiring too much debt to pay for items and activities that might have been paid for through saving or investing, and (4) not understanding what is happening in the financial world.

The term "savings" means consuming less in the present in order to consume more in the future (Library of Economics and Liberty, 2007). It involves storing money safely in a bank or credit union for short-term needs, for example, upcoming expenses and emergencies. In contrast, investing is usually done in different ways than savings and for longer periods of time. It also involves taking risk, such as buying a stock or bond and hoping to realize greater long-term returns. Saving and investing are very important actions for helping individuals and households build financial freedom and security, and ensuring that future needs can be met without borrowing. This section outlines saving goals, types of savings accounts, and types of investment opportunities.

Saving and investing goals. Most people who save do so to prepare for specific future events. The purpose for saving or investing may range from purchasing a new toy or a Mother's Day gift, to purchasing a new house or paying for a child's education. The common element is that the saving or investing is done for a specific purpose. Students should learn to set and achieve financial goals—long term, intermediate term, and short term.

Long-term goals. From the perspective of a first-grader, a long-term goal might be saving to buy a special holiday present for a grandparent. The youngster may have to save all year long, a very long time to someone in first grade. For a high school junior, a long-term saving goal might be to purchase a car upon earning a driver's license. A college senior, on the other hand, should have long-term goals that include saving for a home and for retirement.

Medium-term goals. Medium-term savings goals are for items that cost less money and take less time to save for than those listed above. Two examples would be a new bike or a family vacation. For an adult, it might be saving to make a down payment on a house or to invest in a business. Of course, a medium-term goal for a young child would be quite different, maybe to buy a special toy.

Short-term goals. These savings goals are for items that do not cost much money. One can save for these items in a few weeks or a month, depending on one's financial situation; such items may include a new music CD or a simple dinner date.

Types of savings accounts. Savings deposits are put in the safest places, such as banks and credit unions, so they will be secure and easily accessible when needed. The variety of saving opportunities includes:

1. *Savings accounts.* Set up through a bank or credit union, this type of savings account earns a relatively low interest rate and can be accessed whenever the saver needs it.

2. *Interest-bearing checking accounts.* These accounts combine the interest-bearing quality of a savings account with check-writing privileges. Most banks and credit unions offer these accounts, but often require that the saver maintain a minimum balance.

3. *Money market accounts.* These accounts offer higher interest rates than basic savings accounts, and allow for limited check-writing. Most money market accounts are not insured by the Federal Deposit Insurance Corporation (FDIC), so individuals should assess their risk tolerance for potential losses before opening this type of account.

4. *Certificates of deposit.* These are savings accounts that are set up for specific periods of time, e.g. six months. They offer a moderate interest rate and sometimes require minimum deposits. Penalties for early withdrawal may include a loss of some of the interest earned. Certificates of deposit are usually insured by the FDIC up to a value of $100,000.

Types of investment opportunities. Investing is putting money to work for the long term to build wealth and increase financial security. Wealth-building investing involves having an investment plan and buying assets that are expected to be profitable in the long term. Investments opportunities include:

1. *Stocks.* Stocks represent part ownership in a company. A stockholder owns a small share of a company and is sometimes called a shareholder. When the company does well, the stock price increases; when the company does poorly, the stock price falls. If the company goes into bankruptcy or the stockholder has to sell when the price is lower than the purchase price, the stockholder can lose money, including the initial investment. The price of a stock can range from a few cents to several thousands of dollars. The two main types of stocks are common stocks and

preferred stocks. *Common stocks* are the most basic form of ownership of a company. Owners of these stocks can vote on such things as company policies and election of members of the board of directors. However, these are the riskier type of stocks as owners of these stocks are at the bottom of the priority list to receive dividends—return on their investments—and may lose their entire investment if the company goes into bankruptcy. *Preferred stocks,* also called *preference shares,* are higher ranking than common stocks, but have no voting rights. Preferred stocks have priority over common stocks in receiving dividends, and they are less risky.

2. **Bonds.** Buying a bond is making a loan to a company (corporate bond), to the federal government (government bond), or a state or local government agency (municipal bond). The bond has a face value (par value) and a fixed rate of interest called *yield.* Each bond also has a fixed maturity time period: that is, the number of months or years that the investor is expected to keep the bond. There are several types of government bonds, e.g. (1) *Treasury Note,* which has a life (maturity period) of 3 to 10 years; (2) *Treasury Bill,* which matures in 3 to 12 months; and (3) *Treasury Bond,* which matures in 10 to 30 years.

3. **Mutual funds**. A mutual fund is a group of stocks and bonds in a professionally managed portfolio. A person who buys a share in a mutual fund is buying a part of a large, diverse portfolio. On the other hand, stocks are shares in a single company.

Unlike savings accounts, these investments are not FDIC insured, and their values fluctuate with the stock and bond markets.

Teaching Applications, Discussion Questions, and Assessment of Concepts
Students, of all grade levels, can be asked to:

1. List their saving and investing goals—listing those that are most important first. How many years will it take to meet each specific goal? Is it possible to save more to reach these goals sooner?

2. Explain how saving and investing help to meet financial goals and build wealth.

3. Explain what is meant by the *personal saving rate* and why it is better when it is a positive number.

4. Define the following concepts: common stock, preferred stock, blue chip stock, growth stock, value stock and stock split.

Other activities and assessments might include word games, puzzles, simulations, and saving and investment quizzes. Several of these resources can be found online at sites such as the Consumer Credit Counseling Services (www.cccsintl.org), the Association for Financial Professionals (www.afponline.org/pub/res/news/ns_20060106_search1.html), and the Stock Market Game—Vocabulary (www.vocabulary.com/SMGameFITB.html).

Figure 1. The Effect of Compound Interest—Beginning Investment of $1,000

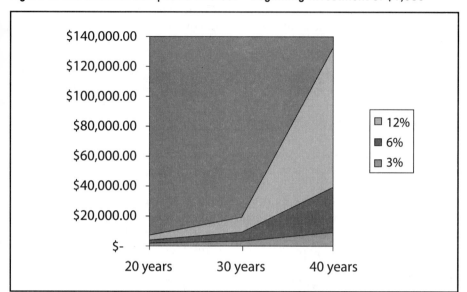

SAVING AND INVESTING DECISIONS

The terms "saving" and "investing" are unique concepts that are often mistakenly used interchangeably. However, they are very different, and it is important for students to understand the key differences. This section discusses the challenges of choosing between saving and investing, and choosing the best saving and investing options.

Choosing Between Saving and Investing

Saving is storing money safely, for short-term needs such as upcoming expenses and emergencies, while *investing* involves buying assets that are expected to yield long-term gains. Investing involves taking risk with some of one's money by purchasing stocks, bonds, and mutual funds, hoping to receive higher rates of return than possible with savings accounts. Over the long term, investments such as stocks, bonds, and mutual funds will earn a high enough return to outpace inflation; however, they may also decline in value from time to time depending on market variables that affect supply and demand for these investments (Kapoor, Dlabay, & Hughes, 2008).

In choosing whether to save or invest, consider (1) the available interest rate on savings, (2) the expected dividend on investments, and (3) whether the saving or investment is for short-term, medium-term, or long-term goals. Also, consider not only the interest rate on savings but also how often the earned interest is added to the account (compounded). Interest is compounded monthly, quarterly, semi-annually, or annually. The more frequently interest on saving is compounded, the faster the account grows in value. For example, $100 saved in a bank account earning an annual interest rate of 5% will become at least $105 at the end of one year. If the $105 is kept in the bank for another year, it will earn another 5% on the $105, assuming that the interest is compounded annually. If the interest is compounded monthly or quarterly the savings will grow even faster. Thus in two years, earnings will be at least $110.25 (Kapoor, Dlabay, & Hughes, 2008). Figure 1 shows what can happen to a lump sum of $1,000 invested for 20, 30, and 40 years at 3%, 6%, and 12% interest rates. This figure demonstrates the magic of compound interest and the value of obtaining the highest possible interest rate on one's savings.

The $1,000 invested grew to over $90,000 over 40 years when the interest rate was 12%, but to only about $30,000 over the same time period when the interest rate was 6%.

With regard to some income-producing stocks that pay dividends, the amount of dividend paid on investments is based on a company's annual earnings and is deter-mined by the company's directors. Choosing the best saving and investing options is very important and may require the advice of a professional financial planner.

Choosing the Best Saving and Investing Options

Selection among the best saving or investment options is influenced by such factors as inflation, liquidity, rate of return, and risk. Other variables inherent in the markets for investment vehicles (such as stocks, bonds, commodities, and derivatives) are beyond the scope of this chapter and may require professional expertise.

Inflation. If the rate of return on investments is not keeping pace with the rate of inflation, the purchasing power of the money invested is reduced. One suggestion is to follow the longstanding suggestion of Bannister and Oatney (1992) to find investments that provide returns that are equal to the inflation rate plus 3%.

Liquidity. How accessible is the money, i.e. how easily can the investment be converted to cash? Some savings plans impose penalties for early withdrawal or have other restrictions. For example, with certificates of deposit, early withdrawals may be penalized by the loss of interest or a lower earnings rate. Consider the degree of liquidity desired in relation to the savings goals. For example, consider whether it would be better to trade liquidity for a higher return rate.

Rate of return. What returns should be expected from investments? Safe invest-ments tend to promise a specific, though smaller return. Investments that involve more risk provide the opportunity to make or lose more money. Using the *Rule of 72* allows one to estimate how long it will take to double savings or investments based on the rate of return. For example, if $4,000 is invested at 10% per year, it will double in just over seven years (72/10), which is the percentage rate of return. Figure 2 provides four additional examples of this calculation.

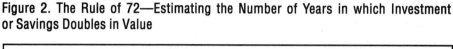

Figure 2. The Rule of 72—Estimating the Number of Years in which Investment or Savings Doubles in Value

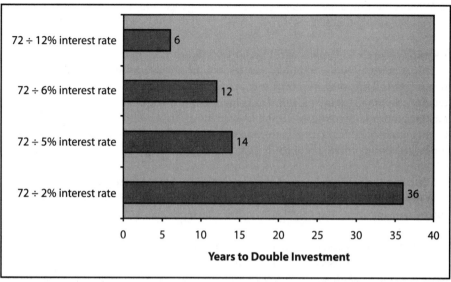

As shown in Figure 2, an investment that pays a 12% rate of return will double in six years and one that pays a 6% rate of return will double in 12 years.

Risk. The biggest risk is the possibility of losing the money invested. Another very important risk is that the investment will not provide enough growth or income to offset the impact of inflation. Investments (stocks, bonds, and mutual funds) involve a higher level of risk than savings. Individuals who are nervous about losing their investment should select savings accounts and low-risk investments such as mutual funds. On the other hand, individuals who are able to be patient and calm through the stock market's ups and downs can put their money in investments that pay better than average returns but carry greater risks (Bannister & Oatney, 1992).

Teaching Applications, Discussion Questions, and Assessment of Concepts
The following activities might be used with students in the middle grades and higher:

1. Have students calculate the following answers following class discussions.

(a) Using the Rule of 72, what interest rate would be needed to double $2,000 in 8 years? (b) In how many years will $2,000 double in value, if the interest rate is 6%?

2. Prepare a chart that compares simple interest and compound interest earned on a set amount of money, e.g. $500, and explain why the account that is earning compound interest has more money.

3. Given a rate of return of 11% for eight years, use a financial calculator to find the end value of $5,000.

4. What is the annual percentage yield for a savings account that earned $56 in interest on $800 during the past 365 days?

INVESTING IN STOCKS, MUTUAL FUNDS, AND BONDS

Stocks, mutual funds, and bonds are among the most popular types of investments. Investors of all income levels can find opportunities in these investments. Many require only small initial outlays of money, and information for effective decision-making among competing investments is readily available. This section discusses how to obtain reliable information in the markets for buying and selling stocks, mutual funds, and bonds and for protecting against catastrophic loss.

Obtaining Reliable Information about the Stock Market

A wealth of investment and company information is available to investors via the Internet, financial media, prospectuses and annual reports, and stock advisory services.

The Internet. To obtain company information, type the company's URL or the name of the fund in a search engine to locate the home page. Usually through links labeled *Investor Relations* or *Investor Information,* the site will have information on the firm's earnings and other data that affect the value of its stock. For mutual funds, it will provide statistical information about performance of individual funds, procedures for opening an account, and different investor services.

Websites, such as Yahoo! Finance (http://finance.yahoo.com), SmartMoney (www.smartmoney.com), and Kiplinger's Personal Finance (www.kiplinger.com), also provide investor information, including current market values, price history, and profiles for various mutual funds and their managers. From the U.S. Securities and Exchange Commission website (www.sec.gov), investors can also obtain financial and other information that corporations have given to the federal government.

Financial media. *The Wall Street Journal, Barron's,* and other newspapers provide information on stocks and mutual funds. Magazines such as *BusinessWeek, Forbes, Fortune,* and *Money* also include information about investing in stocks and mutual funds. However, investors should carefully examine the credibility of the investment source, for example, making sure it is not just an advertisement.

Prospectuses and annual reports. A *prospectus* is a booklet that describes the investment that is for sale. This document contains a statement of objectives of the company or mutual fund as well as a financial statement listing assets and liabilities, types of investments and performances, quality of management, services provided to the investor, and fees for such services. In addition to the prospectus, also read the company's annual report. An annual report may be obtained by visiting the company's website or requesting a copy from its home office.

Stock or professional advisory services. These services provide research and detailed financial reports for investors. Standard and Poor's, Value Line, and Mergent are the three most widely used services for stock investors. Lipper Analytical Services, Morningstar, Inc., and Value Line are three commonly used services for mutual fund investors. In addition, many mutual fund companies provide financial information to investors through newsletters and other publications (Kapoor, Dlabay, & Hughes, 2008).

Buying and Selling Stocks and Mutual Funds

A major part of investing is buying and selling stocks and mutual funds. Potential investors can purchase or sell stocks of a publicly held company. Publicly traded stocks can be purchased through a *stockbroker*—a licensed individual employed with a full-service, discount or online brokerage firm that buys and sells securities for clients.

Once a decision is made to purchase a particular stock, the stockbroker will place the order with the firm's broker on the stock exchange floor. When the broker on the stock exchange floor receives the order, he or she will try to get the best price available and complete the transaction as soon as possible. Payment for the stocks purchased, including the brokers' commission, is generally required within three business days after the transaction. A stock certificate is sent to the purchaser within four to six weeks, unless the certificates are left with the brokerage firm for safekeeping (Kapoor, Dlabay, & Hughes, 2008).

Mutual funds, a popular means of investing, can be purchased as part of a 401(k) or 403(b) retirement account, a Roth IRA, or a traditional IRA, or they can be owned outright. Mutual funds are purchased through an account executive of a brokerage firm, a salesperson who is authorized to sell them, or by contacting the investment company that manages the fund.

Mutual funds can also be purchased through the fund's reinvestment plan. If someone already owns shares in a mutual fund, dividends can be used to purchase additional shares in the fund. In this way shares are purchased without having to pay additional sales charges or commissions. Shares can be sold to the investment company that sponsors the fund by giving proper notification, and the investment company will mail the check.

Buying and Selling Bonds

Investors may also buy and sell various types of bonds. Safety is the main reason that investors purchase corporate and government bonds: Bonds are debt instruments and, in the case of a company's bankruptcy, debts are paid off before ownership shares (stocks). Therefore, bonds are considered to be safer investments than stocks and mutual funds. Investors expect to get their entire principal back with interest. *Treasury securities*, which are government bonds, are issued by the U.S. Treasury Department and can be purchased through the website Treasury Direct (www.treasurydirect.com). Treasury Direct conducts auctions to sell treasury securities, and buyers interested in purchasing these securities at such auctions must have a Treasury Direct account in order to bid. Treasury securities may also be purchased through banks or brokers, who charge commission. Investors may hold the securities until maturity or sell them before they mature. If the securities are sold, the interest earned is exempt from state and local taxes, but is taxable for federal income tax purposes. Treasury Direct is the easiest and least expensive way for individuals to purchase treasury securities.

Most municipal and corporate bonds are purchased through full service, discount, or online brokerage firms. When a discount or online brokerage firm is used, the commission is lower; however, there is still need to do research. As with other investments, when buying bonds it is important to evaluate the potential investment very carefully. Obtain price information and review the ratings for the bond to determine the quality and risk associated with bond issues. For both Moody's and Standard and Poor's, the first four individual categories (AAA, AA, A, and BBB) represent investment-grade securities that are suitable for conservative investors. Bonds in the next two categories (BB and B) are considered speculative investments. Finally, the C and D categories are bonds with poor prospects of repayment or even continued payment of interest. Bonds in these categories may be in default, which means the company fails to pay the interest and/or principal. The rating designations for municipal bonds are similar to corporate bonds described above. Securities issued by the Treasury Department are not graded because they are considered risk-free as they are backed by the federal government (Kapoor, Dlabay, & Hughes, 2008).

Protecting Against Catastrophic Loss

Money that is invested is a greater risk of being lost than is money in savings accounts. One of the best ways to protect against catastrophic loss is to develop an exit strategy when purchasing a stock or mutual fund. In developing an exit strategy, decide how long the stock or mutual fund will be held, how much risk is acceptable and, finally, at what price to sell. In fact, Stocksignalz.com (2005, Introduction) notes that "At no time should you own a stock and not have a standing sell order in place." A *sell order*, also called a *protective stop-loss sell order*, is an order requesting a broker to sell an investment when it reaches a specific price. Its purpose is to limit an investor's loss.

Diversification is another strategy for managing risk. Diversification spreads invested money across a variety of investments, for example stocks, bonds, mutual funds, and regular savings. Diversification is consistent with the statement "Don't put all your eggs in one basket." Diversification does not guarantee against loss, but it lessens the possibility of overall investment loss. One fairly easy way to diversify an investment portfolio is to buy a mutual fund that invests in several stocks, bonds, and cash instead of buying individual stocks. Other ways to protect against investment loss include avoiding investing in new companies that have no performance track record, carefully reviewing the prospectus of any mutual fund plan to purchase, and understanding how to assess price-earnings ratios and other financial data related to stocks and mutual funds.

Teaching Applications, Discussion Questions, and Assessment of Concepts

The following are some activities to help reinforce and assess learning:

1. List some sources of information on the rating of stocks, mutual funds, and bonds.

2. Use the Yahoo! Finance Website (http://finance.yahoo.com) to locate a mutual fund with a Five-Star Morningstar Rating. What does the five-star rating mean?

3. For four years, Mary McEwen invested $4,000 each year in the same company. The stock was selling for $32 per share in 2005, $45 in 2006, $35 in 2007, and $50 in 2008. (a) What is Mary's total investment in the company? (b) After four years, how many shares does Mary own? (c) What is the average cost per share of Mary's investment?

SUMMARY

The chapter describes the critical importance of saving and investing and shares information on several curriculum guides that might be used to infuse them into public school curricula, starting from the early grades. In discussing the U.S. saving and investing rates and their impact on future spending, the importance of saving and investing, and how to make good saving and investing decisions, the chapter also outlines a variety of teaching applications, discussion questions, and assessment concepts.

REFERENCES

Abate, T. (2006). *Americans saving less than nothing.* Retrieved November 8, 2007, from http://www.mindfully.org/Reform/2006/Americans-Saving-Less8jan06.htm

Bannister, R., & Oatney, L. (1992). *Consumer approach to investing: A teaching guide, 2nd ed.* (ERIC Document Reproduction Service No. ED 351 615).

Bigham-Bernstel, J., & Saslav, L. (2000). *Macmillan teach yourself personal finance in 24 hours.* Indianapolis, IN: Pearson Education Macmillan USA.

Dorval, C., & Hubbell, C. (2002). Study finds that many Americans do not expect their children to attend college. *Aegon Institutional Markets.* Retrieved December 24, 2007, from http://www.aegoninstitutional.com/pdfs/College_Savings_Survey.pdf

Guidolin, M., & La Jeunesse, E. A. (2007, November/December). *The decline in the U.S. personal saving rate: Is it real and is it a puzzle?* Federal Reserve Bank of St. Louis *Review* 491. Retrieved November 8, 2007, from http://research.stlouisfed.org/publications/review/07/11/NovDec2007Review.pdf#page=4

Haramis, I. E. C. (2006). *Saving versus investing*. Retrieved December 26, 2007, from http://www.articlecity.com/articles/business_and_finance/article_7853.shtml

Kapoor, J. R., Dlabay, L. R., & Hughes, R. J. (2008). *Focus on personal finance (2nd ed.)*. New York: McGraw-Hill/Irwin.

Library of Economics and Liberty. (2007). *Saving and investing*. Retrieved November 8, 2007, from http://www.econlib.org/library/Topics/HIghSchool/SavingandInvesting.html

Merrill Lynch Retirement Preparedness Survey. (2003). *Merrill Lynch announces results of "Retirement Preparedness Survey."* Retrieved November 8, 2007, from http://www.ml.com/index.asp?id=7695_7696_8149_8688_8570_5868

Mintel International Group. (2004). *Teen spending estimated to top $190 billion by 2006*. Retrieved April 22, 2008, from http://www.marketresearchworld.net/index.php?option=content&task=view&id=615&Itemid=

Money Management. (2004). *Americans saving for a "rainy day." Money saving habits*. Retrieved November 11, 2007, from http://www.emaxhealth.com/10/5534.html

Office of Investor Education and Assistance. (1999). *The facts on saving and investing: Excerpts from recent polls and studies highlighting the need for financial education*. Retrieved December 24, 2007, from http://www.sec.gov/pdf/report99.pdf

Renick, S. X. (2007). *Get kids in the habit of saving early, not late!* Retrieved December 22, 2007, from http://www.stretcher.com/stories/04/04oct04f.cfm

Stocksignalz.com. (2005). *Overview of selling techniques*. Retrieved November 8, 2007, from http://www.stocksignalz.com/stock-selling-tips.html

154

Chapter 11

Buying Goods and Services

Lisa Gueldenzoph Snyder
North Carolina A&T State University
Greensboro, North Carolina

Consumers often are faced with confusing questions: Is it better to lease or buy? How does one mortgage company differ from another? Who sells the best brand of tomato sauce? Some choices about goods and services require major financial decisions, such as buying a car or a house. Others are less significant, such as grocery options, yet they are all economic decisions that require an understanding of economic value and budgeting. Rational decision-making and effective evaluation in personal buying is indispensable in today's marketplace where a vast array of goods and services is available—both locally and online. This chapter addresses several indispensable concepts related to buying goods and services by beginning with an outline of the curriculum standards in economic and personal financial literacy. Then the major concepts related to making wise choices when buying goods and services, selecting purchasing alternatives, and understanding consumer protection issues are addressed. In each section, teaching strategies for integrating these concepts are presented for elementary, secondary, and postsecondary business education classes. The chapter concludes with a description of general teaching resources available from professional organizations, government agencies, and financial institutions.

CURRICULUM STANDARDS

Ben Bernanke, the chairman of the Federal Reserve Board, stated that "in today's complex financial markets, financial education is central to helping consumers make better decisions for themselves and their families" (Federal Reserve Education, 2008a, p. 1). Several organizations provide financial literacy materials, but the three primary curriculum resources for economics and personal finance education are the National Business Education Association, the National Council on Economic Education, and the Jump$tart Coalition for Personal Financial Literacy.

National Business Education Association

The National Business Education Association (NBEA) updated its *National Standards for Business Education* in 2007. NBEA's standards identify performance expectations at three levels for each category of the learning objectives and provide a comprehensive outline of the skills and abilities students should be able to demonstrate. The standards include nine economic and eight personal finance criteria. The concept of "buying goods and services" is listed specifically under personal finance; the achievement standard for this concept is described as the ability to "apply a decision-making model to maximize consumer satisfaction when buying goods and services" (NBEA, 2007, p. 10). Indicators include applying rational decision-making, distinguishing between goods and services, identifying alternative purchasing options, and recognizing consumer rights and protection laws. Faculty designing courses and creating objective statements in this content area will find the NBEA *National Standards for Business Education* a primary resource in their curriculum development process.

National Council on Economic Education

The National Council on Economic Education (NCEE) was established in 1949 to provide economic and personal finance resources to faculty (NCEE, 2008). Its *National Standards* articulate 20 content areas related to economic education, each with dozens of related concepts. Many of the standards apply in some way to "buying goods and services," such as scarcity, marginal cost/benefit, and the role of competition. The standards are linked to related online learning activities that provide hundreds of lesson plans for students at the elementary and secondary levels. Additionally, the lesson plans are searchable by grade, economic concept, and national standard. State affiliates of NCEE and 275 university centers around the country supported by NCEE provide local resources and services for teachers and students. NCEE also offers educational DVD programs that correlate to state standards for elementary, middle, and secondary grades. These resources provide a wealth of curriculum tools and instructional strategies.

Jump$tart Coalition for Personal Financial Literacy

The Jump$tart Coalition for Personal Financial Literacy was founded in 1995. Its mission is to ensure that students graduate from high school with the basic skills needed to manage their personal finances and understand the "principles involved with earning, spending, saving, and investing" their money (Jump$tart Coalition for Personal Financial Literacy, 2007, p. 1). The Jump$tart Coalition published the third edition of its *National Standards in K-12 Personal Finance Education* in 2007. The standards provide a model framework for instruction in both personal finance (managing income and assets) and financial literacy (managing resources for lifetime security). The standards include financial responsibility and decision-making, income and careers, planning and money management, credit and debt, risk management and insurance, and saving and investing. Specific, measurable competencies are outlined at the fourth-, eighth-, and twelfth-grade levels. They also offer a searchable clearinghouse (http://www.jumpstartclearinghouse.org) of educational materials that are categorized by grade level, learning format, and specific content. To help faculty determine the best materials for their students' specific needs, the *National Best Practices Guidelines* (http://www.jumpstart.org/gp.cfm) also offer helpful instructional resources.

The NBEA, NCEE, and Jump$tart Coalition all offer similar standards and resources related to the topic of buying goods and services; however, each entity provides unique learning activities and lesson plans. Instructors are encouraged to utilize all available resources when designing financial literacy curricula and/or preparing classroom experiences to facilitate students' understanding of effectively buying goods and services. To help identify the primary issues related to the concept of buying goods and services, three general topics are addressed in the following sections: goods and services, purchasing alternatives, and consumer protection.

GOODS AND SERVICES

As defined in economic terms, goods and services are the products and fee-for-labor opportunities that are marketed for consumer consumption. Goods include items that focus on the consumer, such as food and clothing, or on the producer, such as raw materials used to make consumer goods. Services vary greatly and include, but are not limited to, "educational, health, communication, transportation, and social services" (Virtual Education, 2008, p. 1). In this section, goods and services are described in terms of making good buying decisions; understanding advertising and marketing; utilizing consumer information; taking time to comparison shop; and buying, renting, or leasing goods and services.

Making Good Buying Decisions

According to the Children's Financial Network (CFN), adolescents spend 98% of the money they accept from gifts, receive as an allowance, and earn from part-time employment (Children's Financial Network, 2008). CFN also reported that 45% of college students are in debt and typically graduate with an average $28,000 debt due to academic loans and credit card bills. To help students avoid debt from overspending, financial literacy education must address not only traditional basic money management issues, but also the significant impact of effective personal decision-making and wise buying choices on their future financial condition. Education that supports students' ability to evaluate choices and make good buying decisions will enable them to make informed choices (Franklin, 2007).

As outlined in Chapter 8, "Personal Decision-Making," young consumers may make quick buying decisions based on external factors, such as peer influence and targeted advertising ploys, rather than a rational decision-making process. When helping students understand how to make good buying decisions, instructors should underscore the criteria that constitute good decision-making. These include defining and clarifying the action (in this case, the good or service that is being considered for purchase), gathering as much information as possible about the good or service, brainstorming purchasing options, comparing the advantages and disadvantages of each option, selecting the best option, and re-evaluating the purchase to reflect upon and learn from the decision (Hermalin & Isen, 2008). As shown in Figure 1, these variables can be presented as a rational five-stage decision-making process (tutor2u, 2008) for maximizing consumer satisfaction when buying goods and services. Although listing pros and cons may seem burdensome for inexpensive purchases and unnecessary for everyday expenses, every penny counts in a budget. Students will be more apt to apply this model to larger expenditures if they make use of the same process for smaller purchases. Each step of the Five-Stage Decision-Making Model is discussed as it relates to understanding advertising and marketing, utilizing consumer information, taking time to comparison shop, and evaluating which purchasing option is most appropriate (e.g., buying, renting, or leasing).

Understanding Advertising and Marketing

Advertising and marketing support the distribution of goods and services to target markets. To help students make wise buying decisions, they need to understand how

Figure 1. The Five-Stage Decision-Making Model

Source: tutor2u (2008). *Buyer behaviour – Decision-making process.* Retrieved May 11, 2008, from http://tutor2u.net/business/marketing/buying_decision_process.asp

advertising and marketing affect their purchasing decisions. When students (as consumers) identify that they want a particular good or service, they consider the first factor in the Five-Stage Decision Making Model, *Need Recognition and Problem Awareness*. Oftentimes, this awareness becomes evident only after seeing an advertisement that makes a logical, emotional, or credible appeal for the good or service. Understanding these methods of persuasion helps students recognize the advertising ploys marketers use to motivate consumers to purchase their goods and services. The Urban Dreams program, funded by a grant through the Oakland Unified School District in California, provides a Critical Consumerism lesson plan collection that focuses on advertising analysis. One of the 50-minute activities addresses the aspects of persuasion and their effect on consumers' purchasing decisions. Students brainstorm their own persuasive habits, such as convincing a parent to grant permission for a special request, and then analyze whether they used logos, pathos, or ethos as a method of persuasion (Urban Dreams, n.d.).

Students may confuse the concept of advertising—the dissemination of information about a product or service by its provider to its existing and potential customers—with marketing—the "processes for creating, communicating, delivering, and exchanging offerings that have value for customers" (American Marketing Association, 2008, p. 1). Simply stated, advertising is one of the many variables of the marketing process. Marketers create a demand for the supply of goods and services that producers want to sell. Competition among producers creates more supply, but also increases the amount of advertising that inundates consumers from a wide variety of media sources. To make sense of the massive amounts of advertising information and move to the second part of the Five-Stage Decision-Making Model, students must effectively utilize consumer information.

Utilizing Consumer Information

Skilled consumers use credible information to make good decisions. The objective is to get students to take the time necessary to research the information and ensure the data they find are credible. Several sources of reliable consumer information are available, such as the federal government's Consumer.gov website, which categorizes content as well as provides a site-based search tool. Additional consumer-based links provide resources for online safety, credit reports, personal privacy, and e-commerce issues. This resource also provides a link to the Federal Citizen Information Center, available at http://pueblo.gsa.gov/teachers/. The site includes several free resources for teachers, including lesson plans for grades 6 through 12, posters, and related print materials (Federal Citizen Information Center, 2008).

Taking Time to Comparison Shop

Even with credible resources at their disposal, well-informed consumers take the additional time necessary to use information to compare goods and services. Taking time to make comparisons among the available goods and services relates to the third stage of the Five-Stage Decision-Making Model, *Evaluation of Alternatives*. Additional resources can help students make accurate comparisons among goods and services. For example, ConsumerWorld.org offers links to find the lowest gas prices, comparable prices for items available online, and information from other entities, such as *Consumer Reports* (Consumer World, 2008). Additionally, its long list of "Consumer Quickies" includes information about tips for saving money when buying car insurance, eating at restaurants, and using coupons. Instructors may find the weekly email newsletter *Consumer World Update* a useful resource when integrating current consumer information into their business education classes.

Because young consumers are often impulse buyers, educational activities that encourage evaluating alternatives and making comparisons can be extremely beneficial to students' development of both personal decision-making and financial literacy. A WebQuest (an online project-based teaching resource) developed by mathematics teachers at Union High School in Iowa provides an interesting activity that requires students to compare three to six automobile options within three different price ranges. Students are given links to several Internet resources, such as a consumer auto guide, payment calculators, and financing and purchasing tips, to assist them in the selection and justification of their choices. This WebQuest is available at http://www.union.k12.ia.us/ukhs/WebQuest/math_car.htm (Gregory & McCright, n.d.).

Buying, Renting, or Leasing

Part of comparison shopping includes decisions about buying, renting, or leasing goods. These options reflect the fourth element of the Five-Stage Decision-Making Model, *Purchase*. These alternatives typically apply to expensive goods, such as buying or leasing a car or buying or renting a house. The Federal Trade Commission (2008a) provides several links related to financing, leasing, or renting automobiles at its consumer-related website (http://www.ftc.gov/bcp/menus/consumer/autos/finance.shtm). Resources include instructions for reading car advertisements, questions to ask when renting a car, and facts about financing and repossession. A WebQuest entitled "Math Models and Economics," developed by the Atwater-Cosmos-Grove City School District in Minnesota, takes students through the process of comparing buying, renting, and leasing options for both cars and homes (Atwater-Cosmos-Grove City School District, 2008). Following the procedures and using the resources outlined in the WebQuest, students create a PowerPoint presentation that displays their choices, justifies their decisions, and shows the math related to bank rates, loan calculations, and interest paid over time (available at http://www.acgc.k12.mn.us/alc/webquest1.ppt).

Teaching Strategies

This section outlines additional teaching strategies to encourage students to make good buying decisions. Based on research related to effective methods of financial literacy (Cook, 2007; Franklin, 2007; Hermalin & Isen, 2008), students of all ages learn the concepts of money management most effectively when they are engaged in activities that mirror actual financial situations. For example, students are better able to understand and appreciate how factors influence their purchasing decisions when they experience the problem solving and critical analysis involved in buying goods and services (Cook, 2007). In many of the available resources, students complete these learning activities collaboratively by using the input from their teammates to define and clarify the good or service, gather information, brainstorm options, compare pros and cons, select an option, and reflect upon the decision (Hermalin & Isen, 2008).

Although many teaching materials are designed for teens and young adults, resources are also available for younger students. To introduce the basics of money management to students at the elementary level, games are popular methods of not only engaging students in learning, but also delivering content. For example, BankSITE offers a Kid's Corner (http://banksite.com/kidscorner/index.htm) that uses an interactive cartoon, "Dollar the Dragon," to teach children foundational concepts, such as the history of money, fun facts, and ideas for making money. The games challenge students to "win" by making decisions that result in a positive cash flow by the end of the game.

Another online project geared for younger learners asks students to help a nine-year-old girl decide if she is ready to buy (and care for) a pet dog. In teams of four, each student is responsible for a different role: the financial advisor determines the expenses (budgeting), the breeder makes decisions about what kind of dog to purchase (comparison shopping), the commitment advisor determines the pros and cons of the purchase (evaluation of alternatives), and the training expert provides information about caring for the pet (post-purchase evaluation). This WebQuest, developed by Doglinks (2008), is available at http://doglinks.co.nz/educatn/dogquest/dogquest.htm.

In summary, the activities described in this section provide students with the opportunities to practice buying goods and services and allow them to reflect on their purchasing decisions, which exemplifies the last variable of the Five-Stage Decision-Making Model, *Post-Purchase Evaluation*. By using learning activities that simulate the step-by-step model, students will be better equipped to make effective decisions about the goods and services they buy. As with any content area, faculty should carefully evaluate age-level appropriateness, the availability of resources, and the usefulness of all learning activities.

PURCHASING ALTERNATIVES

After a good or service is determined to be "the best" option, several purchasing alternatives exist including retail stores, catalogs, e-malls and online venues, and shopping networks. This section outlines the differences among these options and provides teaching strategies to help students make good decisions, consider their purchasing alternatives, and identify the most appropriate choice.

Retail Stores

Traditional outlets for purchasing goods and services include the "brick and mortar" options—department stores, pharmacies, lawyers' offices, etc.—that have populated Main Streets across the globe for many years. Today, the number of single proprietary retail stores is declining rapidly, giving way to international franchise enterprises. The unique individualism and personal attention of the "mom and pop" general stores have been replaced by corporations with thousands of chains and subsidiaries that offer bargain basement prices and a wide variety of inventory. Retail stores provide consumers the ability to "touch and feel" the products they offer, allowing side-by-side brand comparison and the capability to read the labels' fine print. In many cases, sales associates are able to provide additional product explanations to assist consumers in their purchasing decisions.

Catalogs

The progression from print advertisements to multiple-page flyers in the 1800s led to the development of the catalog, a hardcopy pictorial inventory of goods offered by a retail store. Mail order merchandising grew with the Homestead Act of 1862, which enabled frontier farmers to develop land in the West where supplies were limited, if available at all. As railroads connected the populated eastern states with the "Wild West," goods were ordered by catalog and shipped by rail. One of the most popular and longest-running catalogs is the Sears Catalog, which was first published in 1888 (Sears, 2004). Catalogs continue to be popular for consumers because they are both convenient (delivered by mail or available online) and easy to use (orders can be placed over the phone, online, or by mail). Although they are not able to "touch and feel" the goods, consumers can compare prices among various brands of products and call customer service representatives to seek assistance.

E-malls and Online Venues

Dating back to the 1920s, shopping malls developed as the modern marketplace. The first enclosed mall opened in 1956 in Minnesota, but it wasn't until the 1980s that the "giant megamalls" became widely accepted as favorable shopping experiences (Pocock, 2007). The convenience of one-stop shopping is still popular today both in traditional mall environments, which also serve as face-to-face social networking venues for teens, as well as online "e-malls" where products from thousands of stores can be compared online. Many e-malls offer products within specific categories, such as BestBuys.com (not the retailer, "Best Buy") that specializes in electronics, and BrandsForLess.com that offers discounted name-brand apparel, such as Calvin Klein and Donna Karan products. Other e-malls offer eclectic groupings of products, such as OnlineShoppingExpress.com, which sells traditional department store products with customer reviews, and LiquidationConnect.com, which provides tax-free shopping.

Online retailers and entrepreneurs benefit from access to an international marketplace, global consumer base, and reduced operating costs (e.g., no overhead).

Customer registration features that store shoppers' preferences and personally welcome online users upon subsequent visits attempt to compensate for the lack of personalized service and attention offered by face-to-face retailers. Online shoppers often are profiled based on their prior purchases. For example, after buying a book from Amazon.com, shoppers will receive suggestions for additional related products that other similar consumers purchased. "Brick and click" stores—those that offer both online and traditional retail purchasing alternatives— provide consumers the opportunity to compare not only the products, but also their purchasing alternatives. They can decide the better option: (1) driving to the store; selecting the item; buying it with cash, check, or credit card; and having it the same day; or (2) going online; selecting the item; buying it with a credit card; and having it delivered (perhaps with a shipping charge). Students can debate these questions during class discussions and identify pros and cons based on several variables, including product categories, personal selection opportunities, and immediacy of use.

Shopping Networks

The literal definition of shopping networks refers to the multi-product retailers who offer their wares through dedicated television programming, such as the Home Shopping Network (http://www.hsn.com) and QVC (http://www.qvc.com). Although most shopping networks' products are also offered online, televised demonstrations coupled with "special deals" for calling to order within a specified timeframe provide incentives for impulse buyers who may be "surfing" through the channels from the comfort of their home.

User-based shopping networks and online auction communities, such as eBay, uBid.com, and WeBidz, provide unique selling and buying opportunities with a worldwide audience. Another form of shopping networks is the unique combination of social networking (e.g., online forums) and online shopping (e.g., e-malls) into social shopping, which consists of "product listings from site users who recommend their favorites, often with a strong emphasis on what's hot, new, and exciting" (Gordon, 2007, p. 1). Other sites, such as Craigslist and local city-based networks, offer free buying and selling opportunities as well as real estate, personals, and employment postings. These sites support social interaction among users in one-on-one formats (such as sales negotiation) and among multi-users (such as discussion forums). Social shopping provides not only consumer information and evaluation of alternatives (the second and third elements, respectively, of The Five-Stage Decision-Making Model), but also the links to purchase the items and the ability to post product reviews (stages four and five, respectively).

Teaching Strategies

To help students understand the factors involved with making alternative purchasing decisions, projects should be assigned that require students to research their options with a variety of products. By assigning different genres to different teams—

such as electronics, name-brand clothing, or jewelry— students can compare the same product availability among retail advertisements, catalogs, traditional online vendors, and shopping networks. Students can "do the math" by identifying the differences in price, including taxes and delivery charges, as well as factoring in the convenience costs of gas/mileage and personal time when choosing "brick" over "click."

Students could also create a buying guide for their peers that outlines the pros and cons of the purchasing alternatives for the goods and services that they deem most applicable for their age group. As a project-based learning activity, the buying guide could be categorized into sections assigned to teams who specialize in specific content areas. This project could be implemented at nearly every grade level. For example, elementary students might focus on games and toys available through local retail stores, catalogs, and online venues. Secondary students would benefit from information about iPods, cell phones, and music downloads. Postsecondary students could address vendor options for textbooks, loan information, and professional clothing or accessories. Regardless of where they buy their goods and services, students should understand the issues related to consumer protection. Careful evaluation of learning activities will ensure that the options and products are aligned with students' age level and abilities.

CONSUMER PROTECTION

The wide variety of goods and services that are available both in traditional environments, such as retail stores and catalogs, as well as technologically supported commercial ventures, such as online stores and shopping networks, create a wealth of options for consumers. However, the old adage of *caveat emptor*—buyer beware—has never been more relevant than in today's Internet age where global purchases are made with the click of a mouse, enabling impulse buying without the limitations of time or geography. As students learn about the goods and services that are available to them via the plethora of purchasing alternatives, they must also become aware of the Consumer Bill of Rights, federal consumer protection laws, and consumer protection resources.

Consumer Bill of Rights

The Consumer Bill of Rights was originally based on President John F. Kennedy's 1962 speech to Congress and was eventually endorsed and expanded upon by the United Nations in 1985 (Lush, 2008). The basic constructs of the bill include consumers' rights to be informed, to be safe, to choose, and to be heard. A consumer's right to information relates to advertising, labeling, and financing; consumers are further protected in these areas by legislation such as the Fair Packaging and Labeling Act (1966), the Truth-in-Lending Act (1968), and the Magnuson-Moss Warranty Act (1975). The right to safety focuses on protection from injury and is supported by the Consumer Product Safety Commission, which has the power to recall potentially hazardous products. Consumer choice relates to the availability of a wide range of products and services and is protected through limitations of patents, mergers, and business practices. Finally, the Consumer Bill of Rights protects the consumer's right to be heard and provides outlets for filing complaints.

Federal Consumer Protection Laws

In addition to the Consumer Bill of Rights and subsequent related legislative acts, the federal government has enacted several laws to protect consumers. For example, the Fair Credit Reporting Act along with the Fair Debt Collection Practices Act protect consumers from the unfair collection, dissemination, and use of their credit information. Consumers should regularly check their credit reports to ensure that their credit history is accurately documented. The Gramm-Leach-Bliley Act, also referred to as the Financial Modernization Act of 1999, "protects consumers' personal financial information held by financial institutions" (Federal Trade Commission, 2008b, p. 1). The Federal Trade Commission's (FTC) Bureau of Consumer Protection provides a wealth of information, including categorical content, publications, and videos (2008a). Instructors may find the videos (available at http://www.ftc.gov/bcp/consumer.shtm) useful classroom tools to help students understand, both visually and conceptually, the importance of consumer safety issues.

Consumer Protection Resources

As Chapter 8 identified, students should be aware of liability costs related to stolen debit and credit cards. The Electronic Fund Transfer Act defines debit card regulations, and the Fair Credit Billing Act outlines resolution procedures for credit card liability. The Fraud Center supported by the National Consumers League (http://www.fraud.org) provides information about fraudulent activities related to telemarketing, business scams, and Internet-related issues. Its resources also include links to online shopping information that focuses on Internet fraud and identity theft. The Better Business Bureau (http://us.bbb.org) offers links that provide information about businesses and charities, allow consumers to file complaints, and enable searches for accredited retailers and service providers by state. These resources can be used in a wide variety of teaching strategies.

Teaching Strategies

Because a large number of consumer protection entities and laws exist, student teams could be assigned to investigate them in detail and identify how they relate to and complement each other. As a continuation of the buying guide activity outlined above, students could create a consumer awareness guide that describes the kinds of protection offered by each act, the steps for reporting unfair practices, and the ramifications (from a business perspective) of violating the laws.

In addition to traditional reporting activities, postsecondary students could be encouraged to analyze their credit report through one of the three credit reporting agencies available at AnnualCreditReport.com. Equifax, TransUnion, and Experian provide free comprehensive credit reports. Each agency allows users to access one credit report each year. For long-term use, students should be advised to check their credit reports three times a year, once from each agency. Because the content includes sensitive information, instructors may not wish to use collaborative or presentation assignments; however, students could be assigned the activity as homework that is documented by the students' reflection of the information provided, rather than their personal content.

TEACHING RESOURCES

Several organizations offer resources related to economic and personal financial literacy that help faculty by providing not only relevant content and instructional materials, but also engaging teaching resources. Many of these activities have been pre-evaluated for their instructional use and are searchable by content area and grade level. The primary outlets include professional organizations, government agencies, and financial institutions.

Professional Organizations

Several professional organizations provide teaching resources about buying goods and services that can be integrated into various levels of business education classes. Teaching resources at the national level are available from the following sources:

- National Association of Economic Educators (http://www.naee.net)

- National Education Association (http://www.nea.org)

- National Endowment for Financial Education (http://www.nefe.org)

- U.S. Academic Decathlon (USAD) Curriculum Content Standards (http://www.usad.org)

At the regional level, most states offer rich resources through their local Councils on Economic Education, such as Illinois (http://econed-il.org/icee/index.shtml), Indiana (http://www.econed-in.org/tsi.asp), Michigan (http://www.mceeonline.org), and Minnesota (http://www.mcee.umn.edu). Instructors are encouraged to search for their closest resource by using the directory services through the National Council on Economic Education at http://www.ncee.net/network/directory.php.

For resources specifically targeted to elementary-aged students, Education World (http://www.educationworld.com) offers links to a wide variety of activities, such as online games like the Lemonade Stand (http://www.classbrain.com) that teaches basic supply and demand concepts. The Educator's Reference Desk (http://askeric.org) lists several economics-based lesson plans from kindergarten (e.g., "Baa, Baa, Black Sheep, Have You Any Goods?") through high school (e.g., "Microeconomics – Personal Budgeting").

Mid-Continent Research for Education and Learning offers lesson plans and related resources for economic education (http://www.mcrel.org/lesson-plans/economics/econlessons.asp). Although its website appears to be geared primarily for the younger grades, the Children's Financial Network (CFN) also provides products and services for adult financial literacy (http://www.childrensfinancialnetwork.com). As a fee-for-service entity, CFN offers keynote presenters, consultants, and public relations programs to help faculty learn about and integrate financial education into their curriculum.

Government Agencies

Government agencies, such as the Federal Trade Commission (FTC), offer consumer awareness and protection resources (Federal Trade Commission, 2008a). As previously stated, the Federal Citizen Information Center offers free printed materials for teachers (http://www.pueblo.gsa.gov/teachers/). The President's Advisory Council on Financial Literacy is a relatively new initiative signed by President Bush as an Executive Order on January 22, 2008. To focus financial education on high school students, the Council created the National Financial Literacy Challenge (http://flc.treas.gov/teacher) that uses online assessments to recognize individual student achievement. Students compete nationally for yearly award medals.

Financial Institutions

Because they benefit most from consumers' wise purchasing decisions, financial institutions also offer extensive teaching resources for faculty at various levels of education. For example, Merrill Lynch sponsored the 2008 Financial Literacy Surveys of High School and College Students, the results of which were presented by the Federal Reserve Board. Ernst & Young supports Moneyopoli$ (http://www.money opolis.com), an interactive game that engages middle school students with concepts about financial planning using math and money skills. The site includes both instructor materials (Teacher Town) and resources for parents (Parent Place).

Money Smart is a financial education program of the Federal Deposit Insurance Corporation (FDIC) that provides links to curriculum content for learners of all ages, including adults (Federal Deposit Insurance Corporation, 2008). As part of the FDIC's *Money Smart* curriculum, Wachovia Bank offers a financial literacy program called Extra Credit^{SM} that focuses on credit and debt management issues (Wachovia, 2008). The program supports both traditional face-to-face classroom environments as well as web-based instruction (requires video capabilities) and includes instructor and participant guides, overhead slides, marketing posters, and student certificates of completion. Wachovia also offers an eCommunities*first*® financial literacy program that sponsors workshops on integrating technology. Six lessons focus on the practical application of PC and Internet skills as they relate to buying goods and services as well as managing financial resources.

The wealth of information provided by curriculum standards and teaching materials from a variety of sources often makes the breadth of economic and personal financial literacy difficult to comprehend, both for students and faculty. Examples of curriculum initiatives in action include Indiana's Networks Personal Financial Literacy initiative that helps ensure students' financial management education through collaborative efforts with schools, businesses, government groups, and nonprofit organizations (Wilhelm & Chao, 2005).

SUMMARY

As indicated throughout this chapter, research indicates that students typically do not make good economic and personal financial decisions; therefore, the integration of financial education is critically important at all levels of education (Cook, 2007; Franklin, 2007; Hermalin & Isen, 2008; Wilhelm & Chao, 2005). Although a wide variety of issues is related to buying goods and services, the curriculum standards outlined by the National Business Education Association, the National Council on Economic Education, and the Jump$tart Coalition for Personal Financial Literacy provide comprehensive lists of learning goals and objectives that can support new financial management educational offerings or be incorporated into existing business education courses. Regardless of the delivery system, these objectives can be applied to realistic buying scenarios by taking students through the practical elements of the Five-Stage Decision-Making Model. Realistic learning activities, such as buying guides that outline purchasing alternatives and consumer protection information, will not only provide critical information to students as they research the content, but also create rich learning artifacts that students can refer to for years to come.

REFERENCES

American Marketing Association (2008). *Marketing definitions.* Retrieved May 11, 2008, from http://www.marketingpower.com/content4620.php

Atwater-Cosmos-Grove City School District (2008). *Math models and economics.* Retrieved May 20, 2008, from http://www.acgc.k12.mn.us/alc/webquest1.ppt

Children's Financial Network (2008). *Welcome to Children's Financial Network, Inc.* Retrieved May 10, 2008, from http://www.childrensfinancialnetwork.com

Consumer World (2008). *Consumer World: Everything consumer.* Retrieved May 20, 2008, from http://consumerworld.org

Cook, S. (2007). Investment clubs teaching financial literacy. *Techniques: Connecting Education and Careers, 62*(7), 26-27.

Doglinks (2008). *WebQuest: Is Kim ready to care for a dog? You decide!* Retrieved May 18, 2008, from http://doglinks.co.nz/educatn/dogquest/dogquest.htm

Federal Citizen Information Center (2008). *FCIC – For teachers.* Retrieved May 16, 2008, from http://pueblo.gsa.gov/teachers/

Federal Deposit Insurance Corporation (2008). *FDIC: Money smart – A financial education program.* Retrieved May 8, 2008, from http://www.fdic.gov/consumers/consumer/ moneysmart/index.html

Federal Reserve Education (2008). *Personal financial education.* Retrieved May 8, 2008, from http://www.federalreserveeducation.org

Federal Trade Commission (2008a). *FTC bureau of consumer protection – Consumer information.* Retrieved May 16, 2008, from http://www.ftc.gov/bcp/consumer.shtm

Federal Trade Commission (2008b). *Privacy initiatives.* Retrieved May 20, 2008, from http://www.ftc.gov/privacy/privacyinitiatives/glbact.html

Franklin, I. E. (2007). Expanded financial literacy unit helps students make wise choices. *Journal of Family and Consumer Sciences, 99*(1), 17-18.

Gregory, M., & McCright, M. (n.d.) *The car project.* Retrieved May 18, 2008, from http://www.union.k12.ia.us/ukhs/WebQuest/math_car.htm

Gordon, K. T. (2007). *The power of social shopping networks.* Retrieved May 18, 2008, from http://www.entrepreneur.com/marketing/onlinemarketing/article174746.html

Hermalin, B. E., & Isen, A. M. (2008). A model of the effect of affect on economic decision making. *Quantitative Marketing and Economics, 6*(1), 17-40.

Jump$tart Coalition for Personal Financial Literacy (2007). *Jump$tart Coalition.* Retrieved May 8, 2008, from http://www.jumpstart.org

Lush, V. (2008). *Consumer Bill of Rights.* Retrieved May 20, 2008, from http://www.book rags.com/research/consumer-bill-of-rights-ebf-01/

National Business Education Association (2007). *National standards for business education: What America's students should know and be able to do in business.* Reston, VA: Author.

National Council on Economic Education (2008). *EconomicsAmerica©: National standards.* Retrieved May 8, 2008, from http://www.ncee.net/ea/standards

Pocock, E. (2007). *Shopping mall history.* Shopping Mall and Shopping Center Studies, American Studies at Eastern Connecticut State University. Retrieved May 18, 2008, from http://www.easternct.edu/depts/amerst/MallsHistory.htm

Sears (2004). *History of the Sears catalog.* Retrieved May 18, 2008, from http://www.searsarchives.com/catalogs/history.htm

tutor2u (2008). *Buyer behaviour – Decision-making process.* Retrieved May 11, 2008, from http://tutor2u.net/business/marketing/buying_decision_process.asp

Urban Dreams (n. d.). *Lesson plan menu: Critical consumerism.* Retrieved May 15, 2008, from http://urbandreams.ousd.k12.ca.us/lessonplans/consumerism/lesson_3.html

Virtual Education (2008). *Goods and services.* Retrieved May 8, 2008, from http://www.virted.org/ECONOMICS/GoodService.html

Wachovia (2008). *Wachovia financial literacy.* Retrieved May 8, 2008, from http://www.wachovia.com/inside/page/0,,139_413_427,00.html

Wilhelm, W. J., & Chao, C. (2005). Personal financial literacy: Shaping education policy. *Delta Pi Epsilon Journal, 67*(1), 20-35.

Banking and Financial Institutions

Tena B. Crews
University of South Carolina
Columbia, South Carolina

Wanda L. Stitt-Gohdes
University of Georgia
Athens, Georgia

This chapter provides the historical context of the development of banks and financial institutions. Banks are defined, types of financial institutions are discussed, and factors to consider in choosing a bank are reviewed. Banking services and international banking practices are also discussed in this chapter.

BANKING BASICS

It is essential to understand what a bank is, how banks are started, and how to choose a bank with which to do business. The information in this chapter provides learning activities for students to understand banking in today's society. With this knowledge, students can become wise consumers by saving money and managing their finances.

What Is a Bank?

A common definition of a bank is "an establishment for the custody, loan, exchange, or issue of money, for the extension of credit, and for facilitating the transmission of funds" (Merriam-Webster, 2007). This definition provides a brief overview of common transactions that occur in financial institutions. Ryan (2006) defines a full-service bank as "one that offers every possible kind of service, from checking accounts to credit cards, safe-deposit boxes, loans, and automated tellers (ATMs)" (p. 213).

Financial institutions also offer many other services such as online banking, certified checks, and debit cards. The Federal Reserve of Boston reported that "banks sell financial services such as car loans, home mortgage loans, business loans, checking accounts, credit card services, certificates of deposit, and individual retirement accounts" (2007, p. 6). Banks are typically insured through the Federal Deposit Insurance Corporation (FDIC) so customers are protected against a loss of their money up to $250,000 per account.

How Banks Are Started

When a group of individuals wants to start a bank, a state banking commission must review the application. The banking commission reviews all charter applications and reviews the financial status of each proposed organization. The commission also reviews the character of the applicants. If the banking commission approves the organization to become a financial institution, the organization is provided with information including the amount of capital that must be raised and a timeline for such funding (Federal Reserve Bank of Boston, 2007). The timeline also includes other key steps that must be completed in a timely manner, such as developing a board of directors (management team) and obtaining FDIC insurance. Upon the completion of all steps and full approval by the banking commission, a bank is established.

U.S. law provides for a dual banking system, so the bank obtains authorization to be either a state or federal agency. Not all financial institutions are affiliated with the Federal Reserve, as other agencies insure money held within banking institutions. The agency (state or federal) with which the bank affiliates is responsible for protecting the public from unsafe banking practices.

Choosing a Bank

Several issues must be considered when a customer chooses a bank. The bank must be insured and offer the services the customer needs. MetLife (2008) offers the following advice: (1) evaluate needs, (2) compare costs of services that meet needs, and (3) consider what is most important in a banking relationship, such as customer service, Internet/electronic options, branch access, and other features.

Banks are not simple businesses, and choosing one to meet one's specific needs may be complicated. A few steps are helpful in making a decision. A prospective customer must ask three specific questions to make sure not too much is paid for services and that one's money is safe: (1) Does the bank pay competitive interest rates? (2) Is the bank insured by FDIC? (3) Does the bank invest in the community? (Federal Reserve of Boston, 2007).

Teaching Application: Banking Basics

To assist middle or high school students in learning key banking terms and to help them develop an understanding of banks in general, it is essential to create an engaging activity to pique their interest. As an example, the following activity can be designed for individual or group work. Each student or group will be given the definition of a bank on an index card. Students will research types of banking services, define each service, and explain any associated fees. As they research, students will create lists containing the information. The teacher will check student work for completeness.

The students will then be instructed to pretend they are going to start a bank, but their bank can only provide five services. Students must decide which services are most important and develop a bank name, logo, vision statement, and rationale for offering only the five services. Students must also rewrite the definition of a bank provided to them earlier so the definition more accurately represents their particular bank. This project may extend over several class periods depending on the amount of research students may complete. The NBEA Banking and Financial Institutions standards (NBEA, 2007) covered in this activity include basic services provided by financial institutions and evaluating services and costs associated with personal banking needs.

Evaluation of the Learning Activity
This section defines what a bank is, provides guides for consumers in choosing a bank, and explains how banks are started. Through teaching applications and evaluation, basic steps are provided to help students understand terms and important concepts related to this section.

Student understanding of the definition of a bank, services provided, and fees that may be affiliated with such services in this project can be demonstrated through group presentations. Student teams must defend their choices of the five services using logical resources and providing adequate explanations of services and associated fees, if applicable. Rubrics can be easily created on the RubiStar Web site (http://rubistar. 4teachers.org/), such as the sample on page 173.

INSTITUTIONS
A variety of banks and financial institutions exist. This section highlights the differences among institutions and explains various controls under which banks operate. While types of financial institutions may vary, each of them is established to provide services to the public under certain controls. One such controlling body is the Federal Reserve. This section provides information about different types of banks in, and controls of, the Federal Reserve System. Through the teaching and evaluation applications, students are provided the opportunity to research these topics and work collaboratively to understand the banking concepts.

Types of Banks and Financial Institutions
Common types of banking institutions include commercial banks, savings banks and credit unions, and savings and loan associations. Commercial banks typically

CATEGORY	2	1	0
Services	Student describes 5 services for the bank.	Student describes 3-4 services for the bank.	Student describes less than 3 services for the bank.
Associated Fees	Student describes associated fee or notes that an associated fee is not applicable for all 5 services.	Student describes associated fee or notes that an associated fee is not applicable for 3-4 services.	Student describes associated fee or notes that an associated fee is not applicable for less than 3 services.
Definition of the Bank	Student provides a well-written rewrite of the definition of a bank.	Student provides a rewrite of the definition of a bank, but is it not well-written.	Student does not provide a rewrite of the definition of a bank.
Preparedness	Student is completely prepared and has obviously rehearsed.	Student seems fairly prepared but more rehearsals would have been beneficial.	Student is not prepared to present.
Speaks Clearly	Speaks clearly and distinctly all (100-95%) the time, and mispronounces no words.	Speaks clearly and distinctly all (94-85%) the time, but mispronounces some words.	Rarely speaks clearly and distinctly, often mumbles, or cannot be understood or mispronounces several words.
Posture and Eye Contact	Stands up straight, looks relaxed and confident. Establishes eye contact with everyone in the room during the presentation.	Sometimes stands up straight and establishes eye contact most of the time.	Slouches and/or does not look at the audience during the presentation.
Vocabulary	Uses vocabulary appropriate for the audience. Extends audience vocabulary by defining words that might be new to most of the audience.	Uses vocabulary appropriate for the audience. Includes 1-2 words that might be new to most of the audience, but does not define them.	Does not include any vocabulary that might be new to the audience.

specialize in helping businesses with investments. Credit unions, initially developed to help consumers save money and earn interest, are member-based organizations established, for example, for members of a union, educational facility, or other organization. Savings and loan associations, on the other hand, were initially developed to obtain deposits from consumers and to use the money to make loans to other consumers to purchase or build homes. Savings and loan associations still specialize in accepting deposits and making mortgage loans, and are required by law to make a certain percentage of home mortgage loans.

Not all types of banks are the same. Some banks may meet customer needs better than other institutions, depending on the services offered. Several types of banks offer many of the same services, but banking institutions may have different missions. For example, a commercial bank and credit union have different missions as stated above.

Controls of Banks and Financial Institutions

The Federal Reserve is the central banking system of the United States. It influences the U.S. economy as it regulates the amount of money and credit available, and regulates banking institutions. As described by the Federal Reserve Bank of St. Louis, "The Federal Reserve was created in 1913 in response to the nation's recurring banking panics; its mission has since expanded into fostering a healthy economy" (Federal Reserve Bank of St. Louis, 2008, p. 5). The Federal Reserve was designed to protect consumers and maintain a stable financial system throughout the nation. The Federal Reserve is a bank for the U.S. government and a bank for other banks across the nation. It does not serve as a bank to consumers directly and does not loan money to private borrowers; however, it does have the right to loan money to banks if necessary. The federal government has recently begun lending to large investment banks to help prevent a financial "meltdown" due to the subprime mortgage losses. Chapter 5 discusses the role of the federal government and Federal Reserve monetary and fiscal policy in more detail.

The Federal Reserve is divided into 12 districts representing regions within the country. Each district has its own Federal Reserve Bank to meet the needs of banks in its area. The Federal Reserve is accountable for U.S. monetary policy, and interest rates fluctuate based on this policy. The Federal Reserve supervises banks and regulates their business to ensure safety for the consumer.

Teaching Applications: Institutions

To provide students the opportunity to understand types of banks and the Federal Reserve System, student research must be completed. Using the jigsaw cooperative-learning technique (Library of Congress, 2002), an advanced middle school or high school class would be divided into three "home" groups. One group is responsible for researching commercial banks, one group could research savings banks and credit unions, and one group could research savings and loan associations. Each group should identify the institutional mission, steps to open an account, opportunities for electronic transfers, and three Federal Reserve System regulations for its type of financial institution. Within each group, each student should be given a specific task, i.e. each will become a *specialist* with regard to his or her specific task. Each student specialist (with the same specific task) from the various groups should work together to complete their task.

Student specialists then choose the most important information to share with their own home group. They return to their home groups and share the information. Once each home group compiles the research, the members collaborate to develop one presentation with all the relevant information gathered on their type of bank. The class as a whole will view one presentation on commercial banks, one on savings banks and credit unions, and one on savings and loan associations. NBEA Banking and Financial Institutions standards (2007) covered in this activity include those dealing with checking accounts, electronic transactions, and the Federal Reserve System.

Evaluation of the Learning Activity
Evaluation of the preceding activity would be based on the research conducted and presentation by the groups. The rubric on page 176 could guide student work and evaluate the information researched.

BANKING SERVICES
Banking services available in the United States include checking, saving, electronic banking, and various types of credit. These services are relevant to all populations in the United States, including immigrant consumers. Associated fees and penalties may be involved with certain types of accounts. Security is also an important concern for banks and account holders. These topics, as well as credit debt, are described in this section.

Checking
In the electronic, technology-driven world of today, many believe a checking account is archaic. Actually, nothing could be further from the truth. In 2001, the dollar amount of checks written totaled $47.4 trillion (Swann, 2003). Checking accounts offer a basic way of keeping track of an individual's money. Opening a checking account provides an initial relationship with a bank, helps establish good credit for later borrowing, provides a method for recording all cash transactions (including checks, deposits, ATM/debit card transactions, online bill payments, and automatic deductions), and helps the account holder determine errors they or the bank may have made with regard to money transfers and payment transactions (Pascal, 2007).

Consumers must also be aware of *electronic check conversion*, which occurs when a merchant uses information contained on a check to make a one-time electronic fund

CATEGORY	2	1	0
Mission	Student completely describes the mission of the financial institution in clear, concise, and grammatically correct language.	Student describes the mission of the financial institution in clear, concise, and grammatically correct language, but the description is not complete.	Student does not describe the mission of the financial institution.
Steps for Opening an Account	Student completely describes the steps for opening an account.	Student describes the steps for opening an account, but the description is not complete.	Student does not describe the steps for opening an account.
Electronic Monetary Transactions	Student completely identifies opportunities for electronic monetary transactions.	Student identifies a few opportunities for electronic monetary transactions.	Student does not identify opportunities for electronic monetary transactions.
Federal Reserve System Regulations	Student identifies 3-5 Federal Reserve System regulations.	Student identifies 1-2 Federal Reserve System regulations.	Student does not identify Federal Reserve System regulations.
Speaks Clearly	Speaks clearly and distinctly all (100-95%) the time, and mispronounces no words.	Speaks clearly and distinctly all (94-85%) the time, but mispronounces some words.	Rarely speaks clearly and distinctly, often mumbles or cannot be understood or mispronounces several words.
Posture and Eye Contact	Stands up straight, looks relaxed and confident. Establishes eye contact with everyone in the room during the presentation.	Sometimes stands up straight and establishes eye contact most of the time.	Slouches and/or does not look at the audience during the presentation.
Vocabulary	Uses vocabulary appropriate for the audience. Extends audience vocabulary by defining words that might be new to most of the audience.	Uses vocabulary appropriate for the audience. Includes 1-2 words that might be new to most of the audience, but does not define them.	Does not include any vocabulary that might be new to the audience.

transfer from a checking account. The paper check is no longer the method of payment; instead, the electronic funds transfer has facilitated the transaction so funds are withdrawn faster than with a paper check. The Electronic Fund Transfer Act requires the buyer to receive notification this conversion is occurring (Federal Reserve Board, 2007). Wise consumers research types of checking accounts available and select the best one for their respective needs.

Types of checking accounts. With the variety of checking account types available to consumers, the choice can sometimes be quite complex, especially considering the promotions that many banks use today to attract customers. Choices are complex because of the many features available and associated costs. In addition, banks often use various promotional activities to attract customers, often enticing customers to choose a checking account based on the related promotional item rather than its ability to meet the customer's needs. Bankrate.com (Bankrate, 2006a) provides the following list of popular checking accounts and brief descriptions:

1. Basic: This type is for someone who uses the account to pay bills, with minimal debit card use. This type may require a minimum balance or direct deposit to avoid a monthly maintenance fee and may limit the number of checks written per month with a per-check fee for overage.

2. Express: This type is for someone who does not need the services of a teller for normal banking activities. This account typically provides unlimited check writing, a low required minimum balance, and low or no monthly fees.

3. Free: As the most popular type of checking account, no monthly or per-transaction fees are charged. Of course, fees are charged for a check returned for non-sufficient funds.

4. Interest bearing: This account typically requires a minimum balance to open and to avoid maintenance fees. While the account does earn interest, the rate is quite low.

5. Joint: Two or more people, all of whom have equal access to the account, own this account. Accurate record keeping is crucial with a joint checking account.

6. Lifeline: This is an efficient checking or saving account typically waiving fees and is offered for those with low income and few monthly transactions. These accounts typically have low minimum balance requirements and low monthly fees ranging from $0.00 to $6.00. By law, the following states must offer lifeline accounts: Illinois, Massachusetts, Minnesota, New Jersey, New York, Rhode Island, and Vermont.

7. Money Market: This account requires a higher minimum balance and permits a minimum number of checks per month. However, interest is typically earned.

8. Senior/Student: Banks may provide this type of account for individuals with minimal checking needs. Often special offers are included such as free checking, free ATM use, and a variety of discounts.

These types of accounts are not exclusive, and many may be combined. For example, a customer may open a joint, interest-bearing money market account. Factors to consider when choosing a checking account include the number of checks written each month, minimum balance requirement, and use of a teller versus online banking. For example, a checking account may only allow a certain number of checks to be written before implementing a fee for additional checks or a fee may be charge if a minimum amount is not always sustained in the account.

Associated fees and penalties. One way banks and financial institutions earn revenue is through various fees charged for services provided. Increasingly banks are attracting customers by offering free checking accounts. Genuinely free checking provides a non-interest-earning account that typically also does not require a minimum balance, nor does it typically require any other relationship with the bank such as a bank card or saving account (Bielski, 2004).

When considering a free checking account, the account owner must clearly beware that "free" does not translate into "fee free." One example is the charge banks assess for a non-sufficient funds (NSF) check, which may be as high as $32—and that is only the fee or *penalty* the bank charges (Bielski, 2004). Merchants depositing NSF checks may also assess a fee. Banks frequently use a free checking account as a short-term offer, with various fees charged after the account has been opened for a period of time. Banks may also charge fees for other checking-related services provided, such as ATM use, cashier's checks, or traveler's checks.

Savings

Banks and financial institutions provide a variety of savings opportunities. The three most common are savings accounts, certificates of deposit (CD), and money market accounts.

Savings accounts. Banks and financial institutions offer personal savings accounts. The advantage of opening a savings account and checking account with the same institution is the ability to access funds in both accounts 24 hours a day via ATM banking, and being able to transfer funds electronically between the accounts. The primary disadvantage to a savings account with a mainstream financial institution is the low rate of interest earned. Even though less money may be earned, typically, no fees are associated with withdrawals and money is conveniently available.

Certificates of deposit. Certificates of deposit (CDs) earn relatively high interest rates when compared to savings accounts, but are not *liquid* in that the funds in a CD are invested for a specific period. Typically, a five-year CD would earn a higher interest rate than a three-month CD. When a CD reaches maturity, the financial institution notifies the holder, who then has 10 days in which to either cash in the CD or reinvest it. The holder may also choose to withdraw the interest or reinvest the interest (Bankrate, 2006b). CDs are a good way to save for the future.

Money market accounts. Money market accounts (MM) are a savings vehicle offered by a variety of banks and financial institutions. MM accounts typically require a minimum balance and a maximum of three to five check/transactions each month and offer about double the interest rate of a regular personal savings account (Bankrate, 2006c). Therefore, they provide a method of basic savings typically with a reasonable interest rate.

Comparison of benefits. Wise consumers compare interest rates and terms offered for all savings opportunities. A variety of online comparison tools exist, such as Bankrate.com or Bizrate.com. An online service, YourCheckingIsFree.com, provides a list of various types of accounts to open and institutions with which one may choose to bank. This website provides a wealth of information for comparison shopping for different types of accounts.

Electronic Banking

The term "electronic banking" (or "online banking") describes a method of conducting banking transactions in which a customer does not need to visit a bricks-and-mortar building. Electronic banking has revolutionized the way people manage liquid assets. Long (2007) reported that debit card usage for U.S. consumer purchases is estimated to increase to 22% by 2015 from 12.5% in 2005. Additional transactions facilitated by electronic banking include transferring funds from one account to another, monitoring earnings and spending, and paying bills online.

Security/Encryption. Security is a concern to anyone who uses electronic/online banking. Banks use encryption to safeguard against security breaches. Simply put, encryption is a process whereby information is translated into another format that can only be deciphered by one who has the code. The Financial Crimes Enforcement Network reports (2000) that electronic banking transactions require three levels of security:

> First, an encryption standard, either a Secure Electronic Transaction (SET) or a Secure Sockets Layer (SSL) protocol that assures message integrity . . . and provides confidentiality for the data flow between a Web server and a browser; second, firewalls and filtering routes; and third, an internet operating system that provides protection for stored information (p. 26).

In addition, each electronic banking customer is assigned a personal identification number (PIN) used to access one's account. Security is essential to help alleviate the possibility of identity theft.

Direct deposit/preauthorized payments. Direct deposit enables employers and organizations to deposit salaries paid or funds due to employees directly into checking accounts. This avoids the need for paper checks, associated handling costs, and processing time. Once employees are enrolled in a direct deposit program, they typically receive electronic vouchers or facsimiles of their paychecks, including the amount deposited (Bankrate, 2006d).

Through a similar process, checking account holders can arrange for their bank to make preauthorized payments or withdrawals. Typical preauthorized payments are mortgage payments, car payments, utility payments, or regular deposits into savings accounts (Federal Trade Commission, 2006). While there is no need for any action on the part of the checking account holder once the arrangement has been created, there is a need for them to make note of the transaction in their check register in order to maintain accurate checking account records.

Debit Cards, Point of Sale, and ATM. When customers open checking accounts, the bank may provide a debit card, originally referred to as an automated teller machine (ATM) card. The original cards enabled the cardholder to deposit and withdraw funds from an ATM (Bankrate, 2006b.) Today, however, debit cards may be used in the same fashion as ATM cards and for point-of-sale (POS) transactions. A POS transaction is authorized in one of two ways: a personal identification number (PIN) or a signature. For a PIN debit transaction, the buyer uses a network-branded debit card (such as VISA or MasterCard). After the card is used to activate the machine, the buyer enters a PIN and the buyer's bank account is charged immediately. A PIN transaction carries a higher level of protection since the PIN is required to complete the transaction. With signature transactions, sellers run a debit card through the credit card network, which is then processed at the buyer's bank. The sales total is deducted from buyer accounts, typically within two business days (Borzekowksi, Kiser, & Ahmed, 2008).

Smart Cards. A smart card is a "specially designed integrated circuit chip imbedded" in a bank card (U.S. Department of Treasury, 2000, p. 15). Smart cards may contain an operating system, as well as store and process information in a secure environment (TechFAQ, 2008, para. 1). If a smart card also contains a microprocessor chip, the chip enables the user to increase the monetary value on the card and allows for the automatic deduction of the amount spent.

Lending and Credit

Banks and financial institutions provide a variety of loan and credit services to their customers. Typically, these institutions offer personal loans, mortgages, vehicle loans, second mortgages, and equity lines of credit. All these loan opportunities carry approval processes, a variety of interest rates, and a variety of repayment options.

Advantages and disadvantages of credit debt. An advantage to seeking a mortgage or auto loan with the bank that manages an individual's checking account is that the bank is already acquainted with the individual's financial practices. A disadvantage may be that in some circumstances lower interest rates for loans may be obtained from other lending institutions. For example, if someone has excellent credit, financing provided by an automobile dealership through General Motors Acceptance Corporation (GMAC) or American Honda Finance may yield a lower interest rate than would a mainstream financial institution.

Associated fees. The fees charged by banks and financial institutions are driven by the type of loan for which customers apply. The most extensive fee structure involves obtaining a home mortgage, which often has the following associated fees: loan origination, tax service, administration, processing, application, document review, title insurance, recording, and attorney fees (SunTrust, 2008).

Special Consideration with Regard to Immigrant Consumers
Immigrant banking began during the 1860s. Early immigrant banks primarily operated in urban ethnic neighborhoods (Day, 2002). Today the immigrant market represents a potentially significant market share for both mainstream financial institutions and smaller financial institutions. In fact, a Pew Hispanic Center research study reported, "35 percent of Ecuadorians, 64 percent of Salvadorans, and 75 percent of Mexican immigrants do not have bank accounts" (Appleseed, 2006, p. 1). Because many immigrants have little to no banking experience, knowing the issues relevant to working with immigrant clients is important. These issues include cultural matters, identification, and credit worthiness.

Relevant cultural issues. Immigrant consumers tend to be lower income, typically do not have a banking history, and so are considered "unbanked." They remain unbanked or choose not to participate with mainstream financial institutions for a number of reasons. According to Appleseed (2006, p. 2), "costs of maintaining bank accounts; difficulties overcoming poor credit status; inconvenience of locations, hours, or services; distrust of banks; low levels of financial literacy; perceived cultural differences or language barriers; and a lack of information about appropriate products and services" preclude many immigrants from using mainstream banking services offered in the United States.

While some immigrant consumers may already be using services provided through check-cashing firms or establishments that can transmit money back to their home countries, they may not view these as *banking* services. This lack of confidence in or awareness of all the services provided by a financial institution often results in immigrants carrying large sums of cash, making them extremely vulnerable to robbery.

Identification requirements. An émigré who is a legal resident of the United States will meet the same identification requirements as any other legal resident. However, foreign nationals are treated differently from other émigrés and U.S. citizens. Foreign nationals are individuals who are visiting the United States, but do not have the green card that permits them to work in the United States. Some banks and financial institutions restrict the types of loans available to foreign nationals.

Credit history/worthiness. Because some immigrants have avoided using mainstream financial institutions, establishing a credit history can be a problem. Lenders working regularly with immigrant populations have learned to work with potential customers to establish credit histories and worthiness. One way for immigrants to establish a credit history is to review applicants' international remittance histories to gauge their ability to make consistent payments. The remittance history is the record of applicants' remitting or sending money back to their homelands. Stability in residency and consistent housing payments are the strongest credit indicators for low-income immigrants (Appleseed, 2006).

Loan opportunities. Loan opportunities for immigrant customers vary by financial institution and geographic location. While consumer loans may be available, the biggest barrier is the lack of repayment history for such a loan (Appleseed, 2006). Redlining occurs when banking institutions deny or increase the cost of services, such as banking accounts and mortgages, based on the applicant's race or ethnicity. This is a possibility for immigrant customers.

Teaching Application: Banking Services

To reinforce this section's concepts, advanced-level students must not only apply the knowledge but also use analysis tools. For this activity, students would work in pairs to research three banking/financial institutions: a "bricks and mortar" bank, an online bank, and a credit union/savings and loan. Each pair would be given a scenario: For example, they are recent graduates of college; they are retired and living on a limited fixed income; they are mid-career professionals with children in college; or they are newlyweds. Each scenario would instruct students that they have relocated, are interested in purchasing a home, and are looking for a new bank. Students will use the researched information to choose the best financial institution to meet their needs. Each pair of students reports on saving opportunities, electronic and traditional banking options, security and privacy issues, and interest rates offered for a 15-year and a 30-year fixed rate mortgage. Each group of students will prepare a report in which their choice is presented and justified, given their scenario. NBEA Banking and Financial Institutions standards (2007) covered in this activity include those dealing with electronic monetary transactions; evaluating and comparing services, costs, and online versus traditional banking; and privacy issues.

Evaluation of the Learning Activity

A rubric similar to those shown for the activities described above should be developed for use in evaluating this problem-based assignment. The rubric should include savings opportunities, electronic and traditional banking options, and interest rates.

INTERNATIONAL BANKING

With the increased ease in international travel and individuals living outside their native countries for long periods, understanding international banking practices is an important topic for discussion. This section discusses various money management practices and factors to consider when needing financial services while traveling or living outside the United States. Using ATMs and currency exchange are important topics to discuss for the international traveler. Through the teaching applications and evaluation of the concepts, basic steps are provided to help students understand terms and important concepts related to this section.

Varying Money Management Practices

International financial institutions (IFIs) are organizations typically established (or chartered) by more than one country that must deal with international legal ramifications. According to the New York Federal Reserve, "foreign banking institutions held over one trillion dollars in assets, approximately 11 percent of the total commercial banking assets in the United States" (2007, ¶ 1). The data were provided in December 2006 and indicate the importance foreign banks have on the U.S. financial system. Because of substantial international holdings of assets in the United States, U.S. laws have been passed regulating various types of banking institutions, depending on whether banks are chartered here or in another country.

International banks may offer banking services that provide a full range of options to the consumer. These institutions are typically referred to as retail banks in the international market. However, they may deal with different challenges and limitations than U.S. banks. The amount that may be deposited from U.S. citizens is limited to a certain amount by banking regulations, and is not covered by U.S. deposit insurance such as FDIC.

Traveling Abroad

Electronic banking has considerably eased how international travelers can access their banking accounts. ATMs are used internationally with the same ease as in the United States. In addition, currency exchange and electronic transfer of funds internationally is as easy as in this country.

ATM use. When traveling abroad, ATMs are simple to use to get currency of the country in which one is traveling. The ATM typically provides a choice of languages, an easy transaction process, and typically a better exchange rate than exchanging travelers' checks for local currency. Schlichter (2007) notes that exchange rates are "based on the wholesale exchange rate, which is usually reserved only for very large interbank exchanges" (¶ 1). Basing the exchange rate on the wholesale exchange rate provides a lower exchange rate, typically 2% to 5% lower than the percentage of exchange for traveler's checks. Exchange or service fees may be added by U.S. home banking institutions for international ATM withdrawals.

Currency exchange. When traveling outside of the United States, it is essential to investigate the currency exchange prior to leaving. For example, $1 U.S. is equal to 6.82 Yuan in China (XE Currency Converter, 2008). An item in China that costs 400 Yuan converts to $58.65. Currency converters such as XE – The World Favorite Currency Converter (http://www.xe.com/ucc/ convert.cgi) may be used to convert currency from several countries. Travelers must know how to convert U.S. dollars into another country's currency.

Transferring funds/deposits. Transferring funds between international banks has been streamlined electronically and is common today. Companies and domestic banks have been established to work specifically with international banks to transfer funds. Fees may be assessed for transferring funds. The Federal Reserve has a Division of International Finance that examines issues related to international financial banking markets.

Teaching Application: International Banking

To enhance the understanding of traveling outside the United States and currency exchange, students can create one of two scenarios: (1) choose a country to which they would like to travel or (2) choose a country to be from and pretend to be an immigrant in the United States. Each student would be responsible for finding information about bank and currency exchange access when traveling and for calculating the associated fees for debit and credit card use, if applicable. Students would also investigate whether the country has a cash-based system, or, if pretending to be an immigrant, any fears or concerns they may have about using banks in their country of choice. Students would create a "Tips for the Traveler" document or website containing resources and instructions about banks to help others who might travel to their selected country. The teacher will provide instructions and monitor student work, and should utilize a rubric (as in the examples shown above) for evaluation. NBEA Banking and Financial Institutions standards (2007) covered in this activity include examining the use of financial institutions from a global consumer perspective.

Evaluation of the Learning Activity

Utilizing a rubric (see examples above), the teacher can review the document or website for accuracy and information that is current and helpful. Students may be asked to present the information to the class, the school's Spanish Club (if a country is chosen where Spanish is spoken), or other viable outlets.

SUMMARY

This chapter provides an overview of banking terms and information relating to banking services, types of institutions, and international banking. These components are essential to understanding how to use banks to meet one's needs and key issues to be aware of such as choosing the right bank, service fees, and currency exchange.

REFERENCES

Appleseed. (2006, June). *Expanding immigrant access to mainstream financial services; Positive practices and emerging opportunities from the Latin American immigrant experience.* Washington, DC: Appleseed Network. Retrieved February 15, 2008, from www.appleseednetwork.org

Bankrate. (2006a). *Checking basics: Chapter 1 – Checking account types.* Retrieved February 7, 2008, from http://www.bankrate.com/brm/green/chk/basics1-1a3. asp?caret=2

Bankrate. (2006b). *Investing basics: Chapter 2 – Certificates of deposit.* Retrieved February 11, 2008, from http://www.bankrate.com/brm/green/investing/basics2-1a. asp?caret=8

Bankrate. (2006c). *Investing basics: Chapter 1 – Building liquid savings.* Retrieved February 11, 2008, from http://www.bankrate.com/brm/green/investing/basics1-4a. asp?caret=5

Bankrate. (2006d). *Checking basics – Chapter 1 – Types of checking accounts.* Retrieved February 11, 2008, from http://www.bankrate.com/brm/green/chk/chk8a.asp

Bielski, L. (2004, March). Is free checking worth it? *ABA Banking Journal,* 96, 31-40.

Borzekowski, R., Kiser, E. K., & Ahmed, S. (2008) Consumers' use of debit cards: Patterns, preferences, and price response. *Journal of Money, Credit and Banking,* 40(1), 149-172.

Day, J. (2002). Credit, capital and community: informal banking in immigrant communities in the United States, 1880-1924. *Financial History Review,* 9, 65-78.

Federal Reserve Bank of Boston. (2007). *Banking basics.* Retrieved February 1, 2008, from http://www.bos.frb.org/education/pubs/banking2.pdf

Federal Reserve Bank of St. Louis. (2008). *In plain English: Making sense of the Federal Reserve.* Retrieved February 10, 2008, from http://www.stlouisfed.org/publications/ pleng/PDF/PlainEnglish.pdf

Federal Reserve Board. (2007). *When is your check not a check? Electronic Check Conversion.* Retrieved February 7, 2008, from http://www.federalreserve.gov/pubs/ checkconv/default.htm

Federal Trade Commission. (2006). *FTC facts for consumers: Electronic banking.* Washington, DC: Bureau of Consumer Protection, Division of Consumer and Business Education.

Library of Congress. (2002). *The learning page: Jigsaw lesson plan guide.* Retrieved June 13, 2008, from http://memory.loc.gov/learn/lessons/97/crow/jigsaw.html

Long, K. (2007, May). Reinventing the checking account. *U. S. Banker,* p. 48.

Merriam-Webster Dictionary. (2007). Bank. Retrieved February 10, 2008, from http://www.merriam-webster.com/dictionary

MetLife. (2008). Choosing a bank. Retrieved February 10, 2008, from http://www.met life.com/Applications/Corporate/WPS/CDA/PageGenerator/0,4132,P1628,00.html

National Business Education Association. (2007). *National standards for business education: What America's students should know and be able to do in business.* Reston, VA: Author.

New York Federal Reserve. (2007). Foreign banks and the Federal Reserve. Retrieved February 10, 2008 from http://www.newyorkfed.org/aboutthefed/fedpoint/fed26.html

Pascal, M. C. (2007, August). Financial security and independence start with checking accounts. *Afro-American Red Star*, Washington, DC, p. B3.

Ryan, J. S. (2006). *Managing your personal finances*. Mason, OH: Thomson-South-Western.

Schlichter, S. (2007). Using ATMs abroad: Getting best exchange rates while traveling. Retrieved February 15, 2008, from http://www.msnbc.msn.com/id/16994358

SunTrust. (2008). *Closing cost checklist*. Retrieved February 18, 2008, from http://www.suntrustmortgage.com/closeck.asp?stmleftnav=4.2

Swann, J. (2003). The state of the check. *Community Banker 12*, p. 8, 28.

U.S. Department of Treasury. (2000). *A survey of electronic cash, electronic banking, and Internet gaming*. Washington, DC: Financial Crimes Enforcement Network (FinCEN).

TechFAQ. (2008). What is a smartcard. Retrieved July 8, 2008 from http://www.tech-faq.com/smart-card.shtml

XE Currency Converter (2008). The world's favorite currency site. Retrieved July 12, 2008 from http://www.xe.com/ucc/convert.cgi

Using Credit

Betty J. Brown
George A. Mundrake
Ball State University
Muncie, Indiana

Consumers have developed an attitude toward indebtedness that has led them to accumulate debt at an unprecedented rate. As young people inherit rising expectations for personal wealth, they are vulnerable to overuse of credit to buy the goods and services they are accustomed to having. Young people must learn about the wise use of credit and the consequences of not managing money and debt. This chapter addresses the use of credit with specific attention to credit decisions, types of credit, economics of credit, and applications to assist students to develop personal financial literacy so they can make informed decisions about the use of credit.

CREDIT AND PERSONAL MONEY MANAGEMENT

Most people use credit as a convenient and efficient tool for purchasing goods and services. One of the first major purchasing decisions for many young adults is buying a car. Most young people will finance a car; therefore, they need the skill to evaluate sources of credit to make a good choice. At some time in their lives, they probably will buy a home. To prepare for such purchases, Lewis and Farmer (2004) listed four "rules of thumb" that consumers need to know before buying: how much down payment should be accumulated, what types of financing are available, the advantages and disadvantages of each type of financing, and the cost of credit. Many consumers perceive that everyone else seems to be able to afford much more than they can and see more credit as an answer to their needs and wants. Eventually, many people find themselves in financial difficulty. As Carlson (2004) commented, "Life will conspire to get you off the track of attaining your financial goals" (p. 16).

Life Events and Credit Use

Credit historically was used primarily for "big purchases" such as cars, furniture, and housing. As the U.S. economy grew after World War II, workers began to purchase consumer goods on charge accounts. "Charging" became popular, and consumers bought large-ticket items on credit. Two types of credit were (1) the installment plan, i.e. money that is lent for a good that is sold on condition that the purchaser repays the loan with regular, fixed payments over a specified period; and (2) an array of credit plans from retailers, commercial banks, personal finance companies, and sales finance companies (Calder, 1999). By the 1980s, credit cards were popular for "charging it."

Needs versus Wants

As consumers used credit more and more, their consumption of goods and services became a driving force for credit. During the 1980s, credit card use rapidly expanded into the middle class. As Manning (2000) reported, "Between 1980 and 1990, the charges of the average U.S. household jumped sharply from $885 to $3,753 per year, or more than twice as fast as disposable income" (p. 11). In 2008 the Federal Reserve System reported that a typical card holder carried credit card debt of nearly $5,500 ("Consumer Credit," 2008). Calder (1999) observed that consumption became a means of enhancing personal identities and social status. Financial institutions offered more credit, and credit cards became the most widely accepted means of payment in the U.S. marketplace. For millions of people, debt became a way to achieve a better way of life. When lenders allowed consumers to qualify for credit with fewer restrictions, many consumers assumed too much debt, and bankruptcies and home foreclosures soared beginning in 2007.

Teaching about Credit and Personal Money Management

Personal money management skills can help students evaluate their use of credit in personal money management. The following performance expectations for students studying credit as a part of personal money management are from Standard VII in the Personal Finance content area of the National Standards for Business Education (NBEA, 2007) and can be used to develop objectives for activities for middle school, high school, and postsecondary students:

- Determine the advantages and disadvantages of using credit.

- Research rights and responsibilities of consumers according to credit legislation (e.g., truth-in-lending, fair credit reporting, equal credit opportunity, and fair debt collection).

The instructional activities and techniques described in this chapter meet the objectives for credit and personal money management. The activities are categorized into three levels for middle school students (basic), high school students (intermediate), and postsecondary students (advanced) and are categorized by type: individual, large group, and small group. Online sources of information are listed for some activities. Business teachers can collaborate with teachers in other curriculum areas, especially family and consumer science, mathematics, and social studies, to provide learning activities for acquiring personal financial literacy.

Credit Pyramids: Upside/Downside	Advantages and disadvantages of credit	Level: Basic
		Small Group, Large Group

- Draw three pyramids on the board or on a sheet of paper (small groups) and label them individual, businesses, and society/economy.
- Brainstorm advantages and disadvantages of using credit from the standpoint of individuals, businesses, and society/economy.
- As ideas are developed, place them on the upside or downside of the pyramids and discuss reasons for placement of items.

Marketing and Credit: Co-conspirators?	The role of easy credit in marketing	Level: Basic
		Small Group, Large Group

- Collect advertisements (TV or print ads) that promote easy credit to lure customers to purchase a good or service.
- Create a list of things that may appeal to consumers (e.g., attractive people, freedom, being part of the "in group," vanity, having "nothing to lose," and other tactics).
- Develop consumer purchasing incentives and discuss how easy credit can be a factor to push a consumer to a purchase decision.
- Discuss ramifications of these kinds of decisions.

This Just In	How current events affect credit	Level: Basic
		Small Group, Large Group

- Search for online or print news items about credit to display.
- Report why the news is important, what effect the news will have on credit, and how a consumer may deal with the news.
- ➢ Use online financial news sites such as CNN, FOX, MSNBC, financial magazine sites, or local newspaper sites for current information.

Credit Crosswords	Crossword puzzles to reinforce credit terms and concepts	Level: Basic
		Individual, Small Group, Large Group

- Use online or teacher-generated crossword puzzles for crossword terms.
- Use online puzzles (self-time and self-score).
- ➢ www.in.gov/dfi/education/credit_crossword.htm (credit crossword puzzle)
- ➢ www.education-world.com/a_tech/techtorial/techtorial042.shtml (lesson planning ideas)

For Love and Money	Making personal choices	Level: Basic
		Individual, Small Group, Large Group

- Develop a list of possible scenarios where emotions may be involved in deciding to use credit (e.g., buy something to impress someone, purchase an expensive gift for a certain someone, or overspend on a wedding gift).
- Explore ways to avoid emotion-based credit decisions.

Credit Hot or Not List	Exploration of decision-making	Level: Basic
		Individual, Small Group, Large Group

- Generate a list of "what's hot and what's not" products for teens.
- Discuss which items could be bought on credit and which should not be bought on credit.

Ad Hock?	The role of credit in advertising	Level: Basic
		Small Group

- Examine printed, online, or TV advertisements for products that are usually purchased on credit.
- Identify parts of ads related to credit and evaluate the quality of credit information given.

Credit Bowl	Games to reinforce credit terms and concepts	Level: Intermediate
		Individual, Small Group

- List questions about credit to include in a presentation for students to compete in a quiz bowl.
- Rotate in small groups to compete and self-score performance.

Wonderful World of Wheels: Auto Financing and Ownership	Owning and operating an auto	Level: Intermediate
		Individual, Small Group, Large Group

- Research the price of a dream car (new or used), down payment or trade amount needed, cost of taxes and license tags, and other charges.
- Research loan sources and explore costs such as dealer reserve, credit rating, and sources of a loan.
- Estimate insurance costs, gasoline, and maintenance costs for the vehicle.
- Research the value of the dream car at the end of the loan term to see the effect of depreciation.
- Visit bank, car dealer, and other financial institutions to compare and contrast interest rates between new and used car loans.
- Explore and list reasons for higher rates and differing terms for used car loans.
- ➤ www.kbb.com (Kelley Blue Book for car prices)
- ➤ http://money.aol.com/calculators (online calculators)

Credit Wheel of Fortune or What's In the Cards	Exploration of how life events affect credit decisions	Level: Advanced
		Individual, Small Group, Large Group

- Create a wheel segmented into life events such as going to college, marriage, having a child, buying a car, buying a home, death of a family member, facing a job loss, winning a lottery, and unexpected home or auto repairs. Prepare a deck of cards with these events. Include small ticket items to differentiate when credit is necessary and identify the type of credit needed.
- Spin the wheel or draw a card and then discuss and develop credit strategies for each situation.
- ➤ www.LifeFocus.com (online financial and credit simulation)

Shrinking Credit?: Psychology of Credit, Marketing, and Choice	The psychology of credit, marketing, and personal choice	Level: Advanced
		Small Group, Large Group

- Develop a list of positive and negative feelings (e.g., anger, rejection, hope, depression, happiness).
- Create a second list of common products or services (e.g., washer or dryer, vacuum cleaner, toaster, health club or gym membership).
- For each product and service, list and discuss how each feeling could be used to sell the product or to promote credit so that people will want to buy the goods or services.

| 3 Rs of Credit Rights, Responsibilities, and Risks | Exploration of legal and regulatory aspects of credit | Level: Advanced |
| | | Individual, Small Group, Large Group |

- Search for credit laws, acts, and regulations that relate to credit rights and responsibilities, and report how they can add to or diminish risks of using credit.
- ➤ www.in.gov/dfi/education/pdfs/crights.pdf (Credit Bill of Rights)
- ➤ www.ftc.gov/bcp/conline/pubs/credit/fcb.shtm (Fair Credit Billing)
- ➤ www.usdoj.gov/crt/housing/ecoa.htm (Equal Credit Opportunity Act)

| Consumer Bill of Rights | Consumer rights when using credit | Level: Advanced |
| | | Individual, Small Group, Large Group |

- Examine the Consumer Bill of Rights, available from credit reporting agencies on the Internet, to determine consumer defenses against credit offers (e.g., offers such as "easy credit" to join a club, buy an expensive product, or order online or by mail at a "drastically low price").
- Report on consumers rights and needed action in these situations.
- ➤ www.TransUnion.com, www.Experian.com, and www.Equifax.com (credit reporting agencies)

| Credit Start-Up | Role of credit in starting a business | Level: Advanced |
| | | Small Group |

- Study and discuss printouts from websites or newspaper and magazine clippings about business opportunities.
- Create a scenario that provides a group with a given amount of money and a credit line limit.
- Decide which business opportunity would be the most viable and list the benefits and risks of the venture.

TYPES OF CREDIT

Credit has become indispensable to everyday life. Consumers can borrow money for short or long periods. Credit grantors may require a "guarantee" of repayment in the form of ownership rights to the property (lien) or may grant credit based on the good record of the borrower. Therefore, credit may be secured or unsecured.

Secured Credit

Credit may be extended to consumers with a requirement for collateral. This secured credit gives the lender rights to the property bought on credit if the borrower defaults on the loan. Mortgages, vehicle loans, secured credit cards, debit cards, and long-term consumer loans are examples of secured credit. A secured loan is backed by a particular asset; for example, a home bought with a loan from a bank or mortgage institution becomes collateral for the mortgage loan (Goodman & Bloch, 1994). A secured loan requires a down payment, with the rest of the principal financed at a fixed or variable rate of interest. With a secured credit card, a consumer can deposit a certain amount of cash with a bank that issues credit cards in return for a credit line of the same amount. If the borrower charges to the secured credit card and then is unable to make credit card payments, the lender can seize the money on deposit. On the other hand, charges to a debit card or prepaid debit card reduce the account balance immediately. A secured credit line is a good way for students to start their credit history because they must demonstrate the ability to pay with the cash on deposit. Consumers with a poor credit history also can re-establish good credit with a secured loan in this form.

Long-term installment loans are a popular way for consumers to buy large-ticket items such as appliances and furniture. The seller combines the price of the item and interest cost over the life of the loan, divides the total by the number of months for payments, and collects a payment each month for the life of the loan. A product manufacturer may actually finance the loan instead of the retailer selling the product. The appliance or furniture is collateral for the loan; a retailer could repossess the item in case of failure to pay. For large purchases, borrowing from a bank, credit union, or other financial institution may be an alternative to credit card use.

Unsecured Credit

Revolving charge accounts, unsecured credit cards, short-term consumer loans, and education financing are unsecured loans; lenders do not demand that a specific asset be pledged as collateral. Instead, they extend credit to consumers with a good reputation and a stable income. Interest rates for unsecured credit generally are higher than for secured loans. Unsecured credit is convenient, particularly if a charge card is used—perhaps too convenient. Sullivan, Warren, and Westbrook (2000) observed that "consumers find themselves enjoying more consumer goods but going into debt to enjoy them" (p. 19).

Regular customers of large retailers are often granted a revolving charge account for buying goods and services; they charge purchases to the account and then make regular payments. Customers may choose to pay the entire balance when it comes due or make payments over time. They are assessed no finance charges if the balance is paid within a grace period, usually 25 days. In 2008, 176 million Americans held 1.5 billion credit cards, or about 8.5 cards per credit card holder. In one year, the average card holder charged just over $10,500 on all cards such as bank cards, phone cards, and credit cards issued by oil companies and department stores ("Consumer Debt Statistics," 2007).

An unsecured credit card has a credit limit based on the card holder's credit record, including such factors as stability and amount of income, other credit cards held, past payment record, and credit rating. Finance charges vary among card holders based on their credit records. Consumers may obtain a cash advance on a credit card and use cards as a substitute for cash for almost all purchases. Credit card use is so prevalent, observed Calder (1999), that " . . . it has become virtually impossible to live the American dream *without* access to credit payment methods, as anyone knows who has placed a phone order from a catalog or tried to pay cash for a rental car" (p. 291).

Consumers may need extra money for a short term, perhaps a few months, and can borrow from a bank, credit union, or other financial institution, usually at a higher interest rate than for a secured loan. Banks may offer education financing in conjunction with programs of the federal government such as the Student Loan Marketing Association (known as Sallie Mae). The application and requirements vary with the type of loan. A bank provides the loan and the student begins repayment only upon completion of the educational program.

To choose sources of credit, consumers can use the annual percentage rate (APR) to compare credit costs. Consumers need to know the APRs for purchases, cash advances, and balance transfers. They must understand charges for late payments and minimum payment calculation methods. Lenders are required by the Truth in Lending Act to quote APR to potential borrowers (Pritchard, n.d.). The APR allows a consumer to evaluate the cost of a loan or credit card interest in terms of a percentage, a yearly interest rate. Even a small difference in APR can be significant in the cost of credit over time. Other things being equal, a consumer wants the loan with the lowest APR. However, the interest cost of a loan as well as fees and other charges may be included in an APR quote. Pritchard described several scenarios that demonstrated the difference in costs. In one example, a stated interest rate of 7% on a mortgage was equal to an APR of 7.0989% when additional costs were added to the mortgage amount.

The APR is especially important for credit card users who carry over a balance from month to month. Since cash advances often have a higher APR than purchases, consumers who expect to use cash advances should look for a credit card with a lower APR and lower fees on cash advances. Consumers who plan to transfer balances among credit cards will find that balance transfers often have a higher APR. The APR may increase if monthly payments are late, and some cards have a variable APR rate that changes from time to time. When selecting a credit card, consumers should also consider the grace period (how many days to pay the bill in full without triggering finance charges) and whether the card has a minimum finance charge and other fees. A lender may charge a minimum amount if a balance is carried over, even if the actual interest charge is less. The method by which finance charges are computed can make a difference in the finance charge. Finance charges are based on the outstanding balance, which may be calculated (1) over one billing cycle or two; (2) using the adjusted balance, average daily balance, or previous balance; and (3) including or excluding new purchases in the balance. These factors are also influenced by the balance carried on the card and the timing of consumer purchases and payments for the card ("Choosing a Credit Card," n.d.).

Teaching about Types of Credit

Because so many types of credit are available to consumers, students should be able to differentiate among types and uses of credit. The following economics and personal finance performance expectations are contained in the NBEA standards (NBEA, 2007) in Standard VII, Using Credit:

- Evaluate the various methods of financing a purchase.

- Analyze credit card features and their impact on personal financial planning.

- Explain how the amount of principal, the period of the loan, and the interest rate affect the amount of interest charged.

- Explain why the interest rate varies with the amount of assumed risk.

- Analyze various sources and types of credit (e.g., short- and long-term) and related costs.

- Select an appropriate form of credit for a particular buying decision.

- Compare and contrast the various aspects of credit cards (e.g., APR, grace period, incentive buying, methods of calculating interest, and fees).

- Compare and contrast the legal aspects of different forms of credit (e.g., title transfer, responsibility limits, collateral requirements, and co-signing).

Middle school students (basic), high school students (intermediate), and post-secondary students (advanced) can engage in these activities in small or large groups or individually to analyze types of credit available to them. With adaptation, activities may be used with students at more than one level.

THE ECONOMICS OF CREDIT

Two financial pitfalls for many U.S. consumers that cause them financial problems are the habit of not saving and overuse of credit. Students can fall into those traps, too, and financial problems can crop up at times when the future looks bright. Sullivan, Warren, and Westbrook (2000) described consumption as "a trait of contemporary American society" (p. 292).

Unlimited Wants, Limited Resources

A basic economic fact of life is that consumers have unlimited wants and limited resources. Credit addresses the problem of limited resources. With the aid of credit, consumers are able to "buy now and pay later." They can use credit for purchases that otherwise would have been postponed. Credit makes it possible for consumers to afford

Credit Type Identifi-cation Brainstorm	Consumer goods and services and type of credit used	Level: Basic
		Small Group, Large Group

- In groups, brainstorm a list of items that are typically purchased on credit.
- Discuss types of credit and credit requirements for each item.
- Select, report, and discuss the appropriate credit type for each item on the list.

Rewards: Points or Punishment?	Rewards and points affect credit decisions	Level: Basic
		Small Group, Large Group

- Prepare a set of questions that would be used to help select a rewards-based credit card (e.g., How often will you use the card? Is there an annual fee?).
- Search for different kinds of reward points or cash-back credit offers and evaluate them.
- Discuss when these cards may have advantages and when they will be costly.

Mailbag Activity	Analyze credit mail	Level: Intermediate
		Individual, Small Group, Large Group

- Bring sanitized (names and information removed) credit-related mail to class; analyze the item(s) such as credit offers, privacy statements, letters outlining changes in credit policy, actual statements, advertisement of items that use credit as a lure, or other letters (e.g., duns, problem resolution, clarification, or collection letters).
- Check items for interest rates, charges, and other terms and conditions. In the case of letters, discuss steps to take to remedy a problem.
- Use a prepared checklist of content or develop a list prior to examining the mail items.

Credit Sleuth–Searching for Hidden Costs	Reading and interpreting a credit card statement	Level: Intermediate
		Small Group, Large Group

- Use sanitized (names and information removed) credit card statements or go to a credit grantor's website for samples.
- Isolate the data and compute the monthly interest using average balances and different rates for different offers or types of purchases.
- Examine statements that include a "how to read your statement" flyer for advice to consumers.

Can You Fix a Broken ARM?	Changing adjustable rate mortgages to fixed rates	Level: Advanced
		Small Group, Large Group

- Research and report on the difference between fixed rate and adjustable rate mortgages (ARM).
- Brainstorm a list of reasons or situations to use both types of mortgages.
- Use online calculators or create a 12-month amortization table to compare the effects of ARM interest rate changes.
- Create amortization tables using spreadsheet software.

Credit Life Insurance: Safeguard or Soaking?	Alternatives to credit life insurance based on benefits and costs	Level: Advanced
		Individual, Small Group

- Research offers for credit life insurance and its advantages and disadvantages.
- Search for term life rates for a given loan amount.
- Set up problems using information for comparing differences in the costs of credit life insurance and term life insurance.
- ➤ http://www.ins.state.ny.us/que_top10/que_life_cre.htm (site lists criteria for selecting credit life insurance)

Online Calculator Search	Online calculators for different kinds of loans	Level: Advanced
		Individual, Small Group, Large Group

- List loan types (e.g., mortgage, auto, RV, consolidation), and search websites for banks, automobile dealerships, and other businesses for loan calculators for specific types of loans.
- Report rates, loan requirements, and interest calculation methods.
- ➢ Financial institution websites (local banks)
- ➢ http://money.aol.com/calculators (financial calculators)

The Loan Arranger: I Owe Silver!	Research mortgage loans from local and national sources	Level: Advanced
		Small Group

- Research local banks and financial institutions and nationwide mortgage carriers on the Internet.
- Create a scenario for a group with a given amount of money and a credit line limit.
- Decide which business source for loans would be the most viable and list the benefits and risks of the venture.
- Design a competition of groups (teams) to obtain the best loan terms
- ➢ Financial institution websites (local banks and nationwide mortgage companies)

some items that otherwise would not be possible. They can finance the cost of higher education and training, a necessity for many careers. Relatively few families save enough money to pay cash for a young person's education beyond high school. The federal government and the financial services industry recognized the opportunity to promote education and established student grant and loan programs. The financial services industry then provided organization and management for those loan programs.

On the other hand, problems with credit can lead to financial disaster. Consumers may become overcommitted to credit payments, may lose their jobs, or may be forced into employment at lower-paying jobs resulting in serious financial difficulties. Consumers need guidance in financial management to function successfully in a financial world, to help them make wise choices, and to live within their means.

Consumers are bombarded with offers for all types of credit, and they need to think critically about any credit offers, the financial terms, and how appropriate credit offers may be for meeting their particular credit needs. Haynes and Bailey (2003) outlined a process for helping students to think critically that can be used for evaluating credit offers. They recommended that "a person should filter the flow of information so that only key ideas, statistics, and evidence end up in the mix" (p. 34). They recommended that students select an issue and compare and contrast opposing perspectives. This technique can be used effectively for studying consumer credit issues, particularly consumer problems with credit use.

Davis and Carnes (2005) surveyed employers to identify their expectations of employees' personal financial skills and their opinions about where strong personal financial literacy skills could be developed. Executives rated the importance of two components of financial literacy needed by employees: credit/spending skills and money management skills. Executives rated credit card use highest in the list of financial skills. Four reasons for employees' lack of personal financial skills were "easy access to credit in the form of credit cards, an increasing need for instant gratification, a lack of role modeling and guidance in the homes related to financial matters and inexperience in handling financial responsibilities" (p. 16).

A Credit History

A credit history is a report of all credit cards, loans, and other credit obligations that a person has assumed over a period of time. The history shows how much was borrowed (or the amount of the credit limit), the number of payments made, and whether the consumer met the schedule for repayment. Three major credit reporting agencies (Equifax, Experian, and TransUnion) maintain credit histories and make them available to businesses that are considering granting credit to consumers. A credit score computed from the credit record affects a consumer's ability to obtain credit and favorable credit terms. That score (often based on the Fair Isaac Company model, or FICO) is widely used among lenders for consistency in evaluating credit applications ("Understanding Your FICO Score," 2006, p. 1). The FICO score is based on five factors: punctuality of payment in the past, amount of debt, length of credit history, types of credit used, and amount of credit obtained recently. A bad credit score for a consumer can result in companies that use the three credit reporting services rejecting the consumer for future credit, insurance, employment, or even leases.

Students must be aware that their spending and payment habits affect their financial well-being well into the future. Building a good credit history over time can mean favorable interest rates for consumer credit and business credit, favorable rates for auto and homeowner insurance, and even good employment opportunities. Students should understand that failure to make timely payments on an account not only adversely affects their credit history, but also can cause interest charges on the account to skyrocket. Consumers can check their credit histories in order to prevent credit problems, identity theft, denial of loans, or other problems that affect credit.

Credit Problems and Remedies

Problems with credit occur for various reasons. Consumers may just fall a little further behind on payments every month until they are deeply in debt, or they may manage their debt until something goes wrong and causes unforeseen expenses. Because of poor record-keeping, they can become overwhelmed with no hope of managing the debt. In other instances, someone other than the credit card holder may use their card, yet the card holder becomes liable for the charges. A small business owner may use personal credit to finance a business and then become unable to manage the debt because the business does not survive (Sullivan, Warren, & Westbrook, 2000).

Identity theft. A growing problem for anyone, no matter what age or circumstance, is identity theft. Even a small child's identity may be stolen, and that identity can be used by an identity thief for loans, credit card applications, and purchases of all kinds. Identity theft can occur when a person loses a credit card, visits an online site that is hacked and personal information is stolen, or loses identification materials (wallet or purse, for example) that enable someone else to access their records. When consumers discover the theft, they often already have incurred unexpected credit charges, damage to their credit standing, and major expenses to try to correct the problem. They also must reestablish their accounts and correct their credit reports—often a daunting task.

Thieves steal identities in various ways. They look through trash for paper with personal information; "phish" online for personal information, pretending to be a financial institution; steal credit/debit card numbers when processing a customer's credit card; file a change of address for a consumer to divert billing statements; and steal wallets, purses, mail, pre-approved credit card offers, and new checks or tax information. When thieves acquire someone's identity, they find ways to acquire goods and services and charge the cost to the person from whom they stole the identity. They can open new credit card accounts in that person's name and charge to the accounts. They may open phone or utility accounts with that person's identity. They can create counterfeit checks, write bad checks on an account they have opened, or make electronic withdrawals or take out loans in that person's name. They can acquire government documents, such as a driver's license, by fraud. They can get a job, rent a house, get medical services, or use another person's name if they are arrested. All of these frauds can cost the victim money, time, and effort to try to remedy the situation. The effects of identity theft may linger for years ("2006 Identity Theft Report," n.d.).

Students can participate in class activities that help them to think critically about ways to handle personal information. Moore (2002) described a case study method that allows students to understand and visualize what it would be like to be part of the business sector. This method would work well with students as they learn about the effect of credit problems. They can study cases about consumers' experiences with such sources as "payday loans" that charge excessive interest; credit problems such as identity theft; unauthorized credit card use; or damaging information on a credit record. Students can also learn about the mathematics of credit by computing costs for different kinds of credit. Moore recommended that teachers use the *National Standards for Business Education* (NBEA, 2007) as the foundation for developing a case.

Financial disasters. An unexpected downsizing or job loss, a major illness or accident, unexpected expenses for car or appliance repair or replacement, or personal difficulties such as divorce—all of these can bring about a financial crisis. Many consumers believe that they just cannot save enough money for a "rainy day" to cover such emergencies. Systematic saving over a long period of time can be a comforting shelter against financial problems. Stanley and Danko (1996) interviewed people they identified as millionaires and found a common characteristic among their interviewees —"frugal, frugal, frugal" (p. 28). Further, they identified their interviewees as people who invested first (a minimum of 15% of their annual income) and spent the balance of their income and who had clearly defined goals.

Consumers can get control of their finances with a personal evaluation. They can track monthly income and monthly expenses and ask themselves the following questions: What exactly are their income and assets and liabilities? Which assets (such as a car, furniture, appliances, and home) have been given as security for a debt? Which assets could be sold to pay down a debt if necessary? (Nickel, 2003).

Consumers should ask themselves where they can get credit from reasonable and reputable lenders. Usurious lenders may grant easy credit at very high cost. Payday lending stores that grant short-term loans have earned their name by helping consumers "get by until the next payday" by borrowing against their next paycheck, usually at exorbitant rates.

Overextended personal debt. Some people believe that they should have no debt except a mortgage and perhaps a car loan. Others believe that a high credit card balance is acceptable. Who is right? The answer depends on individual values and decisions. Carlson (2004) listed these warning signs of too much debt: (1) a card holder can pay only the minimum amount due on the credit card each month; (2) the consumer has reached the limit on several credit cards and applies for new cards to continue spending; (3) the card holder applies for new cards and transfers the balance of one overextended card to the new cards; (4) credit card companies have raised the interest rates or have cut the credit limits for the cards; or (5) the card holder is receiving calls about late bill payments from companies or from collection agencies. All of these danger signals can mean that the consumer is teetering on the brink of financial disaster if a job loss, medical emergency, or unexpected major expense occurs.

How can consumers get control of spending and debt? They must assess their financial situation and make a realistic inventory of their debt. They need to find ways to cut credit debt and stop using credit cards if credit card debt has become a problem. A solution may be to pay only cash for all purchases and concentrate on paying down the credit card balances. A second strategy is to switch to secured credit cards, which require that money must be deposited before the card is used and the balance deposited becomes the credit limit. If credit debt has become overwhelming, a consumer can request help from credit counseling services. A credit counseling service works with consumers and creditors to arrange financial plans and payments so that consumers can pay off their debts and get control of their spending.

A last-resort solution may be bankruptcy, which is a difficult decision. Bankruptcy has a serious and lasting impact on a consumer's finances for several years, and the consumer must pay attorney fees and court costs for bankruptcy proceedings. In case of overwhelming debt, bankruptcy may appear to be the only solution—an easy answer for credit problems. However, bankruptcy often still means repayment of debts. Typically consumers struggle for years with their finances before giving in to bankruptcy; they do not file bankruptcy on the spur of the moment. Data from the Federal Reserve System showed that two out of three bankruptcy filers in 2006 had lost a job; half had experienced a serious health problem. Only less than 9% had not suffered a job loss, a catastrophic medical event, or divorce that led to their financial dilemmas ("Helping People Get a Fresh Financial Start," 2007).

The Bankruptcy Abuse Prevention and Consumer Protection Act of 2005 made bankruptcy filing more difficult (Grabianowski & Silverman, n.d.). The intent of the law is to stem a rising tide of bankruptcy filings and divert higher-income bankruptcy filers into repayment plans rather than a liquidation of their debts. Bankruptcy filers must participate in credit counseling before proceeding with their cases. Filers must pay a fee for that credit counseling, and they usually must pay attorney fees for the bankruptcy process. Bankruptcy is not an "easy out."

Teaching about the Economics of Credit

Students must understand the role and uses of credit in our economic system. The following personal finance performance expectations from the NBEA National Standards (2007) for Standard VII, Using Credit, are related to the economics of credit.

- Define interest as a cost of credit and explain why it is charged.

- Examine the use of credit from a global consumer perspective (e.g., immigrants to the U.S., family history, cash-based systems of other countries, ease of overextension of credit).

- Explain the need for a sound credit rating.

- Calculate the payment schedule for a loan.

- Identify strategies for effective debt management.

- Analyze the sources of assistance for debt management.

- Identify specific steps a consumer can take to minimize their exposure to identity theft.

- Identify specific steps that should be taken by a victim of identity theft.

- Explain the implications of bankruptcy.

- Explain credit ratings and credit reports and describe why they are important to consumers.

- Describe the relationship between a credit rating and the cost of credit.

- Describe legal and illegal types of credit that carry high rates of interest (e.g., payday loans, rent-to-buy agreements, and loan sharking).

- Identify the components listed on a credit report and explain how that information is used and how it is received by and reported from credit reporting agencies.

Middle school students (basic), high school students (intermediate), and postsecondary students (advanced) should understand how credit is a part of a market system. These activities illustrate the economics of credit and its role in our economy.

Emancipation Consolidation?	Recovery from a financial setback	Level: Basic
		Small Group, Large Group
<td colspan=3><ul><li>Create case studies about people in financial trouble.</li><li>Create a narrative of the situation, along with information about future income, a list of accounts payable, and possible sources of credit (e.g., a spreadsheet of accounts).</li><li>Analyze the information and report possible solutions to improve the situation.</li><li>List steps to avoid the financial setbacks or to recover from them.</li></ul></td>		
Treating Tribulations	Ways to resolve credit problems	Level: Basic
		Individual, Small Group
<td colspan=3><ul><li>Prepare a list of "bad news" scenarios and put each on a card or in a presentation (e.g., declined credit, a dun, over-limit, error in billing, late charge fee dispute, or wrong name or account).</li><li>Distribute cards to small groups to discuss and report possible resolution steps.</li></ul></td>		
Credit Worthiness: Knowledge is Power	Factors that affect a credit report	Level: Intermediate
		Individual, Small Group, Large Group
<td colspan=3><ul><li>Visit credit reporting websites to determine the factors used to compute a credit score.</li><li>Compile a list of these factors and develop and report a strategy to create and maintain a good credit score.</li></ul>> www.TransUnion.com, www.Experian.com, and www.Equifax.com (credit reporting agencies)</td>		
Finding Yourself Again	Steps for recovering your identity	Level: Intermediate
		Small Group
<td colspan=3><ul><li>Present a scenario about a friend or family member's stolen identity.</li><li>Visit online sites and research steps that individuals can take to recover from stolen identity.</li><li>List steps to prevent or lessen the burden of identity theft on the individual in the future.</li><li>In groups, present steps and suggestions for preventing identity theft.</li></ul></td>		
Is Advice Really Worth What You Pay For It?	Practices of for-pay credit restoration companies	Level: Intermediate
		Small Group
<td colspan=3><ul><li>Visit websites of companies that specialize in "credit restoration."</li><li>Explore services rendered and fees of these companies.</li><li>Create a list of services and steps that consumers can take to restore credit.</li><li>Contrast and compare different online companies that provide credit restoration assistance for a fee.</li></ul></td>		

Credit Makes the World Go 'Round	World credit markets and their effects on domestic credit and the economy	Level: Intermediate
		Individual, Small Group, Large Group

- Research articles and/or websites that deal with world credit markets.
- Prepare a report summarizing the article and report implications that may affect individuals.
- Discuss other ramifications of world credit markets and their effect on our economy

Who Were You?	How identities are stolen	Level: Advanced
		Small Group, Large Group

- Use Internet searches, articles, and news items to list ways that identities are stolen.
- Synthesize the list into major categories such as credit card fraud, hacking, and theft of identification materials.
- From the list, develop a list of ways to prevent identity theft.

Payday or Heyday?	Payday loan rates and fees	Level: Advanced
		Small Group, Large Group

- Visit a payday loan office or go online to gather information about payday loans (e.g., loan application, information about terms and conditions, and repayment options).
- Explore and analyze the information and report on actual APR and fees associated with payday loans.
- Discuss whether procedures for payday loans use legal, illegal, or unethical tactics.
- Discuss other ramifications of using this type of service.

Loan Amortization Calculation	Using spreadsheets to compute loan amortizations	Level: Advanced
		Individual, Small Group

- Provide algebraic formulas for computation of monthly interest.
- Create a spreadsheet that computes payment amounts, monthly interest, balance, and total interest and amount paid for a loan.
- Enter different scenarios to compare interest outcomes.
- Create a side-by-side loan comparison spreadsheet with computations for two or three loans.

SUMMARY

Credit is a tool for handling finances, acquiring goods and services, and obtaining large-ticket items such as a home. Individual, small-group, and large-group activities can be used in business and other curriculum areas to develop knowledge about all types of credit and the role of credit in a market system. Business teachers can collaborate with teachers in mathematics, family and consumer sciences, and social studies, particularly, to assist students to develop personal finance literacy about credit. The activities provided in this chapter for students will reinforce their understanding of the role of credit in personal financial management.

REFERENCES

Calder, L. (1999). *Financing the American dream: A cultural history of consumer credit.* Princeton, NJ: Princeton University Press.

Carlson, R. (2004). *The don't sweat guide to your finances: Planning, saving, and spending stress-free*. New York: Hyperion.

Choosing a credit card. Retrieved January 30, 2008, from http://www.federalreserve.gov/Pubs/shop/

Consumer credit. Retrieved May 12, 2008, from http://www.federalreserve.gov/releases/g19/Current

Consumer debt statistics (2007). Retrieved February 15, 2008, from http://www.money-zine.com/Financial-Planning/Debt-Consolidation/Consumer-Debt-Statistics/

Davis, R., & Carnes, L. (2005). Employers perspectives of employees personal financial literacy. *The Delta Pi Epsilon Journal, 47*(4), 11-19.

Goodman, J., & Bloch, J. (1994). *Everyone's money book*. Chicago: Dearborn Financial Publishers.

Grabianowski, E., & Silverman, J. How bankruptcy works. Retrieved January 24, 2008, from http://money.howstuffworks.com/bankruptcy.htm/

Haynes, T., & Bailey, G. (2003). Are you and your basic business students asking the right questions? *Business Education Forum, 57*(3), 33-37.

Helping people get a fresh financial start. Retrieved January 15, 2008, from http://www.bankruptcyaction.com/Usbankstats.com

Lewis, S., & Farmer, L. (2004). Enhancing financial literacy: Integrating math into the secondary basic business curriculum. *Business Education Forum, 58*(4), 34-36.

Manning, R. (2000). Credit card nation: The consequences of America's addiction to credit. New York: Basic Books.

Moore, W. (2002). Economics brought to life. *Business Education Forum, 57*(2), 36-37.

National Business Education Association. (2007). *National standards for business education: What America's students should know and be able to do in business*. Reston, VA: Author.

Nickel, G. (2003). *Credit smart: Your step-by-step guide to establishing or reestablishing good credit*. Naperville, IL: Sphinx Publishing.

Pritchard, J. (n.d.). Annual percentage rate (APR). Retrieved on January 30, 2008, from http://banking.about.com/od/loans/a/calculateapr.htm

Stanley, T., & Danko, W. (1996). *The millionaire next door: The surprising secrets of America's wealthy*. Atlanta: Longstreet Press.

Sullivan, T., Warren, E., & Westbrook, J. (2000). *The fragile middle class: Americans in debt*. New Haven, CT: Yale University Press.

2006 identity theft survey report. Retrieved January 28, 2008, from www.ftc.gov/bcp/edu/microsites/idtheft//

Understanding your FICO score. (2006). Retrieved May 12, 2008, from www.nasfaa.org/subhomes/annualconference2006/handouts2006/s065privateloansandcreditscores2.pdf

Protecting Against Risk

Judith P. Sams
Virginia Department of Education
Richmond, Virginia

Natural or human-made disasters can wipe out a lifetime of work and savings in short order. There are, however, ways to shift the risk of such potential losses from the owner of the assets to a third party; all adults should be equipped with the knowledge of how to affordably shift a substantial portion of life's risks to avoid personal financial catastrophe. This chapter examines methods that business teachers can use to help students identify risks they will face that can be mitigated with proper insurance coverage and how an individual's risks and insurance needs are likely to change throughout life. Also included are insurance-specific terminology, possible reduction of insurance premiums, and how individuals can alleviate risk through other methods such as emergency cash reserves, loss control through security measures, and non-insurance transfer, such as renting or leasing instead of purchasing.

THE ROLE OF INSURANCE IN FINANCIAL LITERACY

Financial education is essential to help consumers understand how to prevent becoming involved in transactions that are financially destructive, how to avoid becoming victims of fraud, and how to exercise their consumer rights.

Impact of Financial Literacy Education

According to the National Strategy for Financial Literacy (2006), financial literacy empowers consumers to be better shoppers, allowing them to obtain goods and services at lower cost. Comprehensive education can help provide individuals with the financial knowledge necessary to meet near-term obligations and to maximize their longer-term financial well-being. Recognizing the importance of insurance and developing a comprehensive insurance program that is compatible with lifestyle changes can help to protect one from financial loss. Today's increasingly complex financial services market offers consumers an unprecedented number of products, services, and providers from which to choose to meet their financial needs. It also requires that they be equipped with the information, knowledge, and skills to evaluate these options and identify those that best suit their needs and circumstances, especially for populations that have traditionally been underserved by our financial system.

Changing Attitudes about Insurance

Considerable evidence exists that documents the public's negative image of and attitude about the insurance industry. According to Bankrate.com, 8% of Americans state that insurance is a waste of money, 44% state that it is a necessary evil, 44% indicate that insurance is essential, and 3% have no opinion about insurance. Negative attitudes about insurance, in large measure, can be attributed to a lack of knowledge about insurance products and practices (Barrese, 1998).

An existing insurance education program from the Insurance Education Institutes (IEI) has had a positive impact on student and teacher attitudes toward insurance, as will be discussed below. Also, improvements in attitudes and understanding seem to facilitate one another; as attitudes change, so do perceptions about understanding and vice versa (Barrese, 1998). IEI training across the United States allows educator-participants to study with other teachers and to interact with insurance experts, gather teaching resources, earn graduate credit for the course, and, according to a presentation by IEI at the Annual Conference on Financial Education in 2007, become more effective in teaching insurance. One of the resources made available at the Institutes, *Risk, Responsibility, Reality: How Insurance Works* (n.d.), is an educational program from the Griffith Insurance Education Foundation that allows teachers to introduce students to concepts and strategies to support the insurance curriculum through three humorous vignettes included on a DVD and teacher's guide.

Tammi Riddle-Metz, risk management, insurance & financial planning program director of Mississippi State University, states that insurance is a key function of all personal finance and business decisions, and it is crucial to help students learn as much about the insurance environment as possible. Riddle-Metz says that after attending an Insurance Education Institute, teachers feel confident when incorporating risk management and insurance topics into the high school curriculum (Riddle-Metz, personal communication, January 11, 2008).

NATIONAL EDUCATION STANDARDS

Progress continues to be made in teaching economics and personal finance in the nation's schools. However, more progress needs to take place. According to the National Council on Economic Education's *Survey of the States* (2007), 41 states now require economics standards to be implemented. However, only 22 states require the testing of student knowledge in economics. Personal finance, a newer subject in comparison with economics, is now included to some extent in the educational standards of 40 states. However, only seven states require students to take a personal finance course as a high school graduation requirement, and only nine states require the testing of student knowledge in personal finance.

The *National Standards for Business Education* developed by the National Business Education Association (NBEA, 2007) emphasizes the need for students to understand how to evaluate the financial decisions that they will have to make throughout their lives. One personal financial management category contained in the standards (Standard VIII, Protecting against Risk) emphasizes the need for young people to understand risk and how to mitigate it.

DEFINING RISK AND RISK MANAGEMENT

The terminology that is associated with insurance is probably responsible for part of the negative perception of the insurance industry—terms such as risk, hazard, and peril—conjure up feelings of despair and negativity. However, these important terms have a distinct and special meaning in the study of insurance.

Risk

A thorough understanding of the following terms helps to alleviate the possible negativity associated with them. For example, *insurance* is simply protection against possible financial loss, thus imbuing that term with a positive rather than a negative connotation. A *risk* is the chance of incurring a loss or injury. *Perils* are anything that may possibly cause a loss. A *hazard* is a condition that increases the likelihood of loss—a trampoline, for example.

Negligence and *speculative risks* (i.e., a risk that may result in a gain as well as a loss) always add interest to the classroom discussion of the basics of insurance terminology. By asking students to bring in articles about accidents that occur as a result of someone's negligence and generating a list of examples of negligence they observed in their homes and/or communities, there will be an interesting knowledge base upon which definitions of terms and discussions about risk mitigation take place.

Risk Management

Many people think of buying insurance as the only type of risk management strategy. However, several other logical approaches to risk management include avoiding risk, reducing risk, assuming risk, and shifting risk. *Avoiding* risk often involves trade-offs. By refusing to drive to work, one avoids the risk of an automobile accident on the way to work, but the trade-off is that the person either does not go to work or relies on a less convenient mode of transportation. If someone chooses to walk or take public transportation to work, they are simply exchanging one risk for another. *Reducing* risk decreases the likelihood of a loss. If one chooses to drive to work, the driver can observe the speed limit, wear a seat belt, keep the vehicle in good repair, and drive responsibly in order to reduce risk. If drivers *assume* the risk, they take responsibility for potential loss by having a cash reserve fund or self-insurance to cover a potential financial loss. The most common method of dealing with risk is to *shift* it—or transfer it to an insurance company. By viewing different types of insurance as the logical methods for *shifting* risk, a detailed discussion of insurance coverage used to mitigate risks is ready to begin.

TYPES OF INSURANCE COVERAGE

Many types of insurance coverage are available to shift the risk of loss from the insured to the insurer. Insurance can be purchased to insure against all types of business and personal risk. A discussion of the basic types of personal insurance that all young people need to be familiar with follows.

Automobile Insurance

The person who causes an accident or injury may be responsible for the losses to other people involved, and claims for property damage, medical expenses, lost wages, and pain and suffering or even lawsuits may result. Without insurance, anything of value that is owned, including a home, savings, future wages, and other assets, may be taken to pay for those losses. According to a Commonwealth of Virginia's Bureau of Insurance publication, *Auto Insurance Consumer's Guide* (2006), some states, including Virginia, have a financial responsibility law to keep drivers off the highway if they cannot bear the cost of injuries or damage that they cause.

Automobile insurance pools the risks of many drivers so no one individual has to bear the entire cost of an accident. Accident claims are paid from the combined premiums of all insured in the pool. In order to register a vehicle in most states, owners must certify that their vehicles are covered by a minimum amount of liability insurance purchased from a licensed insurer. Alternatively, individuals may opt to pay an uninsured motor vehicle fee. The fee, however, does not eliminate potential liability for negligence; an individual is still personally liable for the negligent use of an automobile. The uninsured motor vehicle fee, however, does allow an individual to register a vehicle and drive it without the benefit of liability insurance. Upon vehicle registration expiration and renewal, the owner can usually pay another fee or provide proof of insurance.

Most automobile insurance policies contain three major insuring agreements—(1) liability insurance for bodily injury, (2) liability insurance for property damage, and (3) uninsured/underinsured motorist liability coverage (Commonwealth of Virginia, Bureau of Insurance, 2007). When determining how much insurance one needs, a reputable insurance agent can explain coverage options.

Risk classification factors that influence automobile insurance premiums include gender; age; marital status; driving record; and type, use, and location of the vehicle. Discounts are typically available for good students, completion of driver training and defensive driving courses, good driving records, mature drivers, multi-vehicle coverage, and safety devices such as air bags and anti-theft systems. Not all insurers offer these discounts, and not all states permit them. Unlike federally established banking regulations, insurance regulations vary from state to state and are enforced by each state's insurance commission.

Insurance premiums may determine whether a young person can even afford a vehicle. In *Financial Literacy for Teens*, Chad Foster (2005) stresses the importance of insurance in financial literacy when he talks of the "FIRM Factor" in determining if a teen can afford a car or an apartment—FIRM meaning Fuel, Insurance, Repairs, and Maintenance. "Think of FIRM in the same way as renter's insurance; if you can't afford the renter's insurance policy, then you can't afford the rent. The deal on cars is the same; if you can't afford the FIRM, then you can't afford the vehicle" (Foster, 2005, p.87).

Rarely mentioned in vehicle insurance discussions is the credit rating of the policyholder. An insurance company can refuse to issue a policy or can increase the premium if the policyholder or someone in the household has bad credit, but the insurance company cannot fail to renew a policy solely on the basis of a credit report. If an insurance company takes an adverse action based in whole or in part on an individual's credit report, the insurance company must disclose the primary charac-teristics that were used as the basis for the adverse action or inform the applicant of the right to request this information, according to the *Auto Insurance Consumer's Guide* (2006).

Instructional Strategies for Teaching about Vehicle Insurance
Vehicle insurance is usually the most popular insurance topic taught at the secondary level because of the interest of this age group in cars and the timeliness as far as students obtaining their drivers licenses and/or their first vehicles. There is no shortage of teaching materials, videos, games, handouts, speakers, and interactive classroom activities for teaching about vehicle insurance—the only problem with teaching resources for insurance is deciding which to use.

A successful classroom activity dealing with automobile insurance involves contacting several local automobile dealerships to bring a variety of automobiles and trucks to the student parking lot during the class period. The class has the opportunity to examine the vehicles, hear the sales pitch and prices, and decide which vehicle they want "to purchase." Upon returning to the classroom, each student researches the cost and availability of a loan, payment amounts, safety rating of the vehicle, gas mileage and annual maintenance and operation cost of the vehicle, and the cost of insurance on that particular vehicle. The cost of insurance is usually the biggest surprise, because the other information is often freely disclosed by the automobile dealers. Students often change their minds from a bright red sports car to a more mundane sedan when they learn of the cost of insurance. A worthwhile follow-up to the parking lot display of cars would be a visit from a local insurance agent to answer student questions about automobile insurance and to provide a sample insurance application for students to complete.

The natural connection between teens and cars was the basis for the *Money Talks* curriculum, developed as the result of a survey of 323 teens in the fall of 1998 (Varcoe, Martin, Devitto, & Go, 2005). Based on the results of this study, a workgroup developed a series of four newsletters, called *Money Talks*, with hands-on activities and teacher's guides containing background information, key points, learning objectives, group activities, pre- and post-tests, and resource websites. After participating in *Money Talks,* teens demonstrated significantly more knowledge about how to save money on car insurance.

Property Insurance
Many secondary school students may decide they have no need to study property insurance because they do not own anything of value, but teachers can dispel that idea quickly by giving basic facts about what is covered in property insurance and how different types of policies fit every housing situation.

A homeowners policy can protect the owner if someone is hurt or has property damaged because of something that caused the damage that existed on the property of the insured. Also, insurance is needed to protect the lender if money has been borrowed to purchase a home, according to the *Homeowners Insurance Consumer's Guide* (2006).

The homeowners insurance policy is a package policy that combines more than one type of insurance coverage in a single policy; the cost of the package policy is usually less expensive than if all types of property coverage were bought separately. As outlined in the *Homeowners Insurance Consumer's Guide* (2006), there are basically four types of coverage in the standard homeowners policy:

- Property damage coverage to protect the home or belongings if they are damaged or destroyed

- Liability coverage if the insured causes another person to be injured or another person's property to be damaged or destroyed

- Medical payments coverage for medical treatment for certain persons injured in an accident in the home of the insured and certain situations away from the home

- Additional living expenses coverage to pay for living expenses when the insured cannot live in their home because of covered damage.

The different types of homeowner's policies vary according to the types of property they cover and the number of perils they cover. Policies may be of the "named peril" type, the "open perils" type, or a combination of the two types.

The most common mistake made by people buying homeowners insurance is not buying enough coverage. "It is very easy to continue buying the same amount of insurance year after year even though the value of the home is increasing due to inflation and improvements which have been made," states the *Homeowners Insurance Consumers Guide* (2006, p. 14).

A 2006 Insurance Research Council poll found that 96% of homeowners had home-owner's insurance, while only 43% of renters had renter's insurance (*The Insurance Fact Book*, 2007). The secondary student quickly pays attention when the teacher talks about students' first apartments and the fact that their property is no longer covered under their parents' homeowners policies. The values listed on the inventory completed at the beginning of the study of insurance make students realize that the average premiums for renters insurance, which range from about $135 to $275 per year (*The Insurance Fact Book*, 2007), make it one of the best bargains in a new apartment.

Instructional Strategies for Property Insurance
To help dispel the idea that students do not need to know anything about property insurance, the teacher may begin the unit by instructing students to write down all the items they own or have in their bedroom at home and collect the papers at the end of a class period. That evening, each student is to make a list of anything of any value in their room or that belongs to them and is located elsewhere. The next day, students can compare the two lists and find that they do, indeed, own property of significant value. The instructor can build on this activity as an effective means for introducing the topic of property insurance to students.

Insurance education cannot be limited to the traditional public school setting, but it must transcend all barriers and challenges. Virginia has a unique situation for providing education to state inmates as the only state with a separate state agency to accomplish the education requirements of inmates at both the juvenile and adult levels in all Virginia prisons. Virginia works closely with the Department of Corrections and the Department of Juvenile Services in this undertaking. A recent classroom survey by a women's correctional center instructor indicated that the women felt less knowledgeable about homeowners/renters insurance than any other insurance. The overall score for knowledge of homeowners/ renters insurance was 2.3 on a 10-point scale, compared with 3.5 for automobile, 4.1 for health, and 3.2 for life insurance (F. Geissler, personal communication, December 15, 2007).

In stressing the need for insurance education, Geissler stated that prior to their incarceration, "Many of those surveyed were at or below poverty and did not understand nor have the time to get better educated in these areas. If inmates being released from prison to be reintegrated into society are not given as much education as possible to help them become and remain successful, they will become another statistic in the high recidivism rates" (personal communication, December 15, 2007).

Regardless of the makeup of the student population, instructors are always faced with the issue of being able to easily find interesting, verifiable facts that are relevant to an insurance discussion. Where could an instructor find the 25 biggest insured property losses in the United States to use for classroom discussion? Insurance figures heavily in many classic movie plots, but where could one find several "leads" to use as jumpstarts in the classroom? Which state generates the most premiums? The answers to these and other questions to enliven a discussion are in *The Guide to Understanding the Insurance Industry* (A.M. Best Company, 2006-2007).

Life Insurance

Traditional life insurance policies continue to be an important part of the life insurance business and can be sold on an individual basis (referred to as "ordinary life") or to groups, such as employees of the same company. Ordinary life insurance can be "term," which provides financial protection for a specific period of time, or "permanent," which provides long-term financial protection and builds up a cash value. Most group policies provide term coverage (*The Insurance Fact Book*, 2007). Life insurance is essentially an investment of savings that offers a tax-free sum of money to the beneficiary at some point in the future. Besides annuities and life insurance, life insurers may offer health insurance and other financial services such as asset management (*The Insurance Fact Book*, 2007). Annuities now account for 51% of the life/health business, followed by life insurance products (26%) and accident and health products (22%).

Instructional Strategies for Teaching about Life Insurance

The Missouri Department of Insurance has created *Quick Facts for Teens* (2007). These worksheets give teens the opportunity to use their knowledge of insurance and learn the importance of insurance coverage through crossword puzzles, word searches, and facts sheets. Teachers also have access to sample lesson plans and teacher-specific links and educator resources at http://insurance.mo.gov/consumer/teens/index.htm.

Some resources listed come with teacher guides and teaching resources. The *LifeGuide Series Life Insurance* is one of a series of insurance-specific booklets from the USAA Educational Foundation. It offers a frank discussion of who needs life insurance, how much coverage a person needs, and how to compare and review policies throughout one's life (USAA Educational Foundation, 2006). The *Virginia Life Insurance Consumer's Guide* (2006), prepared by the Virginia Bureau of Insurance, provides easy-to-understand definitions of key insurance terms and comes with a teaching guide about life insurance that helps teachers answer frequently asked questions, identify problems, and offer solutions. *The Graduate's Independent Guide to Insurance* (2004) from the Independent Insurance Agents of America (or downloadable from http://na.iiaa.org/TrustedChoice/NewWebPage/gradguide04.pdf) is a free, easy-to-read guide concentrating on the types of insurance high school seniors need to consider after graduation.

Health Insurance

Health care costs are high and getting higher, and it is more important than ever for consumers to understand how health insurance works and which health coverage is best for their particular situations. Financially stable baby boomers who retire at a young age or need coverage after a corporate downsizing or supplemental insurance after they turn 65 and become eligible for Medicare benefits are driving this push, experts say ("U.S. Health Insurers Set Sights," 2007). High medical bills that some people accrue without having health insurance trigger about half of all personal bankruptcies.

According to *Virginia Health Insurance Guide for Consumers* (2003), one of the most important things to understand is the difference between traditional health insurance and managed-care health insurance plans when selecting or purchasing health care coverage. Traditional insurance plans generally allow individuals to go to the providers of their choice but require that they pay for the services and file claims for reimbursement. Managed care health insurance plans use networks of selected doctors and other providers to provide health services. In return for using the network of providers, individuals typically pay less for medical care than they would with traditional health insurance.

Health maintenance organizations (HMOs) are the most familiar form of managed care. HMO members pay a fixed dollar amount, which gives them access to a wide range of healthcare services by paying a predetermined fee or co-payment for each hospital visit, doctor visit, or emergency room visit, and for prescription drugs. HMOs generally eliminate the need to file claims (*Virginia Health Insurance Guide for*

Consumers, 2003). Because health insurance plans vary as to coverage, cost, and limitations, it is recommended that the insured take the time to familiarize themselves with the benefits and coverage before there is a claim. In addition to types of coverage, the terminology used in health insurance is so specific that policies usually have one section focused on defining terms and answering questions (such as the meaning of disability, pre-existing illness, major medical, group coverage, coordination of benefits, and COBRA).

The federal Health Insurance Portability and Accountability Act of 1996 (HIPAA) made important changes regarding health insurance in the United States and provided important protections. HIPAA and state laws are complex, and consumers are encouraged to contact the Bureau of Insurance in their own state to discuss the services and protections available to them (*Virginia Health Insurance Guide for Consumers*, 2003).

Government-provided health care is often the subject of heated debate in Congress, in living rooms, and also in classrooms throughout the United States. *Medicare* is a federally administered health insurance program that covers the cost of hospitalization, medical care, and some related services for most people over age 65, people receiving Social Security Disability Insurance payments, and people with End Stage Renal Disease (ESRD). Premiums are subsidized by the government so that individuals pay only a portion of the actual cost of the program. Medicare Supplemental Insurance, or "Medigap," is insurance coverage sold on an individual or group basis that helps to fill the gap between the Medicare payments and the total medical bills due. *Medicaid* is a joint state and federal public assistance program that pays for health care services for low-income or disabled persons. (Virginia Health Insurance Guide, 2003).

Instructional Strategies for Teaching about Other Types of Insurance

Insurance coverage can be purchased for almost any imaginable risk if one is willing to explore the possibilities and pay the premiums. Students love to research and make presentations on unusual types of insurance coverage such as the legs of a dancer or professional athlete, a singer's voice, the hands of a pianist, wedding insurance, rain insurance, or even pet insurance. The high school classroom lends itself perfectly to bulletin boards prepared by students on these interesting topics, a newspaper search for unusual insurance-related events, student-prepared board games such as Monopoly or Insurance Jeopardy, or a lively teacher-monitored game of "Are You Smarter than a Fifth Grader?" with all questions centered around unusual insurance coverage.

DISASTERS AND FINANCIAL PLANNING

Disasters, whether natural or human-made, usually strike quickly, without warning, and with little or no time to decide what to do next. Taking measures to avoid or prepare for a disaster in advance—called "mitigation" in technical terms—reduces the likelihood of injury, loss of life, and property damage far more than anything that can be done after a disaster strikes. An excellent discussion about mitigating the risks associated with natural disasters can be found in *Disasters and Financial Planning: A Guide for Preparedness*, published as a public service by the American Institute of Certified Public Accountants (ACIPA) Foundation, American Red Cross, and National Endowment for Financial Education (NEFE). The booklet answers many questions and can help individuals to avoid a financial crisis if a disaster strikes (NEFE, 2004).

Following the Hurricane Katrina disaster in 2005, the Federal Reserve Bank of Atlanta designed a DVD-based curriculum to teach students about financial readiness during an emergency and in everyday life. *Katrina's Classroom: Financial Lessons from a Hurricane* (2007) provides lessons and detailed information about the risks and effects of natural disasters such as hurricanes. In addition, *Building Wealth: A Beginner's Guide to Securing Your Financial Future* (2007), distributed by the Federal Reserve Bank of Dallas, features videos, interactive worksheets and calculators, tips to avoid identity theft, basics on insurance and wealth protection, and links to web resources.

LIFE CHANGES THAT AFFECT RISKS AND RISK MITIGATION
Students must be made aware that their insurance needs will change as life changes occur. Job changes, marriage, divorce, spousal death, children, a home purchase, relocation, adverse health conditions, additional financial responsibilities, and retirement all have an impact on individual insurance needs. Through classroom training, students become aware that these changes require life-long learning and awareness about financial issues and emphasize the need to have a reputable, competent insurance agent to answer questions and help evaluate life changes.

Many insurance companies believe that credit scores help them underwrite better because insurance companies have shown that a direct relationship exists between a person's credit score and that person's likelihood to file a claim. In other words, the better the credit score, the fewer the claims filed. However, the State Corporation Commission's *Credit Scoring: How It Affects Your Automobile and Homeowners Insurance* (2004) clarified that each insurance company customizes the weights it places on the different aspects of an insured's credit report based on the company's loss experience. Some insurance companies use credit scores to determine the amount of the premiums or which company within their group of companies will insure the applicant. Students should be made aware of the relationship between credit scores and insurance premiums.

THE ROLE OF ETHICS IN INSURANCE
Small-business employers and individuals searching for affordable health insurance increasingly are falling victim to scams and misleading offers. More than 200,000 businesses and individuals in the United States have purchased phony insurance since the decade began, and victims have been left with hundreds of millions of dollars in

unpaid medical claims, according to Mila Kofman, an associate professor at University of Georgia (McQueen, 2007). The bogus insurers collect premiums but pay no claims, or they sell medical discount cards that are often misrepresented as insurance by unscrupulous agents and websites (McQueen, 2007). In the newest twist, telemarketers are selling fake Medicare prescription-drug plans and Medicare Advantage policies to seniors, says Kim Holland, insurance commissioner of Oklahoma. Some fraudulent telemarketers are also using the calls as a pretext to glean confidential information for identity theft, she says (McQueen, 2007).

Professional ethics and claims of unethical practices within the insurance industry are handled through different channels in each state. In Virginia, the State Corporation Commission's Bureau of Insurance responds to thousands of individual consumer inquiries and complaints each year. It is vital for every citizen to become aware of how to address questions and complaints about insurance in their individual state. Most of the state insurance regulation agencies have free speakers, brochures, and websites available to help consumers become aware of ethical issues, possible scams, and questionable industry tactics.

SUMMARY
Despite the fact that considerable evidence exists to document the public's negative image of the insurance industry, instruction in the secondary classroom can do much to reverse that negative image. An examination of the fact that natural or human-made disasters can wipe out a lifetime of work and savings in short order, and the fact that there are ways to shift the risk of potential losses from the owner of the assets to a third party, will help young adults become motivated to equip themselves with the knowledge of how to affordably make that shift in risk. This may help individuals to avoid personal financial catastrophe, but it requires that they be equipped with the information, knowledge, and skills to evaluate insurance options and identify those that best suit their needs and circumstances.

There is no shortage of teaching resources and prepared curriculum materials for instruction about insurance for individuals, and the use of these resources is only limited by the creativity and ingenuity of the teacher. Many of the best resources are free to educators and are often available online or through a clearinghouse of resources or education websites.

REFERENCES
A. M. Best Company (2006-2007). *Best's Review: The guide to understanding the insurance industry.* Oldwick, NJ: A. M. Best Company.
Auto Insurance Consumer's Guide. (2006). Commonwealth of Virginia, Bureau of Insurance. Richmond, VA.

Barrese, J., Gardner, L., & Thrower, E. (1998). Changing attitudes about insurance through education. *CPCU Journal, 41*(3). Fall 1998.

Building Wealth: A beginner's guide to securing your financial future. (2007). Federal Reserve Bank of Dallas.

Credit scoring: How it affects your automobile and homeowners insurance. (2004) Commonwealth of Virginia, Bureau of Insurance, Richmond, VA.

Foster, C. (2005). *Financial literacy for teens.* Conyers, GA: Rising Books.

Katrina's classroom: Financial lessons from a hurricane. (2006). Federal Reserve Bank of Atlanta.

McQueen, M. P. (2007, November). *Health insurance scam.* Richmond Times-Dispatch, Richmond, VA. p. D5.

National Business Education Association. *National Standards for Business Education: What America's students should know and be able to do in business* (2007). Reston, VA: Author.

National Endowment for Financial Education. (2004). *Disasters and financial planning: A guide for preparedness.* New York: Author.

Quick facts for teens. Missouri Department of Insurance. Retrieved August 22, 2007, from http://insurance.mo.gov/consumer/teens/index.htm

Risk, responsibility, reality: How insurance works. (n.d.) Insurance Education Foundation, Indianapolis, IN. Retrieved July 3, 2008, from http://career-connections.info/en/ic/rrr_links.html

Survey of the states: Economic and personal finance education in our nation's schools in 2007—A report card. (2007). New York: National Council on Economic Education.

The Graduate's Independent Guide to Insurance. (2004). Independent Insurance Agents of America, Alexandria, VA.

The National Strategy for Financial Literacy. (2006). *Taking ownership of the future.* Financial Literacy and Education Commission. Retrieved December 5, 2007, from http://www.mymoney.gov/pdfs/ownership.pdf.

USAA Educational Foundation. (2006). *LifeGuide series insurance.* Retrieved September 10, 2007, from www.usaaedfoundation.org

Varcoe, K., Martin, A., Devitto, Z., & Go, C. *Using a financial education curriculum for teens.* (2005). Northridge, CA: Association for Financial Counseling and Planning Education.

Virginia health insurance guide for consumers. (2003). Richmond, VA: Virginia State Corporation Commission, Bureau of Insurance.

Virginia life insurance consumer's guide. (2006). Richmond, VA: Virginia State Corporation Commission, Bureau of Insurance.

What do you want to be when you grow up? (2006). InVESTprogram.org. Alexandria, VA.

Economics and Personal Finance Education

Economics and Personal Finance Education